Praise fo

‖‖‖‖‖‖‖‖‖‖‖‖‖‖‖‖‖‖‖‖
T0035567

A BURNING IN MY BONES

"In the time of a generation-wide breakdown in trust with leaders in every sphere of society, Eugene's quiet life of deep integrity and gospel purpose is a bright light against a dark backdrop. For years his life has been the North Star for my life and pastoral call. This seminal biography is an unmistakable call to quiet resistance against the way of the world and, when necessary, the way of the church. Only read this book if you're ready to live differently."
—JOHN MARK COMER, pastor for teaching and vision at Bridgetown Church and author of *The Ruthless Elimination of Hurry*

"Winn Collier captures Eugene Peterson's sense of wonder over the presence of God and the radiance of Scripture. Through *A Burning in My Bones*, you'll learn to experience life through Eugene's eyes: dig deep, look for what is real, find the sacred in the rough and ordinary, and live like God is real."
—MARK BATTERSON, *New York Times* bestselling author of *The Circle Maker* and lead pastor of National Community Church

"How do you reduce into words the vital reality of this man, scholar, searcher, teacher, and faithful friend? Eugene was a man who brought Scripture to fresh life for me and millions of others— who else would invite the phrase *Holy Luck* into a retelling of the Beatitudes? Winn Collier's skilled storytelling weaves the threads of Eugene's life into something fitting, like the prayer shawl he wore in his study every day."
—LUCI SHAW, Regent College writer in residence and author of *The Generosity* poems

"I knew Eugene Peterson for thirty years, or at least I thought I did. He didn't talk much, especially about himself. I knew nothing about his mouse tattoo, his Pentecostal mother's radio program, the abysmal failure of his first church plant attempt, his friendship with a young Pat Robertson, or his square dancing prowess. Somehow Winn Collier ferreted out the little known facts about Eugene that, taken together, complete the picture of a humble, gentle giant who brought the Bible to new life for millions and became an inspirational model for beleaguered pastors everywhere."

—PHILIP YANCEY, author of
What's So Amazing About Grace

"Captivating from the first page, Collier's artful storytelling immerses us into the life of a spiritual sage. With a gentle hand, he weaves together moments and words and letters and prayers, drawing out themes like threads in a tapestry, never imposing a narrative. In these pages, we go beyond *The Message* and the pastor, and meet the human in all his earthiness and holiness. This is a work of art worthy of the man who wanted to be a saint."

—GLENN PACKIAM, associate senior pastor of
New Life Church and author of *Blessed Broken Given*

"Eugene Peterson indelibly marked both me and *Leadership Journal*, the publication I edited for thirty-four years. In an era fascinated by leadership techniques, he insisted that the essence of pastoral ministry was not 'running a church' (to which many ministers defaulted) but 'curing souls.' This outstanding biography tells the story of how Eugene developed his unique and prophetic voice."

—MARSHALL SHELLEY, director of the Doctor of Ministry
program at Denver Seminary and coauthor of
The Leadership Secrets of Billy Graham

"When a book begins with a map, you know it's going to be good. When it's a biography of a Christian thinker, it's even better. A map means place and embodied experience are going to be part of his story of faith. In the same way Peterson's words welcomed us to walk in the world of the Bible, Collier's words welcome us into Peterson's world, with warmth and generosity. As we spend time in the presence of Peterson, we catch glimpses of the Presence that animated his entire life."

—MANDY SMITH, author of *The Vulnerable Pastor*
and pastor of University Christian Church

"Eugene Peterson was my friend. I miss his voice: his warmth, wisdom, and vulnerability. My deepest gratitude to Winn Collier for evoking the pastor's heart so beautifully throughout these pages. And for the miracle of deepening our intimacy with him even beyond the veil!"

—BRADLEY JERSAK, author of *The Pastor: A Crisis*

"Eugene Peterson's was a momentous life. He held together so much we pull apart: academia and the church, the liberal mainline and evangelicalism, the mystical and the rustic, Hebrew grammar and Dostoyevsky, Jesus and his creation. Now Eugene's life has a suitably momentous biography—an unassuming setting from which this jewel of a life shines. Whether you are a Peterson junkie or have never bought one of his twenty-two million books sold (to date), you will find yourself drawn in and delighted."

—JASON BYASSEE, Butler Chair in Homiletics and Biblical
Interpretation at Vancouver School of Theology and editor,
with Roger Owens, of *Pastoral Work: Engagements with
the Vision of Eugene Peterson*

"This book pulses with life on every page—it's expansive and energetic, deeply human, at times painfully honest, and a call to blaz-

ing holiness. Winn Collier has given us a biography befitting a
beautiful man."

—DANIEL GROTHE, associate senior pastor of
New Life Church and author of *Chasing Wisdom*

"Annie Dillard noted, 'How we spend our days is, of course, how
we spend our lives.' Winn Collier, in *A Burning in My Bones*, offers us a vulnerable look into the life of Eugene Peterson, who
spent his days in pursuit of becoming a saint. Collier fills in the
gaps of Peterson's life, showing us his struggles to live this holy
ambition and revealing a man who wrestled deeply yet who was
able to explore the expansive and generous geography of the kingdom of God. This is a candid picture of a pastor who found that
God's holiness can never be experienced abstractly but only lived
in dogged commitment to one's place and people."

—TRYGVE D. JOHNSON, Hinga-Boersma Dean of
the Chapel, Hope College, Holland, Michigan, and
author of *The Preacher as Liturgical Artist: Metaphor,
Identity, and the Vicarious Humanity of Christ*

"*A Burning in My Bones* is an intimate portrait of one of the greatest spiritual writers of a generation. But in these pages, Eugene
Peterson isn't enshrined. To read Collier's sweeping biography is
to understand Peterson's faithfulness as something earthy, even
imitable. Every chapter inspires our own courage for the long
obedience of faith. In short, this isn't a book that simply sketches
a life; it's a book that makes one long to be saint."

—JEN POLLOCK MICHEL, author of *Surprised by Paradox*

"*A Burning in My Bones* beautifully reminds us that we are shaped,
as are our expectations, by the people and places we relationally
inhabit—as habitations of God's presence. Collier invites us to
walk with Eugene, from his early days of walking the hills of

Montana to pastorally walking alongside followers of Jesus throughout his adult life, with the expectation that one experiences extraordinary holiness in a holy, wholly ordinary, Presence-filled life."

—CHERITH FEE NORDLING, associate professor at the
Robert E. Webber Institute for Worship Studies

"In my years spent trying to bring people of different ethnicities together in the context of the local church, I picked up quickly that labels were not my friend. I guess that's why I've always been drawn to Eugene Peterson. What exactly was he? Trying to define (or confine) him is like trying to squeeze too many clothes in a trunk: something is bound to, well, not fit. The only label all of Eugene Peterson nestled neatly in is the Greatest Commandment. He loved God with all of his being, and his neighbor—even his ethnically-other neighbor during Jim Crow—as himself. At a time of deep label-wearing partisanship, we need books like *A Burning in My Bones* to remind us of what really matters."

—BRYAN LORITTS, teaching pastor at the Summit Church
and author of *The Dad Difference*

"In the midst of increasing attention, Eugene Peterson assiduously avoided being made into a hero. He wanted people to engage directly with Jesus. During his last years, he invited Winn Collier to journey with him and his beloved wife, Jan. This intimate and insightful account is the fruit of that friendship. Though vivid and flowing prose, Collier unfolds Peterson's earthy spirituality in a way that is not only inspirational but accessible. The book captures a life rooted deeply in Christ."

—WALTER KIM, president of the National Association of
Evangelicals and pastor for leadership
at Trinity Presbyterian Church

"*A Burning in My Bones* presents Eugene Peterson as a man of imagination, ambition, and arresting humility: an earthy mystic and transgressor of sectarian boundaries whose roaming intellect and gift for language made him, eventually and inevitably, a reluctant public figure. With an old friend's affection and a novelist's eye, Winn Collier carves out Peterson's place among the other writers and thinkers quoted herein: Thomas Merton, Walker Percy, Wendell Berry, Wallace Stegner, and yes, Bono. If you ever wondered what sort of person undertakes the riskiest job in publishing—writing a new translation of the Bible—you'll be glad Winn Collier wondered too."

—LEIF ENGER, author of *Peace Like a River*
and *Virgil Wander*

"The soulful son of a hardworking butcher and a preaching mother, Eugene Peterson grew into the man he most longed to be: 'a saint without any trappings.' Winn Collier's exquisitely rendered portrait delivers the wild beauty of Montana skies, the tenderness of honest confession, and the steadfast wisdom of a life lived on holy ground."

—KAREN WRIGHT MARSH, director of Theological Horizons
and author of *Vintage Saints and Sinners: 25 Christians
Who Transformed My Faith*

"The greatest praise I can give Winn Collier's portrait of Eugene Peterson is that its intimate conversations and testimonies draw me nearer not only to Pastor Pete but to the Jesus he loved above all. I am spellbound by the surprises in these stories: Collier's questions lead us beyond the borders of Peterson's memoir to unexpected treasure. He writes with a poet's imagination about a poetry-loving pastor. And on delicate matters—Peterson's pastoral or marital struggles, *The Message*'s 'koine American' paraphrases, or late controversies about same-sex relationships in the church—he works with a surgeon's precision, revealing wisdom that comforts the afflicted and afflicts those who misguidedly appoint themselves 'God's policemen.' As I miss my friend and counselor, this book brings him right back into the room, a radiant icon, still speaking with inimitable humility and joy."

—Jeffrey Overstreet, assistant professor of English and writing at Seattle Pacific University and author of *Through a Screen Darkly* and *Auralia's Colors*

"*A Burning in My Bones* is the book we need so desperately today. Far from the cacophonous crowd of celebrity megapastors, Eugene Peterson modeled humility of heart and quiet wisdom. While the world grew more stridently polarized, Peterson illuminated the way of love and joy and generosity. As countless influencers were setting about building their platforms, Peterson showed that the only platform for the follower of Jesus is the Cross. And of course in a world of instant gratification, Peterson demonstrated a long obedience in the same direction. He was the God-ordained messenger of *The Message,* and his slow and careful work has shaped the lives of countless millions. Winn Collier's telling of Eugene Peterson's story is elegant and profound, richly researched and thoughtfully composed. It draws on the experiences and narratives of countless people who can attest to the transformative power of one person who was willing to follow Jesus and feed his sheep. If you want to remind yourself in this distressing time what it means to be wise and generous and good, I cannot recommend a better book."

—Timothy Dalrymple, CEO of *Christianity Today*

A BURNING IN
MY BONES

A BURNING IN
MY BONES

The Authorized Biography
of Eugene H. Peterson

WINN COLLIER

WATERBROOK

A Burning in My Bones

Scripture quotations marked (KJV) are taken from the King James Version.
Scripture quotations marked (MSG) are taken from The Message. Copyright ©
1993, 2002, 2018 by Eugene H. Peterson. Used by permission of NavPress.
All rights reserved. Represented by Tyndale House Publishers, a division of
Tyndale House Ministries. Scripture quotations marked (NIV) are taken from
the Holy Bible, New International Version®, NIV®. Copyright © 1973, 1978,
1984, 2011 by Biblica Inc.™ Used by permission of Zondervan. All rights
reserved worldwide. (www.zondervan.com). The "NIV" and "New
International Version" are trademarks registered in the United States
Patent and Trademark Office by Biblica Inc.™

Published in the United States by WaterBrook, an imprint of
Random House, a division of Penguin Random House LLC.

WATERBROOK® and its deer colophon are registered
trademarks of Penguin Random House LLC.

Author is represented by Alive Literary Agency, 7680 Goddard Street,
Suite 200, Colorado Springs, Colorado 80920, www.aliveliterary.com.

All photographs, with the exception of those credited,
are courtesy of the Eugene Peterson estate.

Paperback ISBN 978-0-7352-9164-5

The Library of Congress has cataloged the hardcover edition as follows:

LIBRARY OF CONGRESS CATALOGING-IN-PUBLICATION DATA
Names: Collier, Winn, author.
Title: A burning in my bones : the authorized biography of
Eugene H. Peterson, translator of The message / by Winn Collier.
Description: First edition. | Colorado Springs, Colorado : WaterBrook, 2021. |
Includes bibliographical references.
Identifiers: LCCN 2020015342 | ISBN 9780735291621 (hardcover) |
ISBN 9780735291638 (ebook)
Subjects: LCSH: Peterson, Eugene H., 1932– 2018.
Classification: LCC BX9225.P466 C65 2021 | DDC 285.092 [B]—dc23
LC record available at https://lccn.loc.gov/2020015342

Printed in the United States of America on acid-free paper

waterbrookmultnomah.com

2nd Printing

First Trade Paperback Edition

Book design by Dana Leigh Blanchette

SPECIAL SALES
Most WaterBrook books are available at special quantity
discounts when purchased in bulk by corporations, organizations,
and special-interest groups. Custom imprinting or excerpting can
also be done to fit special needs. For information, please email
specialmarketscms@penguinrandomhouse.com.

To John Collier, my dad.

The words are fire in my belly,
a burning in my bones.

—Jeremiah 20:9, MSG

Preface

On the flight home from Montana in October 2016, I assumed I'd seen Eugene and Jan for the last time. He was drawing his circle close, severely limiting any commitments so he could devote his diminishing energy to Jan and the family. I began to ponder how one day Eugene's story would be told, reflecting on how I hoped the telling would do more than outline the facts and highlights but would give a sense of the man, a personal encounter, even if only through ink and paper. At the encouragement of a friend, I wrote Eugene, telling him my thoughts. A couple of weeks later, I picked up the phone and heard Eugene's soft, raspy voice on the line. There was nothing Eugene was less interested in than a biography ("The thought of it makes me tired," he said at first), but the more we talked, the more I heard energy rising in his voice. "Okay," he said after fifteen or twenty minutes. "I think you should do this, Winn. I'll help you." And he did. Eugene gave me complete access to himself, his family, and eight decades of papers and journals and manuscripts and letters. And for three and a half years, I've known the joy (and the trepidation) of researching and writing Eugene's story. I am so very grateful.

This story leans heavily on Eugene's papers and journals, as well as scores of personal interviews. Whenever I cite a published work, you will find it in the notes section, which is organized by chapter at the back of the book (to keep the narrative flow intact and to honor Eugene's aversion to chopping up literary beauty with clunky notation). For the most part, Eugene's unpublished written words (journal entries and letters) will appear in italics and without quotation marks. The many quotations from Eugene that are not cited in endnotes are taken from oral interviews I had with him (and all other interviews are offered in the same way).

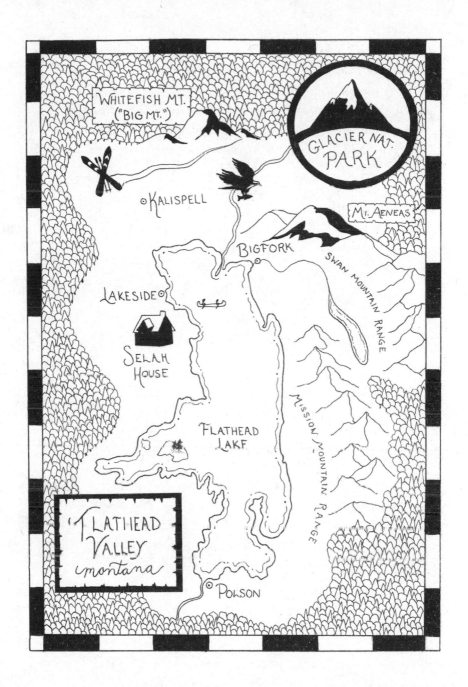

Contents

Introduction

They become what they behold.
—William Blake, *Jerusalem: The Emanation
of the Giant Albion*

A few minutes after 7:00 a.m., with sun streaming through her kitchen windows on a fresh Maryland day, Jan Peterson scooped hot eggs onto five plates, next to scrapple and fried apple rings. "Eric," she called, "go tell Dad breakfast is ready."

"Yes ma'am," Eric answered. The oldest Peterson boy ran to the top of the stairs that led down to his father's home study and stopped short. His dad would be intensely focused and immersed in quiet. With a nine-year-old's mischief, Eric tiptoed down. The basement smelled of must and old print. He stepped onto the chilly tiled floor and cat-walked, with a burglar's stealth, to his dad's study door.

Most days, Eugene spent an hour before daybreak reading Scripture and a second hour reading commentaries. A hand-me-down desk sat under a single window, beside a long bookshelf, packed to the ceiling. Its books were arranged mostly by author: Barth, Dostoevsky, Newman, Teresa of Avila. A rocking chair, the favorite seat for reading, sat in the corner. Fluorescent lights hung from the ceiling, but Eugene rarely flipped on the cold bulbs—a lamp on the desk shed a warmer glow. The old communion table from their church, Christ Our King, sat against the wall, holding a pottery chalice and paten ready for wine and bread. Alongside the Eucharist dishes sat an Italian fiasco, long emptied of Chianti, holding a single white candle, with a year's worth of wax splattered over the straw basket covering the dark glass. A monk's cell. Dad's space—Gene's space—Pastor Pete's space.

Eric turned the knob slowly, silently. He peered through the crack. And even now, Eric's eyes turn moist as he tells me the memory while we sit together. A small woven rug lay on the tile floor before his dad's desk. Candlelight flickered from the wine bottle. Eugene rested on his knees with a tallit—the tasseled Jewish prayer shawl—wrapped around his shoulders, a Hebrew Psalter splayed in front of him. He rocked gently, engrossed in the world of the Scriptures, surrendering to ancient prayers.

Eric watched, hushed. He slowly closed the door and crept back upstairs, to the clink of forks against plates.

Only a boy, but he knew he'd witnessed something holy.

PART ONE

1

Montana

There was nothing but a mercantile and a saloon, one building on either side of the street, and a slow winding river working through the valley (a cow moose and her calf standing in the river behind the mercantile)—and still no sign of life, no people. . . . We knew immediately that this was where we wanted to live, where we had always wanted to live.

We had never felt such magic.

—Rick Bass, *Winter: Notes from Montana*

In 1902, Andre and Juditta Odegard Hoiland loaded their pots and pans, a bundle of clothes, and a few family heirlooms into a trunk and a couple of canvas bags. After wrapping their nine children in heavy coats to shield them from Atlantic winds and the spray of icy salt water, they boarded a steamer in Stavanger, Norway, and watched the coastland cliffs fade to mist. Andre had made this voyage once before, working in the steel mills in Pittsburgh two years earlier to save enough money to move his family. Eugene's maternal grandparents sailed, perhaps on the *Norge* or the *Thingvalla*, to Ellis Island and entered the harbor under the welcome gaze of Lady Liberty. New York City pulsed with the mass of humanity, and the family was immediately exhilarated and unnerved. Pulled by the westward migration, they cobbled

together train passage from New York to Saint Paul, Minnesota,
maneuvering multiple connections. Finally, they boarded the
Great Northern Railway, that massive feat willed into existence
by James Hill, "the Empire Builder." Crammed into their tight
compartment, the eleven Hoilands churned past the lakes of Minnesota, across the plains, and then through the badlands of North
Dakota before they finally stopped fifty miles from the Canadian
border in Kalispell, Montana.

Only a decade old, young Kalispell boasted a train depot for
the Saint Paul, Minneapolis, and Manitoba Railway, the Mill
Creek sawmill, the West Hotel (rooms for two dollars per night),
a livery, and the Conrad National Bank. Harry Stanford, Kalispell's first chief of police, listed "23 saloons, half a dozen gam-
bling joints and a like number of honky-tonks, two Chinese
laundries and the same number of Chinese restaurants, and four
general stores." Early one Fourth of July morning, George Stan-
nard, a local gunsmith, rolled a 220-pound cannon lifted from
Fort Benton into the thoroughfare and lit the fuse, causing pan-
icked neighbors to run out of their houses in their bathrobes.
However, the allure for the Hoilands was primal, with the granite
mountains' jagged spires piercing the skies, the winter white
clinging to the frozen earth, the summer's verdant forests and
azure lake. It was as if they'd come home. Andre, a cement worker,
poured Kalispell's first sidewalks and also served as a pastor, helping form Kalispell's first Assemblies of God church. In addition,
he was a writer, penning pastoral articles for Norwegian newspa-
pers in Norway, Montana, and Seattle.

When Andre and Juditta Hoiland first cast their eyes on the
vast and magnificent Flathead Valley, however, they couldn't
have imagined how this place would shape the generations to
follow, how this ground would form their grandson Eugene.
This wild country—with craggy, impenetrable terrain and a history of vigilante justice, raucous mining camps, and violence

between encroaching settlers and indigenous nations (Bitter-root Salish, Kootenai, and Pend d'Oreilles)—buried many settlers.

Kalispell was still a tough frontier outpost, with all the hard, sordid characters you'd imagine. Several years after the Hoilands arrived, Fred LeBeau held up William Yoakum and his son Riley on their homestead, intending to loot their guns and provisions. However, when the Yoakums didn't cooperate, he shot both men in the gut. After a guilty verdict, the sheriff hung LeBeau on a gallows outside the county jail, with the *Kalispell Bee* offering this headline: "Execution of Fred LeBeau Was Not at All Exciting—No Thrills and Mighty Few Kicks by the Victim of Law's Revenge."

A rough place. But the land's natural beauty overwhelmed the more sordid human elements. Flathead, a lake carved by a melting glacier and tucked into the Mission Range of the Rocky Mountains, cast an enchanting spell. The valley emanated stunning beauty. Early pioneers from the East wrote home describing Flathead Valley as "the Garden of Eden." In 1830, Joshua Pilcher, a frontiersman who walked alone across the expanse of western Canada through waist-high snowdrifts in the brutal winter, penned a letter that eventually landed on President Jackson's desk. Pilcher described the wonders: "The Flathead Lake and its rich and beautiful valley . . . vie in appearance with the beautiful lakes and valleys of Switzerland." The Hoilands considered Norway's magnificence the appropriate rival, but the effect was the same. This was a land expansive and hopeful, a land that matched their souls.

William Blake believed that we become what we behold. The words could not be truer than with Eugene. This Montana landscape—the place Eugene loved, wandered in, and marveled at his entire life—fashioned him as surely as meltwater carved the basin between the mountains. The breathtaking beauty, immense solitude, and sheer physicality of the valley forged in Eugene a visceral sense of place. An *earthiness,* to use a word that would become one of his favorites.

He traversed deep into his surroundings, spending long days exploring. As a boy, he struck out on his own on Saturdays with boiled eggs, bacon, and an occasional biscuit in his pack, "looking for Indians and looking for arrowheads." The splendid grandeur of this feral country, with all the wonder and holiness it evoked, nurtured a spiritual imagination in him that was every bit as formative as what he found in his childhood Pentecostal church. Maybe more. David McCullough, Harry Truman's biographer, explained how "if you want to understand Harry Truman you'd better know a good deal about Jackson County, Missouri." Likewise, if you want to understand Eugene Peterson, you'd better know a good deal about Montana's Flathead Valley.

Late in his life, as I sat to hear Eugene describe how much time he spent wandering alone under that expansive sky, it became clear how the land's stark, solitary beauty shaped him, grounding him in a rich silence of soul. As Eugene saw it, to be a boy of Montana stock—birthed out of such grand country and immersed in the lives and histories of ordinary, hardworking people who lived close to the land without pretense— was not a mere biographical detail but an elemental piece of his life.

Decades before he admired Gregory of Nyssa or Ephraim the Syrian or any of the other great Eastern fathers and mothers of Christianity, Eugene experienced what Russian Orthodox Paul Evdokimov called "the immanence of God at work in creation."

Throughout his writings, Eugene belligerently resisted the common modern habit of severing earth from heaven, splitting the physical world from the spiritual. These convictions would come to be grounded in deep theology but were first felt as a boy as he feasted on the infinite Montana sky, inhaled the scent of aspen and Engelmann spruce, and drank crisp water from rushing streams. Montana was Eugene's birthplace. And it became his catechism.

In this way, Eugene began his life immersed in the reality of what he would one day call "the Presence." This sense of encounter had an epicenter: "two acres of holy ground" perched at the edge of Flathead Lake's "*sacred* waters." This place enveloped Eugene in the vibrant reality of a living, present God.

His dad had purchased these two acres, and this land and the cabin his dad built there rooted Eugene's young faith, baptizing him within a "sacred place where 'on earth as it is in heaven' could be prayed and practiced." And in the large view of his life, everything Eugene became flowed from that place. In his own words, this "Flathead Valley geography . . . became as important in orienting me . . . as theology and the Bible did. . . . This was the geography of my imagination." It was precisely this attention to particularity, to honoring the presence of God made visible in one place, that would later fuel his revulsion toward the commodification of church, the abstractions of impersonal life and worship, and the disembodied, mechanized approaches to the pastoral vocation.

In a meadow only a few hundred yards from his family's lakeside acres, early trappers discovered evidence of a Kootenai medicine site, "a place of visions and healings." Eugene had heard tales of supposed holy sites in the Christian tradition, "holy ground . . . soaked in the sacred where conditions were propitious for cultivating the presence of God." While Eugene didn't know what to make of such stories, he always knew the area he grew up in pulsed with a sacred beauty. "In my adolescence," Eugene wrote in his memoir, "I sometimes wondered if something like that could be going on in this place. I sometimes wonder still."

2

Mother: Those Winter Sundays

You believed in all the beauties and strengths and human associations of place; my father believed only in movement. You believed in a life of giving, he in a life of getting. . . .

"All you can do is try," you used to tell me when I was scared of undertaking something. You got me to undertake many things I would not have dared undertake without your encouragement. You also taught me how to take defeat when it came, and it was bound to now and then. You taught me that if it hadn't killed me it was probably good for me.

I can hear you laugh while you say it.

—Wallace Stegner, "Letter, Much Too Late"

Evelyn perched little Eugene on a stool in the radio booth next to her. She donned headphones and clicked on the mic, launching her Saturday program on KGEZ radio. Evelyn sang on air, played gospel music from vinyls, and vividly recounted Bible stories as if she'd witnessed them herself. Meadowlarks always sat and sang just outside, and his mom insisted they leave the studio window open so they could "get the Lord's song in a strange land." The crackling airwaves carried Evelyn's calming, melodic voice, peppered with fervent conviction, over the entire valley.

Evelyn Peterson was gregarious, passionate, lively. An emotionally sensitive woman, she abounded with energy. "She was very good looking," Eugene said, exuding warmth, "very cheerful, very hospitable." In her younger years, Evelyn was restless, always itching for a move to a new house, a move to Seattle, a different ministry or vocational challenge.

Evelyn never met anyone she considered a stranger. She constantly welcomed people into their home, inviting an incessant string of wandering souls to live with them for stretches of time. She drew and charmed people with her warmth and magnetism.

Though women rarely preached in their Pentecostal circles, Evelyn's charisma would not be contained. In addition to her duties at KGEZ, she grew a popular Sunday Bible class at Kalispell's First Assembly of God—the church her father, Andre, helped form in 1915. Evelyn's leadership and spiritual vitality drew a crowd, and she eventually formed several small Sunday evening congregations that met in Grange halls scattered throughout the valley. Loggers and miners filled these rough-hewn, makeshift churches as the men tried to hold together the thin threads of life during the ravages of the Great Depression. There they would pause for a couple of hours to hear Evelyn proclaim the good news: God had not forgotten them.

In later years, Eugene could not remember a single woman other than his mother at the meetings. Just rows of men sitting on backless benches. Many spat tobacco juice out an open window and often missed. They gathered to hear this young woman with her small boy in tow offer bold prayers, heartfelt music, and words of hope for their weary bodies and souls. Evelyn mesmerized them with her haunting contralto folk singer's voice, playing "Life Is Like a Mountain Railroad" or "When the Roll Is Called Up Yonder" on her guitar or accordion as the "lumberjacks and miners in their clomping hobnail boots, bib overalls, and flannel shirts sang along." The men "wept, honking into their red bandannas, wiping their tears without embarrassment."

It was an odd, cantankerous world in those Montana Granges. But when Evelyn opened the Bible to preach, something altogether different took place. A natural storyteller with a colorful imagination, she wove the Scriptures seamlessly into the hardscrabble life of these men who spent their days covered in soot, snow, and sawdust. And her inventive passion careened off the page. Her embellishments were so lively that years later Eugene remembered reading the Scriptures on his own and being "frequently surprised by glaring omissions in the text. The Holy Spirit left out some of the best parts." When his mother really hit her stride, her words were inflamed, poetic, rhythmic. It would be years later, when he sat under preaching in African American churches, that Eugene would hear such marvelous sermons again.

Eugene enjoyed the winter Sunday evenings best, wind pounding the walls of the rickety buildings as a barrel stove labored against the icy chill. Eugene often tended the fire while his mother tended souls. Some evenings as they left for home, with the Montana wind blasting white powder, their car would spin out in the snowdrifts. A crowd of men, eager to help the woman preacher, would push the car back onto the road, grunting and releasing blue streaks of profanity in the frigid air, then instantly turning red and stumbling over themselves with apologies.

"I heard the best preaching of my lifetime those nights—and the most colorful cursing," Eugene said. Ken, Eugene's younger brother, agreed. "I loved her preaching. I still think of her as one of the greatest preachers. She could work a phrase, *sing* through a sermon. A wonderful storyteller—dramatic. She was top notch. Even without any training." Evelyn's preaching was personal, holding listeners at the edge of their pews. She never pulled an illustration out of some glossy pastor's reference book, instead offering stories from her own experience, her life in *that* place among *those* people. It was intimate. And it made an impression on young Eugene as he fed logs to the stove on those cold nights. "My mother, without knowing what she was doing, was developing an imagination in me for being a pastor."

But the potency wasn't always easy to live with. Evelyn's spiritual fervor could be intense. This was perfectly suited to the Pentecostal tandem of emotional passion and cultural austerity—in her exuberant faith, she was determined to live free from worldly snares. But these snares were odd and erratic. As a boy, for instance, Eugene never had a birthday cake and was not allowed to listen to "dancing music." Evelyn's quest for biblical purity struck particularly hard the Christmas of 1939.

Every year in early December, Eugene's dad sharpened his axe and loaded the family (including Brownie, the spaniel) into their Ford Model A pickup for the drive to Lake Blaine in the Swan Range. Eugene picked a Douglas fir, and with only a few sharp swings, the green prize crashed to the snow. After his dad dragged the tree through the front door of the family home, Eugene pulled boxes of lights and tinsel down from the attic. They trimmed the tree, the familiar scent of evergreen filling the house. Then the crowning moment of holiday cheer arrived as Eugene ran out into the dark and across the street to feast on the glow emanating from the radiant tree in the living room window.

But 1939 was different. Unfortunately, his mother had noticed words in Jeremiah she'd never read closely before: "The customs of the people are vain: for one cutteth a tree out of the forest, the work of the hands of the workman, with the axe. They deck it with silver and with gold; they fasten it with nails and with hammers, that it move not."

The prophet had peered through the telescope of history and indicted, with precision, the Petersons' American Christmas. That year, there was no trip to Lake Blaine, no swinging axe, no tinsel, no Douglas fir lit up for the neighborhood to enjoy. Instead, Evelyn read Eugene and his little sister, Karen, the ominous warning from Jeremiah and left the Bible—open to the Nativity story—on a table in the very corner normally occupied by a glittering evergreen. Every year, the neighborhood boys went house to house, inspecting the presents piled under one another's trees. Humiliated, Eugene invented a pile of creative excuses for why he was unavailable.

Though the tree had been canceled, other holiday festivities were in full swing, including the annual gathering where Evelyn's family showed up in droves at the Petersons' for a traditional Norwegian Christmas. Here, the mother tongue and the smells of lutefisk ("cod fish with all the nutrients leached out of it by weeks of baptism in barrels of brine") and lefse ("an unleavened pliable flatbread with the texture and taste of chamois cloth") filled the house.

Uncle Ernie, Eugene's favorite relative, arrived in all his boisterous glory. He was an atheist. Uncle Ernie's irreverence beguiled Eugene. He was the only person Eugene had ever heard curse in his home and certainly the only person he ever heard joke of lifting a twenty from the offering plate at church. Only a few moments after walking through the front door, Uncle Ernie asked the only question that mattered. "Evelyn, where the hell is the Christmas tree? How the hell are we going to have a Norwegian Christmas without a tree?"

"No tree this year, brother. Just Jesus," Evelyn answered. "We are not celebrating a Norwegian Christmas this year; we are celebrating a Christian Christmas." Then, after removing the Bible from the treeless corner, she commenced reading Jeremiah. Uncle Ernie's eyes grew wider with each apocalyptic sentence. His lutefisk-muffled curses lasted throughout the holiday meal. (Without any explanation and to Eugene's profound gratitude, the Christmas tree returned to its rightful corner the following year.)

But for all her harsh literalism, Evelyn was no dour killjoy. She filled the home with laughter and energy and music. Eugene's mom played the accordion, and his dad played the tenor sax. Each Sunday afternoon at five, Evelyn would gather the family for a little ritual: listening to Charles Fuller's *Old Fashioned Revival Hour.* "I was always a little bored with Charles Fuller's preaching," Eugene recalled, "and thought the weekly reading of letters by Charles's wife 'Honey' was tedious, but it was all redeemed when the quartet sang. And I loved when Rudy Atwood hit the piano, playing 'This World Is Not My Home' and 'Old Ark's a Moverin'.'"

Evelyn was also the disciplinarian. She hung a paddle (aptly named "Old Man Paddler") on the wall so the kids could keep a leery eye on their nemesis. One of Eugene's neighborhood pals, apparently an expert on trips to the woodshed, told Eugene the secret to dodging the worst. "Just put a small shingle in your pants," his friend explained. "It softens the whack." Unfortunately, his mom wasn't fooled. "Then she really spanked me," Eugene remembered, chuckling.

What all the Peterson children remember most vividly was Evelyn's rich life of prayer. She had a closet where she spent chunks of time tucked away, on her knees. She would spend whole days of the week focusing her prayer on one of her children. Mondays were for Eugene. Tuesdays for Karen. Wednesdays for Ken. However, what made an impression wasn't only their mother's discipline of prayer but also how her conversations with God were integrated with everything she did. "Mom was very vocal," Ken remembers. "'Praise the Lord' and 'Thank you, Jesus' around the house. It freaked out some of my friends."

In 2003, Eugene, reflecting on his lifetime in the parish, wrote in his journal,

> *Mother's birthday—I almost continually have the sense that I am living out her legacy, nearly everything I do con-*

*gruent with her aspirations and passions. But I got free of
the sectarian ghetto and have had so much more* room, *such
a much larger circle of friends . . . across so many boundaries.*

And again, another entry:

*My mother's birthday—how much of her life am I living,
continuing, extending? I am immensely grateful. . . . But
sometimes I am sad over the unhappiness that she lived
with. The cramped church. The narrow marriage. With her
legacy I've been able to live with far more beauty and love
and joy.*

A legacy yielding beauty, love, and joy. No person—no theologian or intellectual or luminary—influenced Eugene more than his mother, this woman of prayer and fire and compassion. For a lifetime, his mother was the first to come to mind whenever he heard or spoke the word *pastor*.

3

The Butcher's Son

Knowing the story of your people in a kind of gossipy detail means you can name at least some of your most intimate connections to what has been called the blood of things. It means knowing the names of places, and who named them, and what happened there. In this way the incessant world is closer to becoming a territory where you might be able to take some rest.

—William Kittredge, *Hole in the Sky*

Herman and Matilda Peterson, Eugene's Swedish paternal grandparents, also immigrated by passage across the Atlantic. With the promise of jobs, the support of the Scandinavian community gathered around the Ballard neighborhood of Seattle, Washington, and a longing for a familiar expanse of ocean, they put down roots. In 1923, the Ballard Norwegians founded Fremont Tabernacle, an Assemblies of God church in East Stanwood, Washington, where the Petersons had moved. It is likely that signs and wonders occurred under that roof, but possibly none greater than when the stunning, gregarious Evelyn (who had moved to the area) caught the eye of Herman and Matilda's son, Donald. At eighteen, Don was the youngest MacMarr (later Safeway) store manager in the country, but after they married, Evelyn's brother

Harry asked Don to open a butcher shop in his new grocery. So, when Eugene was one, his family returned to Evelyn's hometown.

Don Peterson was a restless, inventive entrepreneur who had a succession of four or five stores before opening the Meat Supply Co., the thriving enterprise he owned until he retired in 1963. Don cobbled his business from nothing and muscled it through the Great Depression. Those lean years were difficult; customers wrote bad checks, and once two hooligans snuck into his red half-ton Dodge while he was making deliveries, then slipped away with a hindquarter of beef that had been perched on the front seat.

Having come from an immigrant family with few resources and then living with the scarcity of the Depression, Don determined he would build his family a solid future. But his business overwhelmed everything else in his life, including family. "Dad was a workaholic," Eugene said. Eugene remembered his dad stopping on the drive home from church on Sundays to check the meat order from the cook at the local diner. "I'll just be a minute," he'd say, dress shoes hitting the gravel as he shut the car door. From the parking lot, the family would watch Don greet the kitchen staff, holding court from a swivel stool at the counter. One of the servers invariably slid a piece of pie and steaming cup of black coffee onto the bar for him. Don joked and glad-handed while his family waited, stomachs grumbling. Finally, Evelyn would send Eugene in to retrieve him.

Beginning at age five, Eugene walked the few blocks from their house to help out at the Meat Supply Co. on Main Street. Every year, his mother made him a fresh apron out of old flour sacks to keep him clean. Eugene polished the glass cases of the shop, swept sawdust from the floor, and carried out the trash. "One of Dad's butchers would pick me up and stand me on an upended orange crate before the big, red Hobart meat grinder," Eugene recalled later, "and I . . . would push chunks of beef into its maw." Eugene had spent several years proving himself dependable, and so Eugene's dad handed him a razor-edged knife and pointed him to a liver for carving. The boy was eventually entrusted with pigs, deer, and sides of beef, trimming and parting them out for packaging with meticulous precision.

The butcher shop introduced Eugene to a way of seeing. Besides allowing him to participate in his father's world, the shop provided companionship and a community where he was seen, tended to, welcomed. The butchers working there were more than his father's employees; they became Eugene's teachers. Eddie Nordcrist, a true craftsman, taught him that if he ever cut himself, it was because he did not "know" his knife. Butchering, Eddie insisted, was an art, requiring patience, attention, and years of practice. "Carving a quarter of beef into roasts and steaks was not a matter of imposing my knife-fortified will on dumb matter," Eugene remembered, "but respectfully and reverently entering into the reality of the material." Those who failed to respect the craft and their tools and the uniqueness of each slab of meat lying on the cutting table in front of them suffered his father's disdain. "Hackers," he'd mutter.

Herb Thiel, however, was Eugene's favorite teacher in the shop, a man with a "flat, expressionless face disfigured by a bad eye, milky and sunken." Since he didn't wear an eye patch, his "face looked like a tombstone, with that dead eye engraved on it, so everyone called him Tombstone." However, his other name, the one preferred among the butchers, was the Killer. The Killer was tough as nails. "There was something rakish about being in the company of a man sometimes called Tombstone and other times the Killer," Eugene said. Once, Eugene stood next to the Killer as he cut pork loin with a band saw. The Killer misjudged the blade and sliced off two of his fingers. Stopping the saw calmly, he looked down at his limp, disconnected appendages. Expressionless and silent, the Killer picked up his fingers, wrapped them in

19

butcher paper, and walked across the street to the doctor's office. "Put 'em back on," he instructed.

The butcher shop flowed with the routines of small-town life and was frequented by common folks without pretension or flowery language. "I didn't grow up with sophisticated language," Eugene said. These earthy and varying influences meant that as the Bible came alive to him, it was not as some Elizabethan artifact but as a living book, appropriate for the gritty lives of butchers, cement layers, radio-preaching mothers, and the drunks who lounged in the alley behind the shop amid empty bottles of Thunderbird whiskey.

"That butcher shop was my introduction into the world of congregation," Eugene said. "The people who came into our shop were not just customers. Something else defined them. It always seemed more like a congregation than a store." And while his father's passive disconnection was palpable at home, in the store Eugene saw him—and learned from him—at his best. His father treated each person with kindness, those who became true friends as well as those who incessantly fussed over the bacon or hovered over the trimming and weighing. Don Peterson welcomed all his customers as they were, valuing them, whether they unfolded crisp bills for the finest rib eyes or fished in their pockets for coins and walked out with packages of hot dogs. He treated each person with dignity, whether an elder from the Methodist church or one of the women from the brothel a couple of blocks away (Eugene remembered making deliveries to Mary, Grace, and Veronica).

Eugene later viewed his father's work as priestly work and considered it one of his dad's great gifts to him. This priestly connection was visceral, as Eugene saw Old Testament images from church (priests slaughtering the sacrifices) woven with the work his father did six days out of the week. The butcher shop was a place, as he would later describe the church, with "a lot of misfits

and oddballs." It placed him, day after day, in a context of un-
spectacular ordinariness—and he learned to see it as holy.

Oddly enough, the one person who didn't seem to fit in the
butcher shop was Eugene's pastor. He didn't visit Don's establishment often, but when he did, he arrived with a sanctimonious air
and put-on language, which were out of place with the plainspo-
ken character of everyone else. Notably, his visits typically happened whenever an itinerant evangelist or missionary visited
town. The pastor would "get [his] father off to the side, put his
arm across his shoulders, and say in the same 'spiritual' voice that
he always used when he prayed, 'Brother Don, the Lord has laid it
on my heart that this poor servant of God hasn't been eating all
that well lately and would be greatly blessed with one of your fine
steaks.'" Eugene recalled how his father, "ever generous, always
gave him two. I never heard my father complain, but I could see
the other meat cutters wink and exchange knowing looks, and I
was embarrassed for my pastor who seemed so out of place in this
holy place of work."

As Don Peterson's business prospered, so did his community commitments. He received an appointment to the board of the Salvation Army, became a board member of Evangel College, and
served for many years with the Gideons. In addition to playing the
tenor sax, Don served the church as Sunday school superintendent. For a brief political stint, he even served as cochair of a
congressional candidate's finance committee.

Don's best energy was always directed somewhere other than
home. His prosperity overshadowed what Eugene most needed: a
dad who knew and loved his son. "I worked for my dad whenever
I could, after school and on weekends," Eugene recalled. "I loved

the work. Dad took care of his help. He was generous and sensitive to his employees. But he wasn't a very good father." Though Eugene was a star athlete in high school, excelling at both track and basketball, his dad never once showed up at the gym on a Friday night or sat in the stands to watch Eugene run. Once, a day after a meet where Eugene broke a long-standing state track record, Eugene and his dad walked down Main Street in Kalispell. A friend jogged up, beaming and eager, and slapped Eugene on the back. "Gene," his friend bellowed, "*that* was an *amazing* race." "Thanks!" Eugene replied.

As his friend walked away, Don was puzzled. "Eugene, what was he talking about?" The question was too much. Eugene's long-simmering resentment seethed, and he walked away, refusing to answer. In later years Eugene mourned the fact that over his father's lifetime, his dad wrote him only one letter—and it was because he was concerned about a disagreement with Eugene's mother and wanted advice. He could not remember his dad hugging him or ever saying "I love you" or "I'm proud of you."

Even after retirement, Don worked real estate part time from a small office downtown. He was always tending to clients, always working the deal. Decades later, Eugene would experience this same compulsion to achieve, would recognize the menace this demand for accomplishment could cast over a life. Like his father, he wanted to win, to accomplish, to be respected as competent and successful—in the center of things. But Eugene, thinking back to the hole where a father's love was supposed to rest, would come to resist with fierceness the depersonalizing, relationship-killing effect that the American business model brought to his soul and to the church. Work and achievement could be a seductive addiction, as burning and deep as a bottle of Thunderbird.

We often parent the way we were parented, and the fact is that Don Peterson's dad was not a very good father either. Don's mother, Matilda, whom he barely remembered, spent years in a mental asylum in Sioux City, Iowa, where she died, mostly wiped clear from the family history. Don's father, Herman, broken himself, nursed his pain with the bottle. Herman was a skilled craftsman, a master carpenter who fashioned beauty out of fir, oak, and spruce, an aptitude passed down to Don and then to Eugene as well. However, Herman stayed sober only for brief stretches. He split his time living in Seattle with his daughter and in Kalispell with Don. Every so often, Don's sister would call. "Come and get Papa," she'd say, explaining how Herman had spiraled down into another bender. Eugene's memories of his grandfather and his dad's brother were that they "were both drunks."

While living with Eugene's family in Kalispell, Grandpa Herman built a garage and enclosed a front porch, with Eugene tagging along and learning the carpenter's trade. Grandpa Herman carried a jackknife, whittling "tops from empty spools of thread and animals from scrap lumber" as gifts for Eugene. He slept in Eugene's room on the bed, while Eugene slept on the floor. Eugene recalled a particularly odorous night when Grandpa Herman came home after many hours belly to the bar. Eugene woke to the stench of vomit and defecation spewed across his floor, with his grandfather lying in his own filth. Holding his nose against the stink, Eugene was overcome—not by disgust but by sorrow for this man he loved.

One early morning, Don received a desperate call from his sister, and he took Eugene with him on the drive to Seattle. When they arrived, Grandpa Herman was dead, the casualty of a drunken brawl. At the funeral, Eugene's aunt Helen "fell on the casket, cradling his face in her hands and sobbing, 'Papa, Papa, Papa, oh, Papa, oh Papa . . .' " Years later, Eugene reflected on the impact: "I think now that every alcoholic I have ever met was my grandpa."

On the drive back to Kalispell, Eugene's dad stared ahead, silent. Eugene, confused and heartbroken, sat in his seat, watching out the window. Two lonely souls drove in silence together across empty miles.

This aloneness—even when they were together—became a theme. Each year, Don gathered friends for a deer hunting trip in the mountains. With tents lined in rows, they sat around the crackling fire, swapping stories. Eugene woke each morning to the aroma of sausage sizzling in the cast-iron skillet and pancakes frying on the griddle. Eugene reveled in these days, but even then, he wandered the silent woods alone. "Nearly every day, I'd spot a deer," Eugene remembered, "but I couldn't bring myself to shoot." Instead, Eugene raised his rifle to the sky and fired, startling the deer into the brush. Each afternoon, he'd stroll back into camp, hanging his head. "It got away from me," he'd say. Eugene never told a soul how he was merely scattering deer for miles around.

Vowing never to repeat his father's tragic life, Don Peterson never picked up the bottle. And alongside industriousness, Don also modeled effusive generosity. Often, when Don heard of people in need of a house, he'd hand stunned neighbors the keys to a small property he'd purchased or rent them the house at slashed rates. But still, the aloneness between Don and Eugene remained.

Once, Don arrived home with a springer spaniel puppy tucked into a cardboard box. To Eugene's dismay, his dad had already named the puppy, and young Eugene hated the name. "A bad name," he recounted. Eugene melted into despair and would not be consoled. After half an hour of protests and tears, his father relented. "Name the dog whatever you like," he said. Brownie became Eugene's constant companion.

It's possible the puppy was a father's attempt to reach out to his son in the midst of heart-shattering grief. When Eugene was four, his two-year-old sister, Lois, contracted pneumonia, enduring agonizing days in the hospital before dying. Eugene adored Lois, entertaining her with flips and handstands in the yard. After Eugene's parents arrived home, heartsick with the horrific news, sadness descended over the house. A few days after his sister's death, his mom found Eugene in the backyard turning flips and somersaults, pausing between gymnastic feats to peer into the sky. He'd wave and call out, "Do you see me, Lois? Do you see me?"

In 1946, Don Peterson bought two acres south of Kalispell on Flathead Lake and began to build the family cabin. Though only thirteen, Eugene loaded supplies from O'Neil Lumber Company into their GMC truck and delivered them to the edge of the cliff. He honed his craft with saw and hammer alongside his father. In the evenings the rest of the family joined them as they laid down their tools and sat overlooking the mirror of water with a spread of chicken and potato salad.

Sitting in that same cabin, his head now gray and hands withered, he recalled that summer spent building with his father as the singular experience when the two of them shared a meaningful connection, shoulder to shoulder through salty sweat and the long Montana summer hours—pausing to catch their breath, to drop their shoulders and look out from that silent, holy place over the magnificent lake and mountains. That summer there were few words, but few were needed. Perhaps that summer offers another reason why the cabin, in such an engrossing way, was always Eugene's true home, always the place where he belonged, always the place where—in need of grounding and in an effort to escape notoriety and other seductions—he returned. Maybe there his connection to his father lingered. Maybe that was some of the peace and connectedness tied to the cabin. Maybe that connection is part of the fabric of the place that would one day be called Selah House.

4

The Nature of the Search

What is the nature of the search? you ask.

Really it is very simple, at least for a fellow like me; so simple that it is easily overlooked.

The search is what anyone would undertake if he were not sunk in the everydayness of his own life. This morning, for example, I felt as if I had come to myself on a strange island. And what does such a castaway do? Why, he pokes around the neighborhood and he doesn't miss a trick.

To become aware of the possibility of the search is to be onto something. Not to be onto something is to be in despair.

—**Walker Percy,** *The Moviegoer*

Two years after the death of little Lois, Eugene, then six, was thrilled when another sister, Karen, was born. Kenneth completed the trio, as Eugene at age twelve found himself with a bright-eyed younger brother.

Eugene enjoyed being the older brother. He delighted in watching out for his siblings. Once, the big brother loaded Karen on the back of his bike for a ride down Kalispell's side streets, pedaling as fast as he dared. But Karen's legs grew tired, and she jammed a foot into the spokes. The bike seized and flung them to the pavement, grinding her bare skin against metal and gravel. "I screamed like I was being killed," Karen recalled. Bits of rock peppered her flesh and a piece of bone poked through as she splayed on the road, screaming and panicking. Eugene scooped her into his arms and carried her the entire way home. That was Eugene the brother, naturally drawn to act in the presence of suffering. He took his role as firstborn seriously, the one to keep watch and care for the family.

This included his mother, whose brave, ebullient exterior obscured a deep well of pain. Though Evelyn brought rich emotional presence into the Peterson home, it did not assuage the ache Eugene felt for his there-but-not-there father. "Even then, I was aware that I would wish for more with my dad, but I never talked to my mom about my dad," Eugene said. Evelyn apparently felt much the same, experiencing deep loneliness in her marriage. When Eugene was ten, Evelyn took Eugene and Karen to Weldon, Saskatchewan, to stay with her sister, a drastic attempt to get her husband's attention. The trip was an adventure but also profoundly unsettling, with their mother enacting a scandalous separation from their dad. Eugene's fifteen-year-old cousin met them at the train station in Prince Albert at midnight and drove them (in a horse-drawn sleigh) to the house—where they stayed for six weeks. "My mother was very sensitive," Eugene told me. "She would talk to me about my dad. He worked long hours, was often home late. He loved working, and having a good business means you work hard." But of course, those hours away inflicted pain at home, and Evelyn's marital loneliness added to Eugene's burden. "At one point in my life I realized that for some time (maybe halfway through high school and into university), she treated me more like a husband than a son: confiding in me, leaning on me for emotional support. I just thought it was natural, what mothers did."

There was a deeper story, of course. Evelyn's heart had been broken by another man, who had abandoned her in a very different way early in her life. While Ernie, the atheist, was Eugene's favorite uncle, he never met his mother's favorite brother, Sven. With her vivid, animated stories, Evelyn painted Sven as a gregarious brother who took her on horseback rides and regaled her with magical tales from Norway. The town milkman, Sven greeted his neighbors with effusive cheer. If it hadn't been for the milk cart, you'd have thought him the mayor.

So, where was he? Dead, and Eugene had so many questions. Eventually, digging past the cloak of grief and secrecy around Sven, Eugene went outside the family for answers. Young Eugene dove into the dusty library stacks in Kalispell, where, in yellowed editions of the *Daily Inter Lake,* he eventually pieced together the story.

Eugene's aunt Myrtle, evidencing a horrific run of fate, endured the death of her first husband, who was murdered on the *Eureka* ferry in California. After selling their property, she gathered her nest egg and made her way to Montana, where she married twenty-three-year-old Sven. Immediately, Sven began burning through Myrtle's money. And once, Myrtle walked in on Sven in bed with another woman. Their wedding night, however, offered an especially bad omen. Sven disappeared, then returned to his angry and distraught bride at 4:00 a.m. He'd been drinking into the wee hours and came home belligerent, with a gun strapped to his belt, and beat his wife. Sven told Myrtle he'd "tame her as he had tamed lots of other women," a threat he made more than once.

They had been married all of six weeks when after a late night at the bar, Sven returned to their room at the Bienz Hotel, soused. And in an especially foul mood. Sven crawled into bed, shoving his revolver under the pillow. Tempers flared. Sven, angry about the money running dry, told Myrtle to get out on the street and use her body to replenish their cash. Myrtle refused. As their fight escalated, Sven punched her. Myrtle grabbed the revolver and fired one shot, slicing Sven's right ear. Blood gushed, Sven charged, and Myrtle fired three more rounds before Sven hit the cold floor. When the sheriff arrived, he found a terrified Myrtle standing in her nightgown over Sven's dead body.

When the trial commenced four months later, the courtroom overflowed, men lining the walls. Judge Thompson cautioned that the testimony would not be "congenial to the finer senses . . . if there are any women present who'd like to leave, now would be the time." Other than one young woman escorted out by the bailiff, the room remained packed, townsfolk leaning forward to hear every scurrilous detail. The jury acquitted Myrtle, and the next day she boarded the first train out of town. The family never heard from her again.

The tragedy revealed shadier parts of Eugene's family history, providing him one of his first close encounters with human complexity: We can be both good and violent at the same time. One person can bring both joy and sadness into the world. In high school, dreaming of becoming a novelist, Eugene thought Sven's story provided the material for an explosive book. While he never wrote a novel, eventually Sven's sad tale did make its way into his work:

> When I finally did become a pastor, I was surprised at how thoroughly Sven had inoculated me against "one answer" systems of spiritual care. . . .
>
> Thanks to Sven, I was being prepared to understand a congregation as a gathering of people that requires a context as large as the Bible itself if we are to deal with the ambiguities of life in the actual circumstances in which peo-

ple live them. . . . For me, my congregation would become a
work-in-progress—a novel in which everyone and everything is connected in a salvation story in which Jesus has the
last word. No reductions to stereotype.

Eugene's care extended beyond his biological family. When he was
a teenager, Eugene's mother drafted him into visiting the elderly
Sister Lydron from their church. Sister Lydron lived in a fern-
covered house with lace curtains and drawn blinds. Evelyn sent
her son to check on the old woman, always with a casserole or
cookies in hand. Eugene recounted, *Once as I sat in her rocking
chair, making small talk—which I was never very good at . . . she
asked me to pray for her. I remember still the sense of "fit"—that
this was what I was made for—that this is who I was at my core
being.* This intimate, unhurried relationship. This ease of prayer
and presence. At a young age, Eugene felt these early stirrings of
who he truly was long before he had any vocabulary to explain it.

Eugene instinctively moved toward people on the fringes. He regularly took the short stroll to Meridian Road to play chess with a
neighbor boy who was wheelchair bound. In church youth group,
Eugene inevitably found himself with whoever was sitting alone.
And he even found his way to the dogs that were outcasts. An old
English bulldog named Sarge always sat in front of the Pastime Bar
on Main Street. Drunks poured Sarge a bowl of beer, and by noon
he'd be as drunk as they were. Whenever Eugene delivered hamburger to the bar, he contrived schemes to rescue the poor dog.

When Eugene was ten, a scandal hit the neighborhood. A man
who lived across the street from the Petersons caught his son in a

sexual interlude with a goat. There were only whispers among Eugene and his friends, but everyone knew the boy's father tore into him with fury. That night, the boy hung himself. Eugene never forgot the story, always saddened when he remembered the boy's isolation and shame. Whereas most young men would mock the tragedy or stuff it down inside, the heartbreak of it stoked compassion in Eugene's young heart.

In high school, every Saturday Eugene loaded the truck with trash from the butcher shop and hauled bloody meat boxes and rolls of soiled butcher paper to the dump. The garbage facility's caretaker was an elderly man with developmental challenges. He lived in a small cabin on site and always invited Eugene in, wanting to show him the trinkets he kept in his one-room shanty. Most Saturdays, Eugene carried a .22 rifle with him for target practice, taking aim at the rats scurrying over mounds of refuse. Eugene shot the rats, and the caretaker cheered. "There was something so childlike about him," Eugene remembered later.

One afternoon the man made a move on Eugene, attempting to touch him sexually. Shocked, Eugene rebuffed the advance. However, he would not reject the lonely man. And, though it was surely unwise and by no means a template for how to engage someone exhibiting predatory behavior, Eugene returned to the dump on occasion, pulling out his .22 to knock off vermin and give the lonely caretaker reason to cheer. "How could you not accept someone like that into your life?" Eugene explained.

Eugene wasn't always so generous, however. Cecil Zachary, the elementary school bully, lived in a log home with a "yard littered with rusted-out pickups and cars," a couple of hundred yards past the Petersons on South Meridian. Eugene had ventured into the Zachary home only once, when Cecil's mother invited Eugene and two friends in from the bitter cold to warm by the woodstove and savor a bowl of moose meat chili. Eugene was in awe of, and slightly terrified by, the older, larger-than-life boy who wore a red flannel even in summer and "walked with something of a swagger that [Eugene] admired and tried to imitate." When Eugene showed up for first grade, Cecil taunted him, cornering him after school and pounding him black and blue. Eugene endured beatings for months, repeating to himself biblical mantras to bless those who persecute you and to turn the other cheek. Finally, one blustery March day when Cecil cornered Eugene yet again in a vacant lot, something exploded inside him.

> That's when it happened. Totally uncalculated. Totally out of character. Something snapped within me. For just a moment the Bible verses disappeared from my consciousness and I grabbed [Cecil]. To my surprise, and his, I realized that I was stronger than he was. I wrestled him to the ground, sat on his chest, and pinned his arms to the ground with my knees. I couldn't believe it—he was helpless under me. At my mercy. It was too good to be true. I hit him in the face with my fists. It felt good, and I hit him again—blood spurted from his nose, a lovely crimson on the snow. By this time all the other children were cheering, egging me on. "Black his eyes!" "Bust his teeth!" A torrent of biblical invective poured from them.

> But the real action was yet to happen.

> I said to [Cecil], "Say 'Uncle.'" He wouldn't say it. I hit him again. More blood. More cheering. Now my audience was bringing the best out of *me*. And then my Christian training reasserted itself. I said, "Say, 'I believe in Jesus Christ as my Lord and Savior.'" He wouldn't say it. I hit him again. More

blood. I tried again, "Say 'I believe in Jesus Christ as my Lord and Savior.'"

And he said it. [Cecil Zachary] was my first Christian convert.

In 2006, Eugene preached at an Episcopal church in Bigfork, Montana, and told the story of his childhood fisticuffs. After the service, a woman approached him and told him that Cecil lived just blocks away and had died six weeks earlier, a faithful Christian. "I felt a little vindicated in my evangelistic strategies," Eugene said. But that would be the first and last time he punched the gospel into someone.

Perhaps Eugene moved toward outsiders because he felt like one himself. From the time he was a boy, he spent vast amounts of time alone, tramping through the woods or curled among the dusty stacks at the redbrick Carnegie Library in Kalispell, one of 2,500 libraries Andrew Carnegie built across the United States. Eugene disliked school, but he loved books, and his curiosity was insatiable. Under the Carnegie's rotunda at age eleven or twelve, he pulled out Kant's *Critique of Practical Reason* and Durant's *Story of Philosophy*. Engrossed, he read for hours. Though he could barely string the words together, the sheer depth and audacity of ideas enchanted him. Eugene discovered the naturalists John Muir and Henry David Thoreau, who gave voice to the depths of spirit encountered in the untamed world. Emily Dickinson launched his lifelong love affair with poetry. And fiction— where to begin? He was captivated. James Fenimore Cooper, Leo Tolstoy, Charles Dickens, A. B. Guthrie Jr., Nathaniel Hawthorne, and Herman Melville. These writers fed a passion for story in young Eugene. For years he imagined himself a budding novelist, weaving stories out of words in his mind. In the Carnegie, Eugene's imagination swept into a vast and wild interior country.

Even as a toddler, Eugene had been drawn to the wild, free Montana landscape, as well as the solitude. When his mother was distracted, he had often slipped out of the yard and wandered through the neighborhood. (Exasperated, his mom eventually devised a plan, attaching a rope from his waist to the clothesline strung post to post. Eugene could ramble the width of the yard but no farther.) After Don built the cabin, with his teenage son by his side, Eugene spent days there alone, with only his thoughts and the lake for company.

In junior high, during one brief year when the family returned to Seattle, Eugene spent his free time catching the bus alone into downtown Seattle. Every Saturday, Eugene pocketed his $1.50 allowance and rode the bus to Smith Tower, a thirty-eight-story skyscraper, the tallest building on the West Coast until Seattle built the Space Needle. Eugene strolled the streets under the tower's shadow, a solitary boy watching the people and feeling the pulse of the city. As he walked through the grand doors of the Bon Marché and past the perfume counters, the haberdashery, and rows and rows of shoes, Eugene's eyes grew wide at the seven stories of glamor and sophistication. Then he continued on to Frederick & Nelson, past glass counters filled with watches and silver earrings, and peeked into the bustling tearoom, ogling stacks of Frango chocolates. Next were the stamp shops, where he added a piece or two to his collection. Then the waterfront to watch the ships. Seattle was a magical world that felt so far from Kalispell, and Eugene experienced it entirely on his own. The urban energy opened his eyes to other cultures and a wider world. As he slipped unnoticed among the mass of people, Seattle also taught him that one doesn't need woods and vast skies to experience interior silence. One can experience solitude even in the midst of the boisterous throng.

The city spoke to something in the boy. But it was always the Montana wild that beckoned him. "I was a roamer," Eugene remembered later, with a glint of the old freedom in his eye. North of Kalispell, a community of indigenous Confederated Salish and Kootenai Tribes camped, attempting to maintain a remnant of what their life was like before whites decimated the buffalo and created the Flathead Reservation.

Rows of hand-fashioned tepees lined the Stillwater River as the community hunted the Mission Range, crafted leather and beaded goods, and traded meat, hides, pelts, and crafts in town. Though these tribes were Eugene's neighbors, wedded to the history of the place long before Kalispell's existence, Eugene remembered the stark divisions. The only Native American Eugene knew by name was Prettyfeather, a woman who came to the butcher shop every Saturday, wearing moccasins on her feet and a handwoven blanket wrapped around her shoulders. Prettyfeather pulled buffalo nickels from the leather pouch hanging from her neck in exchange for pickled pigs' feet, chitlins, blood sausage, pork liver, and ham hocks. This was Eugene's only encounter with the tribes, and his dad had a strict rule: stay away from the camp. But curiosity tugged at him.

One spring afternoon, that curiosity won. Eugene and their pastor's son slipped out of town and pedaled toward the forbidden north, hearts thumping. Stirred up by overactive imaginations steeped in outrageous stereotypes, they were terrified they would be caught and massacred by face-painted warriors. Pushing through their fear, they sneaked close enough to get a peek. After a few minutes of spying on the camp from the cover of trees, they lost their nerve, crawled back to their bikes, and turned toward home. But on the ride back, Eugene was no longer afraid of being

ambushed by warriors. It was the thought of getting caught by his
dad that had him pedaling like mad for home.

Each time a car passed, the boys slowed, squinting to see if it
was Eugene's dad's. If it bore more than a passing resemblance,
they tossed their bikes in the ditch and hopped after them until the
driver motored past. After several scares, another vehicle crested
the horizon. Eugene, eyes straining, saw it was the wrong color.
Relieved, they cycled onward. They couldn't have known that Don's
car was in the shop. He'd borrowed a friend's—and just happened
to be heading to town that same fateful hour. "That's the first time
my dad ever spanked me," Eugene recalled. "Right there on the side
of the road." Eugene paused, remembering the most distressful fact
of all: "But the preacher's kid got off scot-free."

Eugene was always off on some adventure, and he often pulled a
friend along with him. Jerry Olsen was a constant companion
during high school. Jerry was the barber's son, his father an imposing presence who chain-smoked cigarettes while chatting with
customers and snipping sharp scissors round their heads, their
hair falling like leaves. Like the butcher shop, the Olsen barber-
shop was a rough and human place. To Eugene, this made it holy.

Jerry and Eugene were ecstatic when Big Mountain ski resort
opened in Whitefish, twenty-six miles to the north. Eugene drove
a Chevy coupe, fitted with a rumble seat. "I was the only kid
in my crowd who had a car," Eugene said with a little grin. As
soon as Big Mountain opened, Saturdays found Eugene and Jerry
crammed with five other guys in the tiny car, snaking up the icy
roads of the treacherous mountain. Though Big Mountain had
only one run and a single T-bar lift to drag them to the summit,
they skied as often as they could, a pack of pimply madmen flying
down the mountain.

In high school, Eugene had lots of friends and was well liked. He was athletic, friendly, and had the bearing, even then, of a quiet leader. But he never shook the sense of otherness that had been with him since boyhood. He just didn't quite fit.

It wasn't that he was withdrawn. Quite the opposite. He joined the cast of the Flathead High School Yule program. He played cornet in the band. He participated in a mock trial during a school-wide assembly, overseen by the heavy gavel of the Honorable Judge John Engebretson.

And, of course, he was *fast*. He was the star middle-distance runner on the track team, noted by the *Daily Inter Lake* as a champion with "spectacular upsets" in the 440 and 880 at the Polson Invitational. The sports page even mourned Eugene's absence from practice during his trip to Columbus, Ohio, for the annual convention of the Key club (a national student leadership organization). Somehow, Eugene even found time to letter as a guard on the basketball team.

But he still felt like an outsider. This likely was due in part to his rigid Pentecostal upbringing that caused him to view others with suspicion. But it was also *him*. The sense of not quite fitting in was part of his interior reality, an inner quality that would eventually shape his gifting and legacy.

An afternoon of kayaking when Eugene was seventy-three years old returned him to his boyhood.

We took the kayaks to Tally Lake yesterday . . . the deepest lake (500 ft) in Montana. My first visit. . . . When I was a boy all my Boy Scout friends talked of Tally Lake every summer—it's where they went for Boy Scout camp. When Jan asked me why I wanted to visit I spontaneously said, "Because I was always an outsider." I hadn't thought of

*that before. But it rings true—that old Pentecostal outsider
feeling, never being on the "inside"—has never really gone
away. That and my dad's indifference to me, account for a
lot of who I am, of who I've become.*

And he experienced further revelation after his high school's
fortieth class reunion.

*Went to 40th H.S. class reunion last night at Big Mt. . . .
Mingling and making small talk with those old classmates
brought on the old feelings of social devastation—
outsiderness—that I escaped when leaving Kalispell. I
wanted so much to be part of the inner ring—and would
have been welcomed most likely—but the sectarian mind-
set, so etched in me, wouldn't permit it. And so I re-
experienced that isolation and emotional pain—left
outedness. I wonder how much that is in my psyche still—an
outsider's stance, an exile's boundary experience?*

Growing up, Eugene felt a kind of spiritual exile as well. Among
Pentecostals, speaking in tongues (glossolalia) was the touchstone
experience for the truly faithful. And Eugene longed to be faithful. However, despite many attempts, he could not pray in tongues.
His "failure" plagued him.

John Wright Follette, a Pentecostal teacher, stayed with the
Petersons for the summer when Eugene was fifteen. Follette, "a
small, birdlike man," was a Pentecostal mystic, a teacher on deep
matters of the soul and life with God. In awe of Follette, Eugene
told his mother that he wanted to talk to him, and she encouraged
him to go out to where Follette was lying in the hammock. Eugene
timidly approached and asked, "Dr. Follette, how do you pray?"

The teacher didn't even open his eyes. He just grinned and grunted. "I haven't prayed in forty years!"

"That stunned me," Eugene recounted decades later. "I walked off totally puzzled."

Over the years, however, the shock of that moment unfolded profound wisdom.

> You see, anything he had told me I would have imitated. I would have done what he said he did and thought that's what prayer is. He risked something to teach me what prayer was, and I'm glad he did. Prayer wasn't something he did—it was something he was. He lived a life of prayer. It took me about six or seven years to understand what he had done. But it was sure better than wasting time trying to imitate what he did.

The summer before leaving for college in Seattle, Eugene landed a job with the Department of Street Maintenance. Working the night shift alone on the dark streets under the stars, Eugene watered the grassy medians lined with Norway maples and a few cottonwoods, which cut swaths through the main thoroughfares. Occasionally a trucker blew through, ignoring the speed limit, blasting his horn, and sending Eugene diving for the curb. Eugene had only just received his high school diploma, but his spiritual hunger and awareness exposed a remarkable intuitiveness. With these solitary midnight rhythms, it's as though he were a brother keeping hours with the abbot.

> The monks know what they are doing when they get up at two in the morning to pray Lauds. . . . All summer long I kept vigil, took lessons in being a monk, present to hear the first birdsong, catch the first hint of light coming up from behind the Swan Range of the Rocky Mountains.

I never became a monk, but I got a feel for it that summer.

And what was he actually doing those nights as he lugged hoses and sprayed grass? He was memorizing the Psalms, encountering the bleak night as his own version of the Psalter's wasteland, experiencing the sun peeking over the eastern horizon in the same way the psalmist yearned for God to awaken the new dawn. Somehow these texts became more than lines for memorizing or for acquiring some spiritual benefit; they opened an expansive world into which Eugene entered. Like Israel and Judah and Canaan, Kalispell, too, was a holy place.

"When I left home for college after that summer's work," Eugene wrote late in life, "I left a holy land. The streets and trails, the hills and mountains, the rivers and lakes—all were holy ground, the valley that I had grown up in was sacred space. It still is." But Eugene would also find God in a new geography. Seattle would be the next speck of holy ground, the place where his search would continue.

Eugene had heard much about Seattle Pacific College (now Seattle Pacific University). He felt drawn to it. Seattle was familiar—and wondrous—territory. He appreciated that the school had a growing reputation for integrating faith with rigorous study. Though Eugene could not yet name exactly *what* this fire was that burned in his bones, he sensed a magnetic pull toward the truth and beauty he felt must lie at the core of things. He was, as I look back at his life now, searching for something to expand his vistas, something to kindle his yearning to know—no, to *be part of*—what was real.

This yearning for what was real was not for Eugene merely adolescent self-discovery but an essential element of his internal fiber. In these formative years—with his siblings or his friends, with his curiosity about the hardships of life on the reservation, with his questions for Rev. Follette on that hammock, with those boyhood afternoons alone roaming Seattle's swarming streets, with Cecil on that vacant lot—Eugene had an insatiable desire for the real, the concrete. Past any pretenses. Deeper than the surface. Beyond everything trite or theoretical. Eugene was always searching, always open to more, always on a quest for things that were true and solid. Eugene always had more questions—and a deep well of wonder over the many possibilities he might encounter—than answers. This is one reason Eugene was so (frustratingly) reluctant to dispense advice, why he so detested celebrity: he knew these postures of the ego-driven expert were lies and illusions. And this is why Eugene would rather pray with someone than argue theology, why he'd be eager for a call from his neighbor while letting prominent figures go to his answering machine: friendship (with God and one another) is *real*.

Over my years with Eugene, I can't tell you how many times he *didn't* answer some question that I posed, some burning concern that I insisted required resolution. It wasn't so much that Eugene refused to respond, but somehow, we'd always find ourselves talking about something different. Somehow—and I really can't tell you how this happened—a half hour later we'd be talking about another matter altogether. Eugene, I see now, was not being aloof or obstinate but rather was on the search for truer questions, looking for how God was appearing in our actual life, our actual conversation . . . right then, right there. Eugene was on the search, and he wanted to take me with him. One of my favorite images of Eugene is him on their dock, in Bermuda swim trunks, withered skin white as a lily, preparing to dive into the lake. That is how Eugene lived his entire life: diving into the water, headfirst into the deep, into what was real.

But at this juncture, that restless search was just beginning. Eugene's family and Montana home had given him love, along with pain. He'd learned openness and wonder. He knew the ache of longing and the scent of wildness as well as he knew the shape of Mount Aeneas or the smell of pine.

Still he yearned. And the yearning, like the current of a slow but steady stream, carried him on.

5

Great Promise in Seattle

The sky in Seattle is so low, it felt like God had lowered
a silk parachute over us. Every feeling I ever knew was
up in that sky.
—Maria Semple, *Where'd You Go, Bernadette?*

In September 1950, Eugene walked through the chilling wind and
boarded the Great Northern Railway, the same line that had carried his family into Montana nearly half a century earlier. Rum-
bling through vast stretches of rugged land, he watched out the
window, lost in the quiet of his mind, as rhythmic miles clicked
past. Golden plains stretched toward jagged mountains enveloped
in green forest; a yawning blue sky was dotted with puffs of gray
from the engine stack. The severe country, cued by autumn's crisp
air and fleeting sunlight, seemed poised for its annual surrender.
The land, like Eugene, sat at that thin edge, the moment when one
kind of life ends and another begins.

Though classes would not begin until September 27, Seattle
Pacific University (SPU) freshmen were required to arrive early for
the Frosh Week orientation. Eugene, a suitcase in each hand, felt
the crunch of fall leaves as he walked toward Alexander Hall, his
new home. "I knew no one," Eugene recalled later, during his senior year. "There was a big empty feeling inside of me." And yet,
stepping on campus, Eugene already carried a burning question:

I wonder how you become the student body president of this place?

Ken remembers his brother as "full of ambition. He had a large personality." And Eugene's brother-in-law, Miles Finch, assured me that Eugene's humility was "a learned trait." During college, Eugene explained his drive and aspiration: "I like people who act like they know where they're going. I like people who live aggressively—who have a purpose. I want to be that kind of person." And with the new ambition came the slightest personal rebrand. Across the top of his fall 1951 registration card, Eugene scribbled *Eugene Hoiland Peterson*, trying to pivot away from Gene, the name his family and friends knew him by. "Jan's the only one I like to use it," he told me.

These first few weeks at Seattle Pacific were a whirlwind. Campus life, athletics, and an aggressive academic schedule kept his days packed. On top of those commitments, Eugene's classmates elected him as freshman representative to the student council. He played his cornet in the Trumpet Trio. He made the frosh basketball team and immediately made an impression in track with his 440 time. While the world would come to know Eugene as a pastor and writer, college friends remember him as athletic and popular. Eugene's first college yearbook picture bears an uncanny resemblance to the original all-American Archie cartoon: wavy hair, muscular jaw, and a smile that seems to stretch for miles.

Eugene struck a quick friendship with Ben Moring, one of only two black students in their class. Ben grew up on the streets of Philadelphia, where he set up his shoeshine box on the corner, trading a wax and buff for dimes. He'd return home hungry, hands stained brown and black, unable to wash off the sharp smell of polish. Maybe handling so many shoes had some magic in it, because when Ben hit Philadelphia's Central High School, coaches discovered he could fly like the wind. After a disappointing season at Eastern Michigan, Ben landed at SPU. Eugene excelled at the mile, and Ben ruled the 440 and 880. The duo made up two legs of a relay team that achieved legendary status at SPU. Wandering alone onto campus that first semester, they were merely new faces among the crowd—but they found each other.

When Eugene and Ben arrived, SPU had just hired Ken Foreman, a University of Southern California graduate and two-time all-American in gymnastics, to coach basketball, build the track-and-field program, and resurrect an athletic department that was in shambles. That first season, with the arrival of Ben and Eugene and a few other teammates, Foreman knew he had lightning in a bottle, envisioning a reality no one else could see yet. He determined to take his team to the Drake Relays (at the time the premier US track-and-field event) at Drake University in Des Moines, Iowa. However, SPU had no budget for such an elaborate trek. The campus, enthused by the track team's electrifying promise, banded together and collected one hundred yards of pennies, copper-colored rolls lined up end to end. The team made the trip, offsetting costs by arranging with auto dealers to travel all the way to Detroit and pick up vehicles to drive caravan-style back to Des Moines and then all the way back to Seattle. The upstart relay team astounded the track-and-field establishment by finishing fourth in the two-mile relay.

During spring break of his freshman year, Eugene brought a friend home with him: Bob Finney Stiles. Friends called him Finney, though as the towering center on the basketball team, the

student body christened him "Big Fin." Eugene took Finney skiing on Big Mountain, long wooden skis dangling like toothpicks
off Finney's giant frame. Eugene's mom packed roast beef sandwiches, and they sat atop the mountain, inhaling clean mountain
air. Finney bit into his sandwich, surprised to find strawberry jam
oozing from the edges. "I'd never had anything like that," Finney
recalled. Eugene didn't want to lose any ground with training, but
the nights were black as tar. So Finney followed behind Eugene in
the car, headlights piercing the dark, as Eugene worked the miles.

Finney's dad, J. E. Stiles, a prominent figure in the early days of
Pentecostalism, wrote an influential book, *The Gift of the Holy
Spirit,* which introduced many to their first experience of speaking in tongues. Sitting on the lakeside deck, Eugene shared with
Finney that he'd never been able to speak in tongues, and Finney
explained what he knew about glossolalia. Eugene uttered a string
of sounds. His mother was thrilled. "But it just wasn't me,"
Eugene said. "I had the feeling that I was faking it." For years, this
spiritual experience would be complicated for him. "But mainly I
was sad that I disappointed my mother," he reflected.

For Eugene, though, the real spiritual education of his first
year at SPU was the diversity he encountered. Having grown up in
a sectarian world, where everyone outside the Pentecostal sphere
was viewed with suspicion, Eugene found it eye popping to brush
up against Presbyterians and Baptists and Catholics and Methodists. "But the disconcerting thing," he wrote in an article a few
years after college, "was . . . that they were *better* Christians than
I was."

Three weeks before Eugene returned to SPU after his first summer break, tragedy struck Kalispell. At dusk on a crisp Septem-

ber evening, eighteen-year-old Patti Schumacher picked up two friends in her family's sedan. In the waning light, Patti missed a pedestrian crossing, leaving black skid marks and a body on the asphalt. When County Attorney Ed Schroeter charged Schumacher with reckless driving rather than involuntary manslaughter (leveling a $300 fine and thirty days in jail), enraged letters poured into the *Daily Inter Lake*. One editorial, titled "Death's Price Is Lowered," brazenly declared that the "widespread criticism resulting from the handling of this case is [Schroeter's] alone to bear." One incensed reader stoked fears: "The group Patti runs around with have been asking for something like this to happen for the past two years. . . . Now that it has happened it seems she will get away with it. . . . Will the people stand for it?"

Though it was an immense tragedy, Eugene believed Schroeter and Schumacher were both scapegoats, with neighbors reacting out of inflamed passions—and without mercy. Eugene, evidencing the same pastoral instincts he would follow the rest of his life, was leery of the overheated rhetoric and moral certainty and felt compassion for those facing the mob. He was concerned that injustice was being done in the name of justice. At eighteen years old, Eugene delivered his first published writing, a letter to the editor applauding Schroeter's contrarian judgment and vigorously arguing for mercy and grace—a view in contrast with public opinion:

> This is not a defense of County Attorney Ed Schroeter's actions on the Patti Schumacher case; he needs no defense. He rises far above his accusers in his conduct on this issue. It would have been easy to have been swayed by public opinion and sentiment. Prosecution would have been an easy road. But Ed Schroeter forsook those baser elements and made a

brilliant attempt to capture the spirit of the law . . . and succeeded.

This is a commendation of his attitude and actions in these circumstances. His action has cost him popularity, friends and . . . maybe a job. But his integrity has swelled immeasurably. He meted out justice with a measure of mercy and received criticism for a reward. I admire him.

You speak of justice. What is justice? Is it justice to destroy the hope, anticipation, and future of a youth to avenge the involuntary death of another? I am a young man and speak with the perspective of youth. When you destroy future and remove the qualities of hope and ambition, you leave but bitter tragedy. Schroeter left the petty aspects of the letter and caught the deep, purposeful spirit of the law, and then had the courage to carry it through. The honesty and integrity of his motives justifies his action.

When his second year in Seattle began, Eugene unpacked his bags in old wood-slatted army officers' quarters the university had bought as temporary housing. One end of the barracks provided housing for the ground maintenance manager and his family. Eugene's end offered three "bedrooms," ten-by-ten-foot square units with bunk beds shoved against the wall. The accommodations were spartan, with gray linoleum floors and a single shower that most days had warm water. One roommate christened the humble quarters with a sign over the door: The Shed Where You Dread to Lay Your Head. For two pivotal years, Eugene called the drafty shed home.

The shed held some memorable characters: Eugene, Finney, and Ed Dillery, who became Eugene's closest college friend and eventually a US ambassador; the future husband of the first woman in the country to serve as CEO of a major teaching hospital; as well as the future parent of a beloved ABC news anchor; the future mayor of Tempe, Arizona. One of Eugene's roommates evidenced his entrepreneurialism early (later he'd build a massive contracting business) when he purchased one of the first televisions to hit SPU's campus and charged students twenty-five cents per show. The shed was drafty in the Seattle winters, but those old barracks warmed Eugene with laughter and friendship.

Even with all the vigor of budding friendships, the rush of collegiate athletics, and persistent spiritual stimulation, Eugene's soul withered. Eugene blamed the barren desert on exhaustion. Once he breathed Montana air again and feasted on that skyline above the mountains, he'd surely feel the spark again.

But when he was back in Kalispell for the summer, Eugene's numbness only compounded. "I felt dead inside." Convinced something drastic was wrong, Eugene went to his pastor. "He was a young guy, thirty years old, pretty good preacher. I told him how I was feeling and asked if he could help me." Immediately, this young pastor launched into an extended lecture on sex, thinking that every young man's problems somehow had sexual issues lurking at the core. "I didn't mind the sex thing," Eugene remembered, laughing, "but I didn't think that was what was wrong." He returned for a second visit, but after the pastor sprang yet again into another rambling diatribe on sex, Eugene never returned. This guy just didn't get it and wasn't listening enough to try.

One evening, Eugene, weary, pulled his mother aside. "Our pastor doesn't know me at all. He doesn't know what I'm struggling with. What should I do?" Evelyn encouraged him to go see Brother Ned. Forty years earlier, Brother Ned had been shot during a robbery in Cleveland, leaving him with a severed spine. Confined to a wheelchair, he had the reputation of being saintly—a wise and holy fixture in the church. Brother Ned invited Eugene for a visit. "We'll talk about the Bible," he explained. On Wednesdays that summer, Eugene visited Brother Ned, his massive black leather Bible atop the blanket draped over his lap, and they talked through Paul's epistle to the Ephesians. "He looked at me like somebody who didn't know anything, and so he was just going to shovel truth down me," Eugene said. "He talked all the time. He bored me to death. I had no idea that the Bible could be so dull. After three weeks, I thought, *I can't do this.*"

One friend surprised Eugene by suggesting he talk to Reuben Lance, a coarse man with "huge outcroppings of bristle for eyebrows and a wild red beard. He looked mean." Reuben carried his burly frame and surly disposition onto every jobsite: plumbing, carpentry, masonry, and electrical. Reuben could fix anything and could beat most any man into the dust; he was the kind of man you wanted on your side when you confronted hooligans in a dark alley. Reuben was *not* a man you went to with an aching heart. Eugene said, "I was reluctant to risk his scorn of what he would probably see as adolescent silliness draped with the silk veils of a pretentious metaphysics that I had picked up in college. . . . [I was] afraid that he would rip through the pretense with a single sarcastic remark."

Eugene approached Reuben and nervously explained what he was feeling. Could he talk with Reuben? Reuben's answer was brisk. "If that's what you want. Meet me in the church basement after supper on Tuesdays and Thursdays." Reuben Lance, the man who "never smiled . . . never prayed aloud in church . . . [and] was scornful of most of what passed for religion" became Eugene's first spiritual director. For the remaining weeks of that summer, they met twice a week. No pious language. No heavy theology. "He just talked to me. He treated me like a person. And when I got back to school at SPU, I was different."

It would be years before Eugene could describe what he had experienced that summer with Reuben—and years before he had another spiritual director to rival him. During seminary, Eugene wrote the story of his relationship with Reuben for the *Pentecostal Evangel,* describing how an unsophisticated man with no formal theological training, who talked to Eugene mostly about "everyday stuff—tools, work, landscape, school," had such a massive impact. Reuben simply listened and treated Eugene with dignity. Reuben never viewed Eugene as an "opportunity for ministry" but welcomed him with a "stance of wonderment."

Decades later, Eugene's brother-in-law, Miles Finch, a Montana pastor who knew Reuben, gave Eugene Reuben's contact information. Eugene dialed the number, and Reuben, then in his eighties, answered. Eugene explained to Reuben his profound influence, with only long silence coming from the other end of the line. Eventually, Reuben's frail voice broke the stillness. "You know, I'm just sitting here in my bed. I'm very ill and can't do much. And you're telling me that those Thursday nights at the church changed your life? No one's ever said anything like that to me before. They liked me to fix things for them. But they never seemed to want me for much more than that." Then Reuben cried.

Eugene's final two years at Seattle Pacific rushed like spring meltwater down roiling rivers. New responsibilities. New friendships. An eye turning toward the next chapter. Eugene swam in possibilities, looking toward an open horizon—great promise indeed. He even received his sarcastic superlative—Ugliest Man of 1953—with good humor.

His capacious love for words churned too. During his junior

year, Eugene accepted the position of editor in chief of the *Tawahsi,* Seattle Pacific's yearbook. He was recognized as a young man who "combined wit, originality, humor with innumerable man-hours to bring SPC 1953 between Tawahsi covers." Eugene roped Ben Moring into joining him on the yearbook staff, allowing the two friends to pace each other at the typewriter as well as on the track.

And in it all, a romance had been growing. Eugene's roommate Ed was dating a girl named Marita who had been friends with Carol Rueck since boarding school. The foursome played tennis and shared milkshakes in the college café, and quickly Carol and Eugene found themselves together. Their junior year, they were both elected to the student council, and as the 1954 all-school banquet neared, Eugene published a flourish of goofy poetry in the school paper, by way of invitation to Carol:

> *And now my pretty Queen of Hearts,*
> *Maid of Athens and Cupid's darts,*
> *Will you with a word my fetters free,*
> *And go a-banqueting with me?*
>
> *I'll spend my cash and hock*
> *My horse, to hear you say affirmative,*
> *That me you'll choose, and others chuck;*
> *I'll pick you up at half-past five.*

The *Tawahsi* snapped a picture of Eugene and Carol at the banquet. In it, Eugene stands grinning wide, a crisp white shirt under his dark jacket, bow tie askew, a line of white handkerchief peeping from his suit pocket, a white carnation in his lapel. Carol's white dress, with a subtle paisley in the fabric, is an understated backdrop for a spring corsage splashing color across her shoulder. Later, Eugene wrote home, describing Carol on that evening: *sweet, and sensitive and ingenuous . . . a warm, responsive girl.*

The track, however, remained the place where Eugene found immense joy because of the competition but even more because of the connection with his friends. He and Ben cemented their place as a powerful tandem, with Gordon Fee (who would become a renowned New Testament scholar) later joining the team as a hurdler. And the adventures, the *exploits,* they shared! On one of those epic road trips to the Drake Relays (continuing to drive vehicles back to Seattle dealers to offset travel costs), Coach Foreman led the convoy across the flatlands in a red sports car, with five shiny Buicks motoring behind. One afternoon, the boys needed to change clothes for an event, so the caravan pulled over, lining the shoulder of a remote South Dakota highway. With luggage strewn roadside and clothes draped over doors, the boys stripped to their underwear before noticing a truck, with a farmer and his wife in the cab and wide-eyed children in the back, slowly moving toward them. The truck crawled past, then turned around and drove back. The fellows stood there, stunned and bare. The family gawked as the farmer pulled the truck to a stop and asked, "What happened here?"

Perhaps thinking he would be humorous—or maybe not thinking at all—one of the bleach-white fellows blurted, "We are having a funeral here. We ran over an ant and are about to bury it."

The farmer and his family sat in the idling truck, staring. Finally, the woman answered, "That's too bad." The farmer slowly drove on.

Eugene piled up athletic medals, slowly shaving seconds off his mile by running the Queen Anne Bowl, an old Seattle gravel quarry transformed into a park and overrun by seagulls. Eugene

set records in the six-hundred-yard dash and contended for the
National Association of Intercollegiate Athletics championships
in both '53 and '54. Catching the eye of track officials, Eugene
received an invitation to an exhibition in Vancouver to race Roger
Bannister, the first man to break the four-minute mile in Oxford.
Organizers arranged the exhibition as a warm-up event for the
1954 British Empire and Commonwealth Games (memorialized
by the Miracle Mile, the race between Roger Bannister and John
Landy—the first time two sub-four-minute-mile runners faced
off). The tale of Eugene and Bannister's race took on mythical
status years later, with Eugene's legend growing as the man who
"nearly beat Roger Bannister." Eugene laughed at the preposter-
ous idea. "He was forty yards ahead of me."

His senior year, Eugene's classmates elected him prexy—SPU's student body president—fulfilling that hope he voiced his first week
on campus. Each Thursday at twelve thirty, Eugene tapped a spoon
against a half-empty water glass, calling the student council to
order over a lunch of pea soup, strawberry Jell-O, and cold coffee.
Leadership, Eugene discovered, was not about a dynamic personality commandeering resources and manhandling an agenda but
rather like "a coxswain in a crew race, keeping the strokes in synchronized rhythm." That year, Eugene began to think hard about
what it means to be a leader, but the most telling fact, I believe, was
his remarkable commitment to learn the name of every student on
campus—all eight hundred of them. Decades later, Eugene offered
his conviction that a church was healthiest if it could maintain a
manageable size. He suggested that this manageable size might be,
as a rule of thumb, no larger than about the size of his college, the
size where a pastor (or at least a pastor with a memory as sharp as
his) could still memorize everyone's name. However, he remem-

bered the student body as only five hundred. As a result, countless pastors, taking Eugene far more literally than he would ever have wanted, wrung their hands over an unhealthy congregation, when they still had three hundred persons to go.

Providing early cues to Eugene as a writer, the most intriguing remnant from Eugene's stint as student body president is twenty-five articles he authored for "Prexy's Pen," a regular column in the *Falcon*, the college newspaper. We catch glimpses of the poet and preacher he'd become in his later years. But what is apparent most often in these columns is Eugene's sense of humor, his playfulness, his lack of self-consciousness, his goofiness.

In January 1954, for instance, Eugene explained that over the holidays he had been visited by Dickens's Ghost of the Campus Future, who communicated "a solemn syllabus of impending doom directed to Seattle Pacific College" unless swift changes were enacted. Eugene listed the ghost's demands for students verbatim:

I. To pick up all loose papers, gum wrappers and empty sacks and deposit them forthwith in the nearest depositorium.

II. To date at least one girl per quarter for the next two quarters and experience the overpowering joy and good-will that comes with sharing a 10¢ coke (including ice) with a friend.

III. To attend all athletic contests and cheer at the same with uninhibited enthusiasm in order to raise school spirit to unprecedented heights and also to scare the pigeons from the rafters of the gym.

IV. To faithfully inhabit a chapel seat every day of the week. (This by special request of Mr. Dillon at the College Drugstore who has confided to me that the floor joists are beginning to weaken from the stampeding influx of coffee-hounds at ten o'clock every morning.)

V. To open regularly each text-book that I own and expose it to a bright light for at least twenty minutes per day. (The purpose of this is twofold: first to keep the pages from yellowing and second to be sure that there are no lucky dollars secreted among the pages.)

Cross my heart and hope to die, I solemnly swear to abide by these resolutions and disciple those around me to do the same.

<u>(x) signed in blood</u>

The "Prexy's Pen" columns didn't pay, though, and Eugene found himself short on money. He answered the ad for a job at a Laundromat on Queen Anne Hill, squeezing work into the only spare time he had: the graveyard shift from 11:00 p.m. to 7:00 a.m. Into the wee hours, Eugene pounded coffee and fought back yawns as he supplied quarters for customers, sorted abandoned loads, and swept grimy floors.

Perhaps it was one of these late nights, when he was half-drunk due to lack of sleep, that led to Eugene's tattoo. A man who lived full tilt, Coach Foreman had tattoos covering his body—all drawn himself. "He was a wild man," Eugene remembered with a gleam in his eye. Foreman lived on Queen Anne Hill. One Saturday morning, Ben and Eugene were at his house. The coach pulled off his shirt to explain the story behind each piece of artistry. He was especially proud of a mouse he'd sketched. "You want one to match?" he asked, and Eugene and Ben found themselves nodding.

Foreman fetched a tray of needles and ink, waved their shirts off, and turned on the needle. With the needle buzzing and blood dripping from the outline of the little rodent, suddenly the doorbell rang. Looking out the window, Foreman went ashen. The Free

Methodist Sunday school superintendent was standing on his doorstep. "Cover yourselves," Foreman demanded, pushing the supplies out of sight before opening the door. The superintendent yapped on and on while Ben's and Eugene's shoulders oozed and clotted. But mercifully, he eventually left, and Foreman finished the job.

The next day at practice, several players approached Coach Foreman with a bit of gossip: "Ben and Gene went to Pike Street and got tattoos." Foreman shook his head. "You never know what those boys are going to do."

The next time Eugene was home, his mom noticed the black-inked mouse on his shoulder while he was sunbathing by the lake. Without a word, she went in the house and returned with her Bible. She flopped it conveniently in his lap, opened to Leviticus 19:28: "Do not cut your bodies for the dead or put tattoo marks on yourselves. I am the LORD" (NIV).

Eugene stared at the page, then at her wordless face.

"I didn't know it said that," he whispered.

"Well, it does," Evelyn answered. "And now it's too late."

She never mentioned the tattoo again.

The tattoo wasn't the only way ink was getting under young Eugene's skin. Majoring in philosophy, Eugene had uninspiring grades, but he had a voracious mind. He was fascinated with language and crafting sentences, and his expansive reading stoked a writer's fire in his lanky bones. Elva McAllaster, professor of literature, served as faculty adviser for the *Falcon*. Eugene had never taken a writing course, but McAllaster took an interest in him. She became the young writer's first true editor, offering constructive feedback as Eugene clacked away on his typewriter.

In an early column, when Eugene moaned about having to

make a "dismal decision" between "taking Chaucer and calculus," McAllaster took him to task.

"Eugene, have you ever read Chaucer?"

"No," he answered.

McAllaster reached for her bookcase and pulled down *Canterbury Tales*. "Take this. Read it. Don't come back until you have read the *whole thing*." Then she offered a parting (and humbling) shot: "I expect you don't know much about calculus either."

Embarrassed, he read the thick book and returned it a week later, thinking, *Oh, wow, this is not dull!* However, in an article six months later, Eugene again (perhaps merely to get a rise out of Ms. McAllaster) took another sarcastic swipe at the poet: "This is one of these days . . . when the whole world holds the same prospects for adventure and excitement as an anticipated evening in the library, with Chaucer as companion."

Apparently, McAllaster could take a joke. She stayed in touch with Eugene for decades, encouraging him as he deepened his writing skills (and reading list) and commenting on each piece he published.

But maybe Eugene was right to feel Chaucer was dull when compared with a prettier companion. "Rueck and Peterson to Marry," read a spring 1954 headline in the *Falcon*. Swept up in the anticipation of graduation—and the passion of so many friends making plans to tie the knot—Eugene and Carol decided to marry. However, due to their uncertainty of what lay ahead, they didn't set a date or make any more specific plans than the yes.

That was an ominous omen. Eugene had thought little about what came after college. He'd imagined becoming a professor (philosophy, maybe, or literature) but had no money for more school. Two SPU friends, Augustine Njokuobi and Elijah Odajara, approached Eugene and Ben about returning to Nigeria with them to teach at a Christian high school in Lagos. With no other prospects and with things sputtering with Carol (for reasons Eugene could not pinpoint), they both accepted. However, when Ben decided he preferred seminary, Eugene realized he had no desire to go to Nigeria without him.

So, when the big moment came for caps and gowns, Eugene walked across the graduation stage into an unknown future.

6

Go East, Young Man

Keeps moving, changing
pace and approach but
not direction—"every step an arrival."
—Denise Levertov,
"Overland to the Islands"

Fifty-five years after that graduation, Eugene returned to Seattle Pacific to speak at University Presbyterian Church. He was the recipient of *Image* journal's 2009 Levertov Award, and he noted in his journal how meaningful it was to have many of his classmates from so long ago present at the event. Eugene's talk, "Intently Haphazard," echoed a line from a piece of Levertov's "Overland to the Islands" that Eugene returned to over and over again. The poet's picture of a dog following its nose without any clear direction captured him.

The imagery spoke to him so deeply because he had been that dog for decades. His life and work had been more like tracing a scent than following a map. Discovery, not direction. In all those fifty-five years, Eugene had never truly mapped his future, never tried to lay some ordered path toward a clear career goal. Intent? Sure. But haphazard too. The whole meandering journey had been a dog sniffing the wind, the next whiff being the only real clue. And what had been the scent? Holiness? The Presence?

This was nothing new, of course, and the wandering had begun in earnest after college. The year 1954 was an unsettling time to be twenty-one, holding a freshly inked diploma but with no clear direction, particular job skills, or connections that could provide the much-coveted designation of draft deferment. The Korean War had cast a dark shadow over Eugene's student years. He was used to images of caskets draped with the Stars and Stripes as a result of a confusing, faraway war. And just that year alone, the US Selective Service had drafted another 253,000 young men into the fray. Eugene did not want to be one of them.

These blunt realities added a chilling effect to Eugene's graduation—with school behind him, it was entirely possible that the boy who could not kill a deer might find himself sailing for Korea with an M1 Garand on his back. And besides the sheer horror of war, Eugene wrestled with deep questions: *What is a Christian's response to war and violence? What is the threshold that must be met before a Christian is willing to kill?*

All this ambiguity, fear, and confusion hung heavy over him as he packed his Oldsmobile and pulled out of Seattle, bound for Montana. If possible, whatever he did next would be far from Korea. Eugene decided he would go into ministry. The hurdle now was the cash he'd need for whatever would come next. Eugene intended to save every dollar he could possibly earn over the course of that summer to fund his future ministry.

So, when Eugene returned to Kalispell, he sharpened his cleaver and returned to his place behind the counter at the Meat Supply Co., cutting, weighing, wrapping, joking, and, in the lulls of business, staring out the window with big thoughts in his brain.

Hearing Eugene's plans, his mother suggested he talk to Charles Jackson. Jackson lived in Great Falls, serving as superintendent of the Assemblies of God for the state of Montana. (Interestingly, Charles and Elisabeth Jackson's son was NBA Hall of Fame coach Phil Jackson. The Jacksons and Petersons were friends, and Elisabeth called Evelyn one afternoon when the Jacksons were considering lifting the embargo on Phil playing basketball. Elisabeth wanted Evelyn's assurance that her son could play sports, as Eugene had, without searing his soul.)

So Eugene dialed the Jacksons' number, the line ringing until "Hello?" came through the receiver. After pleasantries, Eugene asked if any denominational churches were looking for a pastor. Sure, he didn't have the credentials or experience typically required, but in the Pentecostal world, protocol readily gave way to zeal.

Charles mentally scoured Montana's small towns in search of a suitable outpost. "Well, we don't have any churches looking for a pastor right now, Eugene. But we've been hoping to start a new church—in Townsend maybe, or Fort Benton. You're welcome to give it a try." With no clear reason, Eugene chose Townsend, planning to start his new ministry in September. Before hanging up, Eugene asked, "Do you have any counsel or direction for me?" And while surely a piece of advice or two were offered to the newly minted minister, in later years Eugene remembered mostly silence on the other end of the line.

Come September, Eugene folded his butcher's apron and packed everything he owned for the five-hour trip to Townsend. It was a fledgling town thirty-five miles southeast of Helena. As his first order of business, Eugene located the butcher shop and explained his expertise, immediately securing a job and promising to show up early on Monday. Next, he tracked down a basement apartment for rent. It was a perfect spot to serve as his modest parsonage, a launching pad for the pastoral work he envisioned. Things were looking bright.

He'd been in Townsend only a matter of hours, but with a job and a home, he supposed it was time to find his congregation. He walked door to door through the entire town, introducing himself at each house. "Hello, I'm Eugene Peterson. I've been asked to come here to start an Assemblies of God church. Can I talk to you about it?" The doors closed, both literally and metaphorically. House after house, not a single person agreed to a conversation. The Mormons and Methodists had the town locked down tight.

Eugene ran the gauntlet of slammed doors. Finishing, Eugene stopped at the edge of town, deflated. He had no more doors to knock on. Baffled, he just kept walking, down to the Missouri River. He watched the sun set. *What am I supposed to do?* he pondered. In the twilight, he trudged back to a diner, where he took a booth and eyed the greasy menu. After a hamburger and slice of apple pie, he returned to his "parsonage" and rolled out his sleeping bag. The next morning, he tossed his gear into his car and drove out of town. Eugene had been a pastor for roughly eighteen hours.

By the time Eugene pulled back into Kalispell, he'd decided to do something. A few days earlier it had seemed about as likely as joining the circus, but now he knew it was right. He'd go to seminary and prepare for a future in teaching. Sectarian Pentecostals distrusted seminaries, often calling them *cemeteries* and warning how those cold institutions would ruin fervent hearts. As he pulled into the driveway, his mom met him at the car, confused. "What are you doing here?"

"I'm not going to Townsend," Eugene answered.

"So, what *are* you going to do?"

Eugene paused, only for a moment. "What would you think about me going to seminary?"

"I always thought you'd go to seminary," Evelyn replied easily. Whatever she believed about it, she knew her son needed more.

The only seminary Eugene knew of was Biblical Seminary in New York City (now New York Theological Seminary). A friend and two professors from SPU were alumni, and better yet, Ben Moring had already enrolled. There was just one problem: classes had already begun. One of Eugene's old profs told him he'd put in a call, though, and Eugene should just go to New York.

So, the next day—without ever unpacking—Eugene nosed his Oldsmobile east. Twenty-five hundred miles stretched between Kalispell and the Big Apple. For four days, Eugene drove across the country, pulling over each night to unroll his sleeping bag and stretch out under the stars. The world was wide open.

Then, the city. Eugene dipped into the Holland Tunnel and emerged from under the Hudson River, immediately jolted by the chaos. He'd never seen such energy, such bedlam. He wove through the intricate traffic and throngs of pedestrians. New York teemed and writhed like a massive ant colony—all organized according to some insect logic that eluded him.

Attempting to finagle his car around Central Park, Eugene grew confused. As he tried to get his bearings, he idled in the dead center of Manhattan's afternoon rush. A police officer spotted him holding up traffic and, taking note of the Montana plate, briskly arrived to deliver a loud dose of New York hospitality. With expletives artfully placed before every other word, the officer asked Eugene what *exactly* he thought he was doing. As cabbies lay on their horns, Eugene sat wide eyed while the officer unleashed a torrent of curses he'd never heard, not even among the loggers.

Finally, ears ringing and profanity lexicon expanded, Eugene inched his way to his destination—a twelve-story brown brick building at 235 East Forty-Ninth Street. He walked into the offices and found the dean. "I'm here to go to school," Eugene told her.

She looked over Eugene, worn from a cross-country trip, with dirty jeans and a wrinkled T-shirt and without so much as an application in his hand. "Don't you think that's a little presumptuous?"

"Well, I guess it is," Eugene admitted. "But I'd still like to go to school."

He started classes the next day.

New York was no Townsend, and doors opened for the young seminarian. Eugene landed a job with the YMCA at fifty-five dollars per week, assisting international students arriving in New York. Due to the con artists prowling arrival queues for travelers to swindle, the YMCA welcome program identified international students, helped them ward off trouble, and provided them with reliable transportation to their destinations. The YMCA assigned Eugene a partner, a fellow seminarian who became one of his closest friends during his New York years: a young man named Pat Robertson.

Pat's father was A. Willis Robertson, a prominent senator from Virginia. At first, Eugene didn't make the connection, but he quickly recognized that Pat hailed from an entirely different social stratum than Montana butchers and their kin. While waiting at the airport for students, Pat pointed out movie stars, corporate moguls, and political insiders, explaining who they were and sharing titillating bits of gossip. He seemed to know everyone and everything.

Pat was married to Dede, a nursing student at Yale. Once Pat and Eugene became friends, the young couple invited Eugene to dinner at their apartment in Queens. And this friendly gesture was only the beginning of a rich social life in the city. Pat organized a small circle of friends, including Eugene and Joo Sun Ae (the first female professor of Presbyterian Theological Seminary in Seoul), to gather regularly for prayer at 6:30 a.m. in a seminary dorm room. With the students inflamed by dynamic stories of religious awakening in Korea and Scotland, the prayer gathering stoked fervent interest among Eugene and Pat's seminary circle in revival and the Pentecostal renewal sweeping through numerous denominations.

Pat and Eugene, along with several friends from the prayer meeting, traveled to Connecticut, to land owned by a friend of Pat's, for three days of camping with a focus on prayer and fasting. After setting up their gear, they explored the woods and discovered a plaque fixed to a rough-hewn stack of rocks marking the birthplace of the renowned evangelist Charles Finney. In the weeks prior, the group had been reading Finney's descriptions of his own encounter with the "mighty baptism of the Holy Spirit." Finney's words shook the band of zealous students:

> The Holy Spirit descended upon me in a manner that seemed to go through me, body and soul. I could feel the impression, like a wave of electricity, going through and through me. Indeed it seemed to come in waves of liquid love. . . . It seemed like the very breath of God. I can remember distinctly that it seemed to fan me, like immense wings.
>
> No words can express the wonderful love that was spread abroad in my heart. I wept aloud with joy and love. I literally bellowed out the unspeakable overflow of my heart. These waves came over me, and over me, and over me, one after the other, until I remember crying out, "I shall die if these waves continue to pass over me."

Finney's story fanned the hot embers. And now, here they were, setting up camp at his birthplace? Pat was undone. "It was as though we were on holy ground, and we kicked off our shoes and began laughing and praising God. I knew the Holy Spirit had allowed us to come to this place for a sign. He was about to pour Himself out on us even as He did on Finney."

Pat and Eugene's friendship was close and mutually inspiring. They spent hours in prayer, hours wandering the streets of New York, and hours in conversation, pouring out their souls to each other as they tried to make sense of their histories and their futures.

But as is often the case in life, the intensity of this friendship was not to last. While Eugene wrote of Pat often in his letters home and their friendship extended until graduation, both geography and deviating ideas of ministry sent them away from the city in contrasting trajectories. Nevertheless, there was always mutual affection in remembering their time shared in New York.

In 1960, Pat purchased a small television station in Virginia Beach, Virginia, that would grow into a media empire, the Christian Broadcasting Network (CBN). Pat tried to convince Eugene to join him in his venture, but as I look back now, it's impossible to envision Eugene sitting behind the bright lights and beaming at the camera to the opening music of *The 700 Club*.

The relationships Eugene developed at that time were formative. But he was there to study. Sliding into his desk that first day of class was an encounter that would reshape Eugene's life—and touch millions more. Professor Robert Traina, up in front of the class, had recently published *Methodical Bible Study*, which would become a foundational text for Bible students for at least sixty years. During those early weeks, Traina served as Eugene's guide into the strange, disruptive, *exhilarating* world of the Bible. "I sat in a classroom," Eugene remembered, "led by a professor who over the next three years would profoundly change my perception of the Bible, and me with it, in ways that gave shape to everything I have been doing for the rest of my life. This is not an exaggeration."

Scripture had always been Eugene's spiritual center. For as long as he remembered, he had read Scripture with rigor and discipline, even memorizing vast sections outright. The Bible had been the turf where, as a young Pentecostal, he would spar (good-naturedly) over doctrine with others. But for all its influence, the Bible had always seemed somehow *external* to him. "To tell the truth, I was bored with it," he remembered later.

The Bible—as Eugene had known it—offered principles for moral living, artillery for theological skirmishes, and clichés providing therapeutic salve. His church had implicitly used it as a textbook or occasionally even a weapon, but no one had ever guided him into the wonder, beauty, and artistry of the ancient pages. It had been a thing to use, to master. Under Traina, he saw Scripture as a world to be entered.

Now incrementally, week by week, semester by semester, my reading of the Bible was becoming a conversation. I was no longer reading words—I was listening to voices; I was observing how these words worked in association with all the other words on the page. And I was learning to listen carefully to these voices, these writers who were, well, *writers*. Skilled writers, poets, and storytellers who were artists of language. . . . Words were not just words: words were holy.

This journey into the Bible's world enlarged him as an entire person, opening new possibilities, giving him a fresh, dynamic imagination. The world of Scripture would shape how he understood friendship, how he saw himself as a husband and a father, how he lived as a neighbor and a pastor. Eugene described the transformation under Traina as a seismic paradigm shift, like the move from Ptolemy to Copernicus.

Eugene's story, at least as a theologian, can be traced from that first class in seminary.

I entered seminary with little, if any, interest in theology. In my experience theology was too contaminated with polemics and apologetics to take any pleasure in it. It always left me with a sour taste. The grand and soaring realities of God and the Holy Spirit, scripture and Creation, salvation and a holy life always seemed to get ground down into contentious, mean-spirited arguments: predestination and free will, grace and works, Calvinism and Arminianism, liberal and conservative, supra- and infra-lapsarianism. At my university I had avoided all this by taking refuge in a philosophy major that gave me room and companions for cultivating wonder and exploring meaning. When I arrived in seminary, I continued to keep my distance from theology by plunging into the biblical languages and the English Bible.

Newly awakened to the delight of the Scriptures, Eugene was drawn to the biblical languages of Hebrew and Greek. In the summer of 1955, Eugene worked at the American Bible Society (the premier Bible translation group in the US) on Fifty-Seventh and Park Avenue, getting an immersive orientation in the work of Scripture translation. Walking those halls, Eugene encountered translators poring over texts, working to shape the words of one language into the heart of another.

He didn't know it, but he was getting his first peek into the very work that would one day be his broadest legacy.

Nearby, Madison Avenue Presbyterian Church was a vibrant congregation situated at the crossroads of opulence and dire poverty.
As he joined the life of the church, Eugene met the first pastor
(other than his mother) he had ever truly admired: George Buttrick.

Traina was showing Eugene a new biblical world from the lectern. But Buttrick opened a new universe from his pulpit. He was
a true pastor, a master preacher, and a religious luminary. His
renaissance-pastor skills had turned national heads for years. One
media writer struggled to capture his breadth: "author, scholar,
orator, strenuous day-and-night pastor of New York's largest
Presbyterian church." And it was all true. Buttrick was a prophetic voice who did not mince words to protect the feelings of
his wealthier congregants. When the country descended into the
Great Depression of the 1930s, even after the church's budget
shrank by a third, Buttrick challenged Madison Avenue to redou-
ble its efforts and respond to the gospel's invitation to love the
thousands of hungry and homeless surrounding their affluent
neighborhood. He believed in the vital role of presence in a pastor's work, making roughly twenty-five house visits weekly. He
spent four hours a day in study, ran the church's social-relief op-
erations, taught at Union Theological Seminary, and served as
general editor of *The Interpreter's Bible*. Under his leadership,
Madison Avenue grew to be the largest Presbyterian church in
New York City—with Buttrick considered one of the nation's
most prominent preachers (named by *Life* as one of the twentieth
century's twelve great preachers, alongside voices such as Howard
Thurman, Billy Graham, Robert James McCracken, Fulton J.
Sheen, and Norman Vincent Peale).

Each year, the church picked ten seminarians as interns (five
from Union Seminary and five from Biblical Seminary). Still aiming for teaching and not pastoral ministry, Eugene had no interest
in a ministerial internship, but he discovered, with frustration,

that every seminarian was required to complete church fieldwork. When the seminary pointed Eugene toward Madison Avenue Presbyterian, he strolled the one and a half miles past St. Patrick's Cathedral and the upscale Bonwit Teller department store (the site where Trump Tower now stands) to the church offices. There he underwent a grueling round of interviews: three sessions with three members of the pastoral staff. Montana Pentecostals eyed New York Presbyterians with suspicion, so Eugene seized the opportunity to witness to these unsuspecting pastors, carefully explaining the gospel to each of them and stressing the necessity of conversion. Eugene walked back to the seminary, swelling with evangelistic fervor and daydreaming of how, after demonstrating his biblical prowess, he might be invited to join Buttrick on the Sunday preaching rotation. When the phone rang, the voice on the line detailed his intern assignment: to coach Madison Avenue's men's basketball team in the city's church league. So for the next year, rather than deliver incisive homilies, Eugene ran up and down the court, blowing his whistle as sweaty bodies practiced layups and free throws.

Buttrick's preaching enchanted Eugene. The preacher's tender yet piercing approach to the Scriptures exuded artfulness. He was a poet in the pulpit, a man who revered the holiness of words. Most preachers Eugene had known were flamboyant and loud, often winging it as they unloaded rambling diatribes. Buttrick's sermons were thoughtful, literary, imaginative, and quietly potent. And the words pointed, with conviction, toward God. Reflecting decades later, Eugene still found the man remarkable: "In the year of Sundays I listened to him preach, I don't think I heard a single cliché pass his lips."

Buttrick used unpretentious language, but it cut to the bone. In his book on homiletics, he wrote, "One flashing phrase that cuts like a rapier is better than an orgy of denunciation." While a brilliant preacher, he was not particularly impressive behind the pulpit. There were no mesmerizing theatrics. Buttrick was "a marvelous preacher because he had no finesse," Frederick Buechner remembered. "He plucked at his robes and mumbled his words, which made him all the more powerful." One of Buttrick's students, John Killinger, punctured any notion of an elevated oratory presence, remembering that he "defied all the rules of public speaking, habitually stuttering and wandering about the pulpit and hanging his head when he spoke." But all who were present in that grand sanctuary heard the crackle of fire in the "odd, sandy voice, the voice of an old nurse," as Buechner described it.

Eugene had never known a pastor like this.

Though neither was aware of the other, another young man sitting in a Madison Avenue pew that year was drawn to Buttrick like a thirsty man to water. Frederick Buechner had moved to New York in 1953 to write fiction full time. With his wildly successful debut, *A Long Day's Dying,* followed by a major disappointment, *The Seasons' Difference,* Buechner found his craft, like his life, in disarray.

Unlike Eugene, Buechner was not a man of religious conviction and was not (he thought) looking for God. However, Buechner was adrift and lonely, and after moving into an apartment on the same block as Madison Avenue Presbyterian, he realized he lived next door to a preacher who was apparently causing a stir in town. With nothing better to do on Sundays, Buechner padded out his front door and into the large domed sanctuary flooded with light from the stained glass and filled with swelling music from the massive Opus 1000 pipe organ.

Something about Buttrick—something Buechner could not exactly capture with words—pierced his heart.

It was not just his eloquence that kept me coming back, though he was wonderfully eloquent, literate, imaginative, never letting you guess what he was going to come out with next but twitching with surprises up there in the pulpit, his spectacles a-glitter in the lectern light. What drew me more was whatever it was that his sermons came from and whatever it was in me that they touched so deeply.

One shattering line from Buttrick lit the spark that set young Buechner's heart aflame. On November 15, 1953, Buttrick preached a rousing sermon titled "He Refused to Be King," proclaiming that if we are ever to crown Jesus as king of our hearts, it will happen "among confession and tears and great laughter." It was these final two words, with their unequivocal invitation to *joy*, that struck the flint. With those few syllables, something holy, animated, *penetrating* burst open in Buechner. "For reasons that I have never satisfactorily understood," Buechner wrote later, "the great wall of China crumbled and Atlantis rose up out of the sea, and on Madison Avenue, at 73rd Street, tears leapt from my eyes as though I had been struck across the face."

Eugene and Buechner never met, but Eugene later learned of their shared history. In one of his journals, he pasted Buechner's description of that momentous morning. Eugene recognized in Buechner's recollection his own profound experience sitting in that same sanctuary, his heart moved on some of the same Sundays as he listened to the same sermons.

On Sunday evenings, Buttrick invited the ten seminary interns to a church member's Fifth Avenue penthouse, its grand windows giving a majestic view over Central Park. Buttrick loosened his tie, slipped his brogue leather oxfords off his weary feet, pulled on his slippers, and eased himself down onto the hardwood floor. He leaned against the radiator, which popped and complained as it pumped warm air to fight back the winter swirling outside the paned windows. Buttrick lit his pipe, took a deep pull, and asked, "What do you want to talk about?" The next hour unfolded with free-flowing conversation. No lectures. Rather than unloading a folio of ministerial information, Buttrick simply opened his mind and his life to the students.

On one of these evenings, one of the seminarians asked him something to the effect of "What's the most important thing you do for your sermon preparation each week?" Without hesitation, Buttrick responded,

> For two hours every Tuesday and Thursday afternoon, I walk through the neighborhood and make home visits. There is no way that I can preach the gospel to these people if I don't know how they are living, what they are thinking and talking about. Preaching is proclamation, God's word revealed in Jesus, but only when it gets embedded in conversation, in a listening ear and responding tongue, does it become gospel.

Though Buttrick's church had many members living on the swanky side of town, the blocks east of the church were a hardscrabble neighborhood, with people working their fingers to the bone trying to put potatoes on the table and keep their kids in shoes. If he was going to preach to these people, if he was going to be their pastor, Buttrick knew he had to step into their lives. Sitting on that hardwood floor, he shared his convictions. Eugene was taking notes.

Eugene sent piles of notes home: tales of his many new experiences, paragraphs unfolding his multiplying ideas and questions, and numerous expressions of how much he loved his family and missed Montana. Ken remembers the excitement of receiving Eugene's weekly letter. His mom unfolded the pages and read aloud (with true Evelyn flare) Eugene's eye-popping tales of the big city. Like the time Eugene encountered a forlorn woman intent on ending it all off the Brooklyn Bridge and talked her out of it. And the time he and a couple of buddies had a harrowing stand-off with one of the neighborhood gangs. For Ken, Eugene's letters were better than television.

Evelyn soaked in Eugene's words. She didn't understand all that he was experiencing, all that this new world held out for him. But she was very proud of him. She read the letters with delight in her voice and then tucked them away and kept them close.

Ever since Eugene's graduation, Carol Rueck and Eugene had been writing too, their letters crossing the country to find each other. But by the end of 1955, the relationship was in trouble. Distance had done little to reignite passions that had mostly cooled by the time they said goodbye in Seattle. Their correspondence meandered, tepid and noncommittal.

However, they had planned for Carol to visit New York over Christmas, and they stuck with it (though Eugene wrote home just before the visit, saying "things are . . . nebulous.") He arranged an extravagant tour of the city, hoping the days would bring resolution to the question of whether there could be any future for them. Eugene dazzled Carol with dinner at Rockefeller Center's Cafe Francais. He described for his folks how they sat at the foot of the Promenade "under the great, brilliantly lighted, sixty-foot Christmas tree, and with an interesting view of the ice-skaters just outside." Impressive, but they were just getting started. They enjoyed another dinner at Toffenetti, the one-thousand-seat Times Square "Cathedral of All Restaurants." An evening at Longchamps too, a white-tablecloth bistro serving Nesselrode Pie and Oxtail Ragout. Yet another meal out, this time at Fraunces Tavern, the oldest bar-restaurant in the city, once frequented by George Washington. And all this was leading up to the apex of the gastronomic tour: dinner at the Waldorf Astoria's Peacock Alley. In between meals, they toured the Met and Radio City, visited the Wall Street stock exchange and the Empire State Building. Eugene showed Carol the fine women's shops on Fifth Avenue, followed by a grand stroll through Macy's and Gimbels. They caught a Broadway show, *Plain and Fancy*. The head usher at CBS, a friend of Eugene's, even arranged for them to have front row seats for a broadcast of the *Arthur Godfrey and His Friends* variety show.

However, the most memorable adventure of the trip came on Christmas Day. Having gone together to Washington, DC, to spend Christmas with Ed and Marita Dillery, they woke on Christmas morning and made their way to National Presbyterian Church, joking how they hoped to see the president. They were delighted when ushers directed them *down to almost directly in front of the pulpit*. Then delight turned to astonishment. Eugene wrote home, describing the unreal moment: *Five minutes to eleven who should be ushered into the same row as we were in and across the aisle, but—you guessed it—Ike and Mamie!* The president's son John, in his army dress blues, sat next to them. John Foster Dulles, Eisenhower's secretary of state, sat in the row in front of them. *We couldn't have asked for a better show.*

Returning to New York, Eugene and Carol spent their final evening together in Times Square, ringing in the New Year alongside the raucous throng throwing confetti and singing "Auld Lang Syne." That was the last time Eugene would see Carol. In spite of the lavish holiday, the goodbye at LaGuardia Airport signaled the end of their on-again, off-again relationship.

You can quit praying about this, Eugene wrote to his mom. *I feel released from it.*

New York was the last place Eugene would have expected to find himself. But the teeming life and diverse cultures, the many new friendships, and the way seminary was expanding his theological and biblical imagination all opened up many new, unexpected possibilities. That scent he'd been following was growing stronger, that burning in his bones generating more heat. The direction he'd been stumbling after—and that rarely seems clear except in hindsight—was slowly revealing itself.

7

Getting It Lived

Study and work with people—the dialectical paradox
of Gene Peterson.
—Eugene Peterson, letter home

After his year's internship at Madison Avenue, the seminary
assigned Eugene to West Park Presbyterian, a thriving church
on the corner of Amsterdam Avenue and West Eighty-Sixth
Street. West Park had just welcomed their new pastor, Dr. William B. McAlpin, from Pittsburgh, where he had pastored while
lecturing in philosophy at Pitt. McAlpin was a skilled administrator and commanding figure, puffing a long cigar anytime he
wasn't behind the massive dark oak pulpit. McAlpin became a
prominent religious leader and was honored with an obituary
in the *New York Times* in December 1972, having died three
days before Christmas while still serving as West Park's pastor.
In 1955, when Eugene first stood on the front steps—just across
Central Park from the seminary—he marveled at the stunning
red sandstone tower, topped by a bell-shaped roof soaring upward. In the spacious auditorium, ceiling-high organ pipes
overlooked mahogany pews, all lit through stained glass. The
light shimmered as illuminated fingers gently reached into hallowed space.

For the next two years, in addition to teaching a junior high boys' Sunday school class, Eugene led West Park's ministry to young professionals (the 20–30 Club), mostly artists eking out meager livings with day jobs while trying to catch the eyes of gallery owners or waiting for callbacks from Broadway. The club was a social affair, with few members expressing much interest in faith. However, the church opened its doors on Friday nights, providing space for gatherings—with a smiling Eugene to organize them.

Eugene enjoyed the evenings when they met. Occasionally the group held a square dance, engulfed in melodies any Montana boy would know. They hired a caller and a fiddler and heated up the floor in the fellowship hall with their stomping, swirling choreography—New York dancers ripping loose to backwoods tunes. Though square dancing was frowned on by his Pentecostal pastors, Eugene had, *somehow,* learned all the steps. "I grew up in square dancing country," he told me with a chuckle. "It wasn't really acceptable, but I was quiet about it. I thought I was pretty good."

His cosmopolitan ministry at West Park pulled him into diverse cultures and new questions. Once again, Eugene found his way to the ordinary folks, never content with the comfortable culture of churchgoers and lifelong Christians. He wrote in one letter back home,

> *Yesterday afternoon and evening I spent at the apartment of one of the 20–30 girls. She had quite a number of people over and we ate, drank (coffee) and passed around highbrow dilettante conversation for a good six hours. Most of the people I didn't know. They were quite an international set . . . Egypt, India, China, Europe—and even one rube from Oregon . . . I don't know how he got in. It was inter-*

*esting though, and was a good chance to cultivate some of
the sown seed.*

West Park's primary gift to Eugene was letting him practice
what it meant to be a pastor, to truly *be* with people. He'd watched
Buttrick immerse himself in the lives of his congregation, but his
seminary professors had "no idea what pastors were or did. Only
one had ever been a pastor, and he was an adjunct." West Park
tossed him into the experiences of real people, giving him oppor-
tunities to roll up his sleeves and immerse himself in the grit of
people's lives. Eugene's letters home overflowed with gratitude for
this space, where ideas and books mattered less than relationships
and conversation.

> *I've been up around the church all afternoon calling on peo-
> ple. I like calling quite a bit. I'm always a little apprehensive
> before I go—afraid of the unknown, you know—but when
> I plunge into it I always begin enjoying it immensely. I keep
> a stack of cards of people that I'm supposed to call on my
> desk and whenever I get tired of seminary and begin to get
> that dusty, monk-like perspective, I grab some cards, jump
> on the subway and, presto!—I'm back in a real world again.*

The members of the 20–30 Club welcomed Eugene and considered him a friend. One couple asked him to help with their
wedding—in the kitchen. *I served in the official capacity of wash-
ing dishes at the reception,* he wrote. *What was it that Jesus said
about that you have to wash people's dishes (or was it feet?) before you can lead them?*
Eugene found something he'd always wanted but had not always known how to name: a true joining of his Sunday faith and
weekday world. *I'm having the time of my life talking to all these*

people at West Park and preaching this informal gospel across cof-
fee cups.

But if the pastoral vocation felt in any way rosy to Eugene, a West
Park janitor would soon contribute an unforgettable and haunting image of the dark side of ministry. Willi Ossa mopped the
floors and polished the pews, but this was only how he paid the
bills. He was an artist, a man working magic with paint and canvas. A German, Willi married the daughter of an American officer
during US occupation following World War II. Upon returning to
New York, the couple lived with their six-month-old daughter in
a third-floor apartment only blocks from West Park.

Willi had seen firsthand the harm that could be wreaked from
pulpits. His boyhood pastor had become a fervent Nazi—and all
the German churches he knew had played cozy with the Third
Reich. He had only disgust for the church and considered the
whole lot corrupt. Willi could not comprehend why Eugene—so
obviously a good and sincere young man—would have anything
to do with such a degraded institution. As they grew to know
each other, he persistently warned Eugene that the church would
ruin him. "He told me that churches, all churches, reduced pastors to functionaries in a bureaucracy where labels took the place
of faces and rules trumped relationships. He liked me. He didn't
want his friend destroyed."

Soon, Eugene was eating dinner every Friday with Willi and his
wife, Mary. After a few weeks, Willi asked Eugene to come an
hour earlier so Willi could paint him. Eugene obliged. He sat quietly during his weekly sessions while Willi coaxed the brush and
eyed Eugene, then the canvas, then Eugene again. Willi's cold intensity spilled onto the easel, but the artist would not allow

Eugene to see his progress. Eugene felt that something was off, though. "One afternoon Mary came into the room, looked at the nearly finished portrait, and exclaimed '*Krank! Krank!*'" Eugene knew only a little German, but the word was familiar: "Sick! Sick!" Mary and Willi argued intensely, and Eugene loosely translated Willi's ominous words: "He's not sick now, but that's the way he will look when the compassion is gone, when the mercy gets squeezed out of him."

In the painting, Eugene's gaunt frame is covered by a featureless black robe. A drab backdrop frames the empty space. A long dim cross stands behind Eugene's shoulder. His bony hands cross a red Bible laid across his lap. His eyes are flat, his expression blank. His skin suffers dark splotches. The form is human, but there is no humanity. *Krank* indeed.

After Eugene had shared two years of friendship and Friday dinners with him, Willi divorced Mary and returned to Germany. Eugene and Willi lost touch, but Eugene kept the painting, pulling it out whenever he needed to remember what was possible, what he could become if he did not guard his soul.

Though Eugene had grown wary of theological reading, Karl Barth smashed his reticence. Remarkably, he didn't first encounter Barth through any seminary class but through one of the basketball players he'd coached a year earlier, a graduate student at Columbia—who wasn't even a Christian.

One Saturday evening as they showered and dressed after a game, the student gushed about these strange, intoxicating words he was reading in Barth's *Epistle to the Romans*. Monday morning, Eugene checked out a copy from the library, and the encounter began his lifelong love of the great theologian. "What I had heard and read of theology up until this point was *about* God.

God and the things of God as if they were topics for discussion, things to be figured out; there was no juice in them." Such theology bored Eugene. It struck him as disconnected from genuine life. But this was different.

> In reading Barth, I realized that for most of my life the people I had been living with and who had taught me had been primarily interested in getting the truth of the gospel and the Bible right, explaining it and defending it. (My parents were blessed exceptions to all this.) Barth didn't have much interest in that. He was a witness. . . . Barth wasn't indifferent to "getting it right," but his passion was in "getting it lived."

For sixty years of ministry, Eugene became a deep and persistent student of Barth, reading through the mammoth corpus of *Church Dogmatics* at least twice. However, it was not so much Barth's precise, labyrinthine (if majestic) arguments that compelled Eugene but rather the *way* Barth did theology, the posture he had before God and with others. Eugene once told me that he was undone by Barth's "vision of God and how Barth never took himself very seriously." Eugene imbibed Barth for six decades. In fact, the writing project he was working on before his death—work he left unfinished—was an essay on Barth.

This widening theological world created a profound tension as Eugene began to sift through his Pentecostal heritage. Immersed in philosophical study at SPU, his thin tether to his upbringing frayed. "I began to feel that my background in religion was crude, earthy and rustic. I began to demand logic and reason for all religious practice." Eugene had felt growing disregard for "loud, apparently undirected sessions of prayer and praise, informal testimony services, the emotional freedom, and the practice of speaking in tongues—all common components of a Pentecostal service."

Eugene's love for philosophy never waned (his seminary classmate Sarah Arnold remembered sitting in the seminary stairwell with Eugene and discussing Kierkegaard for hours). However, he also began to feel the pull of the familiar flame, returning with gratitude to his Pentecostal roots. Those rooftop prayer meetings with Pat Robertson and Joo Sun Ae stirred in Eugene a hunger for intimate encounters, for immediacy with God integrated with the full range of human experience. He longed for "a resurgence of power" that he believed was interwoven with the Holy Spirit. Speaking in tongues, always the lightning rod for Pentecostal theology and long a source of questions and discomfort for Eugene, made him ponder long and hard. Tongues—something that had long embarrassed and confused him—now began to offer to him a direct, life-giving encounter with God.

Eugene, demonstrating how his ideas always seemed to find their way to paper, reflected on his journey in a piece he wrote for the *Pentecostal Evangel* titled "Incurably Pentecostal." He explained how he had sifted through his experiences—frustrations and misunderstandings and the seeming inconsistences of Pentecostal thinking—to rediscover abiding truths. However, writing home after a few rounds with the *Evangel* editor, he expressed frustration: *They've taken out all the punch lines and everything that hints even just a little bit of originality and deviation from the "party line"—and the result is a rather common-place, dull article.* It would be fascinating to read the unrevised manuscript. Where did Eugene raise theological concerns? Where did he veer from the party line? In a final wistful flourish, Eugene echoed the voice of every young writer who is certain his literary brilliance suffers from the heartless slashes of a bad editor's pen: *I . . . hope*

that the day will come when I'll be able to have things in print the
way I write them.

But as Eugene started to make peace with his heritage, a renowned Pentecostal's embarrassing public escapades made it
more complicated. The flamboyant Pentecostal evangelist Oral
Roberts incited ecclesiastical gawking and animated conversation
among the seminarians when he elicited international scorn by
paying $40,000 in freight to transport a carnival tent and eighteen
thousand chairs to Australia for his meetings. Eugene wrote
home, annoyed that the word *Pentecostal* would ever be attached
to such a spectacle—a first taste of how chagrined Eugene would
later become over scandals surrounding religious celebrities.

But for all this, Eugene was also deeply irritated by the anti-
Pentecostalism he encountered in seminary—an attitude that he
considered snobby ignorance masquerading as biblical conviction. If there was anything that annoyed Eugene, it was elitism.
When one professor cautioned that Pentecostal practice inher-
ently leads to excesses like Father Divine (a mid-1900s spiritual
leader who claimed to be Jesus Christ), Eugene wrote in a letter
home,

> Boy, did I blow up. I said—I'm Pentecostal and have been all
> my life . . . and have been to camp-meetings and prayer
> meetings as long as I can remember and have yet to worship
> with anybody that does it with such complete expression
> and fullness as the Pentecostals. . . . My blood really riles
> when people make stupid statements like that. It's a good
> thing I'm here to keep these people straightened out, don't
> you think?

Despite his defensive instinct, as seminary progressed, Eugene's
attachment to Pentecostalism cooled. His theology pushed him
outside the "party line," but this shift was also another case of

simply following the scent. The Presbyterians offered him intern-
ships. They continued to welcome him. Meanwhile, the Pentecostals showed little interest, and slight interactions he did have (such
as writing the *Evangel* article) left him unsatisfied. The longer he
worked at West Park, the more his ordination in the New York
presbytery made sense.

He wrote home,

*I've been thinking seriously of . . . becoming Presbyterian
lately. Everything seems to be opening up that way. And I
feel my ministry is just as full and the need is just as great—
and the doors are open. . . . I'm reluctant to make a decision, but am about ready to conclude that the Assemblies is
a dead-end street for me. In things like this I have no doubt
that the Lord will lead me and make the path clear. So I
won't make any forced decisions. But you pray with me
about it.*

Eugene did not think of this as leaving one tradition for another. Rather, he had begun to bridge both worlds, finding his
own way. In a letter only weeks before his seminary graduation,
Eugene wrote vividly about his experiences with the Holy Spirit.
He told a story of a small group meeting with Harald Bredesen, a
Lutheran minister who later became known as "Mr. Charisma"
on Robertson's CBN. At this meeting, a number of Eugene's
friends (and future prominent leaders) felt a deep hunger for the
Holy Spirit.

Later in his ministry, Eugene seemed to forget some of his experiences (or perhaps later in life, he understood them in different
ways), but this was at least one short stretch where glossolalia, so
elusive yet desired in his youth, was part of his spiritual life. At
any rate, here Eugene was, aglow with the winds of the Spirit—
and wanting to draw others into this vibrant life.

I've been meeting early in the mornings with Donn and Dick at their request to pray for the H.S. I agreed to do it only if I could do whatever I felt like—talk in tongues, sing, pray loud . . . anything. Dick had never heard of anything like that but he agreed—we've been doing it for little over a month now. . . . This is a kind of ministry I've been led into—that is, leading men into a deeper experience with the H.S. I'm beginning to find the use of tongues. The last three months I've been cultivating the practice daily in prayer with much enrichment and profit. It had lain dormant for a long time, you'll remember. The Lord has been teaching me much.

The letter concluded with the flourish of a revivalist: *Look for the Holy Spirit to do great things—and expect big reports for the Holy Spirit's working all over the city. Remember these names. They could tear up the city if they were empowered with the Spirit—wait for the headlines.*

Eugene never abandoned the fundamental convictions that he learned in the churches of his youth—and from the fervent faith of his mother. The Spirit-infused mysticism that characterized Eugene's spirituality the rest of his life was deeply Pentecostal:

The move from Pentecostal to Presbyterian didn't seem like a big thing at the time. It still doesn't. Certainly nothing that could be called a crisis. I was not aware that I was changing any part of what I believed, and certainly not how I lived. But was I still a Pentecostal?

I assumed I was. I hadn't renounced anything that I had grown up believing. I wasn't aware that my Christian identity had eroded in any way. . . .

If I were to define what for me makes up the core Pentecostal identity, it is the lived conviction that everything, absolutely everything, in the scriptures is livable. Not just true, but livable. Not just an idea or a cause, but livable in real life. Everything that is revealed in Jesus and the scriptures, the gospel, is there to be lived by ordinary Christians in ordinary times. This is the supernatural core, a lived resurrection and Holy Spirit core, of the Christian life. What Karl Barth expressed dialectically as the "impossible possibility." I had always believed that. I believed it still.

One personal encounter rearranged Eugene's theological categories in ways that would have given his Pentecostal brethren indigestion. Tasked with reflecting on a current religious personality, Eugene picked Harry Emerson Fosdick, a provocative choice. "In my culture, Fosdick was Beelzebub," he said. A lightning rod in the 1920s fundamentalist versus liberal controversy, "Fosdick was the enemy—the incarnation of unbelieving liberalism . . . the Antichrist." However, Eugene had just finished Fosdick's *The Meaning of Prayer,* the best book on prayer he'd read. He was curious, and rather than accepting the inflamed opinions of others, Eugene wanted to meet the man for himself to learn "what was behind, or not behind, all the vicious invective that surrounded the name Fosdick."

Jim, a seminary classmate, told Eugene that Fosdick lived on Long Island, and he kept prodding Eugene to go talk to him. Eugene hesitated, imagining his Pentecostal pastors seething as he descended into the realm of hell for a conversation with the great Satan. However, while Eugene deliberated, one afternoon Jim picked up the directory and dialed Fosdick's number, then shoved the receiver in Eugene's face. After two rings, Eugene heard a weathered voice. "Hello, this is Harry Fosdick."

The two made plans for Eugene to go to Riverside Church,

where Fosdick still kept an office. When Eugene stepped out of the elevator, a slightly chubby, gray-headed man with rosy cheeks and round, thin-rimmed spectacles grabbed his hand and welcomed him with warm cheer. "Hello, Mr. Peterson, I'm Harry."

Settling into Fosdick's study, Eugene confessed the oddity of their meeting. "You aren't a very popular person in the world I grew up in."

"I know," Fosdick answered, then shared a story about a professor at Southern Baptist Theological Seminary in Louisville who brought a letter from Fosdick to class, a letter in which Fosdick gave a rather orthodox summary of his beliefs. One student in the first row pounded his desk. "I don't care if his name is Harry Emerson Fosdick—he's still a Christian!"

Eugene and Fosdick laughed, and for half an hour, their conversation roamed the religious landscape. "Another name crossed off my 'enemy list,'" Eugene later wrote. "By the time the subway had returned me to midtown Manhattan, my Christian and church world had expanded exponentially." In a later conversation, Eugene added more: "I think Fosdick was quite wrong in some of his conclusions, but I also think we were even worse in our vilification."

Another pivotal encounter was with John Oliver Nelson, a professor at Yale Divinity School who founded the Kirkridge Retreat and Study Center in the Poconos. In November 1956, Eugene wrote home, describing how Nelson brought a group of *social radicals together with devotional radicals . . . [to] integrate them . . . [and to build] the committed kind of ministers who would dive head-first into a buzz saw if they thought that was the will of God.* The retreat week began with silence, forcing the thirty seminarians to dislodge any theological posturing. Eugene continued, *After awhile no one knew what anyone's bias was, where he was from, how good he was, because if you can't talk pretty soon you're all equal. After hours of this the experience of the mystic fellowship of the Christian Church began to be felt.* Daily, they shared morning prayers and physical labor, followed by Scripture reading and discussion. This was Eugene's first monastic experience, and it gripped him. This subversive encounter was a precursor to themes that would ultimately define Eugene's ministry: silence as an essential antidote to overly theologized postures (hearing from God is more essential than talking about God) and suspicion toward our ingrained ideas of success (what you know and what you've done say little about who you are before God).

Eugene was drawn to Nelson. He had potency, an intense conviction. *Nelson is an extremely refreshing and witty man—also the exemplar of the non-conformist who is responsibly committed to a radical, revolutionary ministry.* This hunger for something radical—something so true that it burned in his bones—was a constant in Eugene's life. His longing for God ignited a ferocity in his soul. He left that week at Kirkridge aflame. *It was encouraging to know that there were students in other seminaries—not many perhaps, there never is—but they were there, and they were committed to doing Christ's work in revolutionary ways.*

Eugene needed a revolution. The place, as much as anything else, was a drain on the young seminarian's spirit. As stimulating and invigorating as his friendships, work, and classes were, Eugene longed for Montana's contours and natural beauty. New York did not speak the language of his soul. He wrote in a winter letter home,

We're having a rip-roaring Montana snowstorm in New York today. I woke up this morning with big, soft, fat snowflakes drifting down past my window. Then in a couple of hours the winds were whipping down the 49th street wind tunnel and the elements were abusing every building and pedestrian they could find. But somehow the snow isn't as pretty in the city. Snowflakes weren't made to caress steel towers and soulless cement. They only make them look a little more gaunt and make the cold a trifle more severe. Snowflakes were made for rolling meadows and living trees and black earth that teems with life. Snow is winter's robe for sleeping nature. But put the garment on steel stuff and it's like draping a soulless mannequin with the loveliest creation from the Fifth Avenue salons—they don't exactly enhance one another. Snow in the city becomes like the city—dirty, unwanted, with no purpose . . . antithetical to the beautiful. Snow was made for the country where things live and people live and beauty throws garlands all around. Snow was made to blanket rich black earth, and balance delicately on balsam, and drift unmolested. Snow is the enchanted evening dress of nature denuded. But snow is a dull thing in the city.

But even with its shortcomings, New York unleashed something in Eugene, stimulating his mind and imagination. While his grades had been mediocre at SPU—and a number of his marks at Biblical were lackluster as well—Eugene mastered the languages and his archaeology courses, earning straight As in Greek Exegesis, Hebrew Grammar, and Biblical Archaeology. The dustier and more technical the subject, the more it seemed to shift Eugene's brain into high gear. His master's thesis, "The Doctrine of Salvation in the Qumran Community," sifted through fine grains of historical and lexical detail, like a child digging for treasure in a sandbox.

Eugene's innate talent shone bright. He applied to Princeton for doctoral studies, but he wasn't accepted. However, his work had caught the attention of one of his professors, Old Testament scholar Dewey Beegle. Early on, Beegle took Eugene under his wing and was a presence throughout his time in seminary. During Eugene's final year, Beegle pulled him aside and blindsided him with a remarkable offer. He proposed that Eugene could go to Johns Hopkins University to study with William Albright, one of the world's most prominent biblical archaeologists and Semitic scholars. Beegle had studied with Albright and would make the connection. After Johns Hopkins, Eugene would return to join the faculty at Biblical Seminary to teach Hebrew, archaeology, and Greek. The plan seemed perfect, but the offer meant rethinking his trajectory. Eugene wrote home, reeling from the invitation. His heart leaped at the possibilities.

> [I could study with] Dr. Albright—the greatest Old Testament scholar in the last fifty years. . . .
>
> Well, as I said, it knocked me out for a while. I hadn't been thinking about teaching. I was enjoying my work at West-Park and rather looking forward to a pastorate. I've grown to detest the dry, unreal academic life. If there is anything I don't want to be it is a tiresome, tedious, cold, exacting seminary professor. . . . Archaeology and Hebrew of all things! How archaic can you get! And in the past I've had trouble spiritually with such things. When I become too intellectual I sacrifice spiritually—so I've gotten afraid of it.
>
> But . . . the thing that I want to do more than anything else, and of this there is no doubt in my mind, is to deal with people spiritually. I like to teach. Dr. McAlpin spends most of his time nursing old ladies. Dr. Beegle spends most

of his time grappling with students' problems. There are hardly any seminary professors here or anyplace else who deal with people spiritually, or who are even capable of it. God seems to have given me a ministry of digging deeply into certain spiritual issues. A seminary might be a good place to exercise that—the Lord knows there's a need for it. I have been given an open door—this set-up happens to about one student in a thousand—this may be God's leading . . . even though unexpected and revolutionary to my thinking. I don't have to make a decision for three months. So I won't—and we'll all pray.

Eugene ended the letter by asking for advice: *Tell me what you think—it shook me up bad at first but I'm beginning to feel better about it now.*

It wasn't only Eugene's scholarship that was flourishing. Eugene's pen flowed freely as well. Though he'd always dreamed of writing novels, poetry found him first. Effusive, Eugene wrote home explaining an invigorating literary project.

I've had a little secret brewing for a while that you might be interested in. A few around here have encouraged me to write a little more. So I've been pulling a bit of the casual poetry that I sometimes dash off together. Jim Hughes, who is an extraordinary artist, is making charcoal drawings to go with each one, so that facing each poem will be a sketch. If we can ever find anybody to publish it, it would be called "Twentieth Century Psalms," or "A Modern Psalmist," or something like that. Jim says that it's a snap to publish poetry—anybody can do it. So if that's true we might have

some success. . . . I think it's great writing myself—the
problem is to convince the world!

Eugene and Jim never finished the sketches and poetry. Yet it's
remarkable to encounter the seedbed of Eugene's creative impulse
that would come to fruition over forty years later when he would
eventually fashion Psalms into contemporary language, poetry
for the modern ear. There was so much stirring in Eugene, so
much passion and energy, so many possibilities.

During Eugene's last year at seminary, Pastor McAlpin pulled
Eugene into his study. "Eugene, I know you're heading to graduate school and plan to become a professor, not a pastor, but
I'd like to see you get ordained into the Presbyterian ministry."
Eugene listened. "You need a church in which you have peers and
affirm an established theological heritage. Professional ministry,
whether as professor or pastor, is not a place for lone wolves."
With the understanding that he was heading to the academy, not
the church, Eugene agreed and entered the ordination process
that would continue while he commenced his PhD studies. However, his acquiescence had boundaries. Eugene wrote home with
clear instructions.

Don't ever buy me a pulpit robe. That is one thing I have no
desire to possess. If they want me to wear one, they can
provide it—otherwise I preach as I come. If you insist on
getting something for my graduation get a pair of socks
(but no ties please).

With that, Eugene was off to Baltimore. In the fall of 1957, Eugene arrived at Johns Hopkins to study with William Foxwell Albright. Besides being one of the seminal scholars of the twentieth-century biblical archaeology movement, Albright was a character. The son of Methodist missionaries to Chile, Eugene's new teacher had been raised in near poverty and had a reputation for being a bit spartan with money. (The story goes that Albright produced the final typescript for his groundbreaking work, *From the Stone Age to Christianity*, on recycled paper, refusing to trash pages still offering one clean side to type on.)

That frugality extended to medicine, with Albright touting home remedies his mom had relied on as she made do with their meager missionary salary. Albright's favorite cure-all was liniment oil; he pushed the tonic at every hint of illness, provoking behind-the-back snickers from his doctoral students. Once, when Eugene had to spend extended time in the infirmary with a knee injury, Albright visited and, with doctors out of earshot, offered advice. "You know," he said, leaning in as if to share a precious secret, "people don't think I know what I'm talking about, but what you need is . . . *liniment oil*. It'll take care of you."

But the personal quirks only threw his brilliance into sharper relief. An intimidating intellect, he was a "polymath who made contributions in almost every field of Near Eastern studies." Albright's eccentricities made him all the more beloved by his students, who affectionately referred to him as the "Old Man." In Albright, Eugene found "one of the first men I encountered who really lived what they believe, and when you encounter someone like that, you wake up." Eugene admired Albright because he combined a dazzling mind with a profound humility. Albright "was brilliant but untainted with any superficiality."

One morning, Albright entered class after staying up half the night working through a vexing question: the location of Mount

Moriah, where God commanded Abraham to bind Isaac for sacrifice. Albright rushed into class, breathless to share his groundbreaking discovery. Feral with new knowledge, he attacked the
room-wide blackboard, scratching strange linguistics from one
wall to the other. He poured Ugaritic, Arabic, Assyrian, Aramaic,
and Hebrew onto the black space, basking in a monumental triumph. *He had found it.*

Eugene and the rest of the class reeled, trying to keep up
with this explosion of genius. But then, the unthinkable—
Prescott Williams, one of Eugene's friends, interrupted. "But,
Dr. Albright . . ."

The class sat spellbound. *Impossible*—one of their own dis-
agreeing with the master. But Albright listened, stone still and
pondering as Prescott politely walked through his objections to
the argument. Then the room fell silent. The professor picked up
his eraser and slowly wiped vast swaths across the blackboard.
"Forget everything I said," he stated simply. "Prescott is right."

Eugene never forgot it. "The people who stand out in my life,"
he reflected, "are the people who don't flaunt what they are doing
and aren't stuck on who they are." A man who could wipe away a
little of his ego along with the chalk was a man to be respected.
Years later, Prescott Williams, an expert in biblical languages
himself (and also someone Eugene admired for using his intellect
with immense humility), would serve as an exegetical consultant
on *The Message*.

Eugene entered Johns Hopkins with mental energy revving.
Under Albright, he began to see how ideas and knowledge could
be *lived*, a surprising discovery to make in the ivory halls of a top
tier archaeology department.

The world of the intellect came alive for me in those years in
his presence. Knowledge wasn't just storing up information
in a mental warehouse. It was the disciplined practice of

thinking, imagining, formulating, testing for the truth. And teaching wasn't just getting information or data into students' minds. There was something deeply dialogical involved, as words sparked into meaning and started truth fires that blazed with comprehension.

Every week, listening to Professor Albright lecture, sitting with him in his study with five other students reading the Hebrew Bible, drinking coffee with older students in the commons, getting a feel for the immense world of the mind, the aesthetics of the intellect, I began to inhabit a world I never knew existed, a world of learning *embodied*, vibrant with energy.

In this invigorating Hopkins world, Eugene rubbed shoulders with numerous other academics. Like Raymond Brown, one of the most prominent biblical exegetes of the twentieth century, who was finishing his degree under Albright. And Sam Iwry, the eminent Hebrew scholar who helped authenticate the Dead Sea Scrolls (Iwry was a Jewish professor who always referred to Eugene as his "goy student"). And Gus Van Beek, curator of old-world archaeology at the Smithsonian for forty-eight years. And there was Charles Fensham, a Fulbright scholar completing his third PhD, who rescued Eugene most evenings, when, after a grueling day of classes that left Eugene completely lost, Charles "patiently untangled and sorted out the stream-of-consciousness commentary that left me bewildered in the lectures and seminars." Charles, a distinguished professor of Old Testament at the University of Stellenbosch, and Eugene remained friends, writing letters until Charles's death.

However, as stimulating as each friendship and academic course proved to be and as remarkable as it was entering Albright's orbit, none of these offered the encounter that would turn Eugene's world inside out. Not even close.

It's easy to imagine Eugene during those classroom years, reflecting back on the early movements of his life with the old sense of "fit" in mind. This son of a butcher, with mountains in his soul and the wide sky in his squinting smile, had always been looking for his place of belonging. The academy, with its serious ideas and search for truth, had an irresistible allure, but he also eschewed the pretense, the inflated egos, the shallow woodenness. The church was his home, but he often felt at odds there too, with its stale formality and its too-easy disconnect from the grit of life.

Eugene always longed most for relationship, for human connection. "Being a pastor is always relational work," he told me. This longing is why Eugene could know all kinds of VIP figures but never have much to say about any of them. But his friends—the former students, the farmer (Uncle Vern) who provided him produce, a few plain pastors, his parishioners—these were the people he would talk about, the people whose names and phone numbers were scribbled in his little pocket notebook. But there would be one person with whom he would find his true place, his true belonging. Together, they would weave an intimate bond, that connection Eugene had always craved.

PART TWO

8

The Long Married

October is a fine and dangerous season in America. . . .
It is a wonderful time to begin anything at all.
—Thomas Merton, *The Seven Storey Mountain*

As Birmingham's autumn leaves blushed auburn and gold, Vincent Stubbs paced the sterile waiting area of South Highlands Infirmary's maternity ward. When the doctor emerged through the corridor doors, he pumped Vincent's hand. "Congratulations. It's a girl."

October 30, 1935. Janice Endslow Stubbs had arrived.

Jan, with her brother, Vincent Jr. ("Buddy"), and older sister, Nancy, enjoyed a warm, joyful childhood. The Stubbses lived in Edgewood, only five miles south of Birmingham's center but known by locals as "over the mountain." Gentle, tree-lined streets, with only two police officers—the kind of town where you'd walk with your siblings to the drugstore for a soda.

If the walls of the old Stubbs house could talk, they'd recall music and good conversation. Jan's mother, Dorothy, played the piano, and her father made rich discussion an art and a pleasure. "My dad was the last of the southern gentlemen," Jan remembered. "Every evening after supper, after dessert if we had any, we'd sit around the table and talk. Dad would talk about any pressing issues that were happening."

It was wonderful. But Eden always has a serpent or two. Although still too young to articulate the tensions, even as a young girl, Jan recognized the racial divides of the South. One warm, breezy afternoon, Jan played in the backyard as her mom hung clothes on the line. Jan wandered out the gate, around the corner, and down the block. A neighborhood landscaper, a black man named Will, caught her toddling down the sidewalk and scooped her in his arms. "Now, Miss Jan, you're not supposed to run away like that," he told her. Will walked Jan home, carrying her a block, walking hand in hand a block. Jan remembered Will's kindness for the rest of her life, in hindsight understanding she had been protected by a man most of her neighbors treated with contempt.

Another memory of racial disparity stood out after her family moved to Montgomery so her dad could open an office for the United States Fidelity and Guaranty Company. Eleven-year-old Jan walked with her family along Dexter Avenue Square in downtown Montgomery, only blocks from Dexter Avenue Baptist Church and only steps from the bus stop where Rosa Parks would board the Cleveland Avenue bus. A large construction project took over the square, closing the sidewalks. Pine boards ran along the edge of the street, allowing pedestrians to walk single file to stay out of the mud. Jan stepped on one end without noticing a black man on the other end walking toward her. Immediately, he stepped off, yielding. "It hurt me that he felt like he had to be submissive to a white person. I don't know where my feelings came from. I knew something was wrong." That sense of the wrongness of things never left her, always pulling her toward questions of justice.

In Montgomery, the Stubbses lived at 33 Courtland Drive, in a quiet neighborhood lined with small one-story homes, a few blocks from where Hank Williams Sr. lived for a short stretch. Jan attended Sidney Lanier High School, an all-white school with an elaborate culture of secret societies. One of the societies, named "13," recruited her, but both Jan and her mother wanted none of it. The girls (including the governor's daughter) made a hoity-toity circle, with a barbaric sense of social punishment for those who didn't make the guest list for weekend parties. Jan found more kinship in the youth group at Memorial Presbyterian and in regular worship at Trinity Presbyterian.

Jan especially loved when Granddaddy and Grandma Stubbs came to visit. He "was a Quaker, full-on, quiet, dressed conservatively." Her grandparents had owned a farm in Delta, Pennsylvania, passed to her granddaddy Gilp from his father, who was the first store owner and first postmaster in the town—and the man described in 1905 by the *York Daily* as "Delta's most progressive citizen . . ." Jan's grandparents had to sell the farm when all the help shipped off to the First World War, and they moved into town, where Granddaddy Gilp bought a furniture store. But he made most of his money building caskets by hand in a shop at the back. Whenever morticians dropped off a body, the corpse would lie next to Granddaddy's workbench, offering quiet company while he sanded and fitted the raw boards. Anytime Jan was visiting, she snuck to the back, reverently watching her grandpa work the saw and plane and smelling the formaldehyde, glue, and sawdust.

When it came to profound friendships for Jan, none equaled her neighbor Gertrude Floyd. Most summer Saturdays, Gertrude and her husband joined the Stubbses in their backyard for barbecue. When she turned thirteen, Jan began to regularly walk through the gate in her back fence and knock on Gertrude's screen door. Gertrude threw the door open with a smile. "Come in—I'll get us some lemonade. You go on out to the porch." Jan spent countless hours on that veranda, sitting with a woman who offered her both her home and her heart. Later, Jan remembered Gertrude as the woman who introduced her to the hospitality of unhurried conversation—the hospitality that became Jan's life-long gift to the world.

In 1953, Jan entered Alabama College, State College for Women, an all-girls school. "They had to import boys from a navy base in Florida," Jan remembered with a glimmer. Then her mischievous-ness gave way to exasperation: "It became coed *after* I left."

As part of her social work major, one year Jan landed a sum-mer job back in Montgomery with a government program screen-ing for tuberculosis. "Everyone had to have chest X-rays, but in the black neighborhoods, they made them have blood work too. That galled me because they didn't do that in the white neighbor-hoods." One week, Jan's team set up their clinic in the Sunday school rooms of Dexter Avenue Baptist. Unloading supplies, she noticed on the wall a painting of a black Jesus surrounded by black children. "The image startled my prejudice, and I thought, *Oh, yeah, I've got to adjust—this is right, not the way I assume it.*"

All morning, folks from the neighborhood streamed through, scratching their names and family histories on clipboards, then stepping outside into the mobile medical unit. During a lunch break, Jan roamed the hallways, wanting to see the sanctuary, the first black church she'd ever visited. She found the silent space, hazy light filtering through arched windows, bright red carpet running up the center aisle to the pulpit. Entering from the hall adjoining the auditorium, she jolted when she saw a man stand-ing next to the communion table. He said nothing, but there was a weightiness to him. "Oh . . . excuse me." Jan stumbled over her words, feeling like a juggler in a monastery. He glanced, then

The young Peterson family: Eugene (top left), Don (top right), Ken and Karen (middle), Evelyn (front).

Don Peterson (right) and Harry Hoiland in front of their grocery and butcher shop.

Eugene as a toddler, practicing his trademark grin.

Eugene (right), Ben Moring (second from left), and the relay team at SPU.

Haunting portrait of a young Eugene by painter Willie Ossa. For the rest of his life, Eugene kept this image as a reminder of the spiritual danger of the pastoral calling.

Eugene and Jan on their wedding day, August 2, 1958.

Newlyweds Eugene and Jan at Camp Letts, Maryland.

Bono and the pastor.
Photo by Taylor Martyn

The young family, about 1966 (from left: Leif, Grandpa Don Peterson, Karen, Eric, Eugene, and Jan).

Eugene playing banjo for his family.

Breaking ground for Christ Our King Presbyterian Church, Bel Air, Maryland, 1964.

Pastor Eugene in the sanctuary of Christ Our King Presbyterian Church. This building became a physical expression of his pastoral calling and belief about Christian community.

The extended Peterson family gathered at Flathead Lake, Montana.

Christ Our King Presbyterian Church, Bel Air, Maryland.

Eugene and Jan during one of the
many happy summers spent on
Flathead Lake.

Eugene on the dock below the Peterson
home on Flathead Lake, Montana.

Newspaper story of Pastor Eugene
running marathons, showing his
community engagement and humanity.

Eugene teaching at Regent College,
Vancouver, British Columbia.
Photos by Kate Power

Eugene and Jan float
in the Dead Sea during
one of his three trips
to the Holy Land.

Eugene and Jan on
a trip to Scotland,
speaking and
visiting friends.

Eugene with his grandson Drew on
the day of Eric's ordination.
Photo by Todd Holden

Eugene at their Bel Air, Maryland, home.
Photo by Todd Holden

Eugene and Jan with Gisela Kreglinger, one of the many beloved students welcomed into the Petersons' lives.

View of Flathead Lake from Selah House.
Photo by Winn Collier

Eugene at rest in his casket—handmade by his son Eric.
Photo by Winn Collier

Eugene and Jan canoeing on the lake.

looked away. "He acted like he didn't want to see me there, so I walked back out to the education wing, where I was supposed to be anyway."

Several years later, when Jan and Eugene were invited to a somewhat secretive gathering with Dr. Martin Luther King Jr. in Baltimore, she realized whom she had encountered in Dexter Avenue's sanctuary.

After Jan had attended Alabama College for two years, her family moved to Baltimore for her father's work. Wanting to be closer to her family in their new city, Jan transferred to Maryland's State Teachers College at Towson (now Towson University) and switched her major to education. Here, she could save money by living with her folks while finishing her degree.

Eugene was moving to Baltimore for school too, and before leaving New York, Eugene had saved money by selling his Oldsmobile to help with tuition for the PhD program at Johns Hopkins. When not studying with Albright, Eugene lived in a cramped dorm with Bob Morrison, a grad student in geology. Bob, an atheist, detested Christians. But he eventually warmed to Eugene's easy way, and the two spent weekends roaming Baltimore and touring the Piedmont in Bob's Jeep.

On Thanksgiving weekend, a friend on staff at InterVarsity Christian Fellowship invited Eugene to a Saturday gathering hosted at Johns Hopkins Medical School. Knowing Eugene was Pentecostal, his friend assumed he could lead the singing.

It was a momentous invitation. The day of the event, Jan was wrestling with loneliness and an aching heart. She walked into the front entrance of the medical school that day with a prayer: *God, would you please provide someone for me? I want to find love.*

God listened. When Eugene stepped onto the platform to lead

two hundred young adults in rousing choruses, his pulse quick-
ened when he saw an attractive brunette in the sixth row. "We
were almost eye to eye," Jan remembered. "I liked his smile." The
music was only slightly a disaster; Eugene, in spite of being Pentecostal, fought to keep his rhythm and remember lyrics. Jan
found herself distracted too. "Gene was standing right in the center. He seemed so *close* to me. I thought he had blue eyes, and I
was really looking him over. I liked him—he looked like a good
person. I sure stared when he was up on the stage. *Yessireeee.*
Within an hour of praying that prayer, I laid my eyes on the man
I was married to for sixty years."

The service dismissed, and the pair converged briefly in the
jammed aisle. "We had both noticed each other," Jan told me, her
cheeks flushed and eyes bright, a fire freshly kindled. "He was
very shy. And I was very shy. We both said small hellos. Then he
disappeared. A few minutes later, I looked, and he was at the book
table. Of *course* he was." With both their hearts stirred, the evening ended. They slipped into the cool Baltimore night without
another word. On the ride home with her girlfriend, Jan made a
vow: "I'm going to have to start going to InterVarsity more often."

The next evening, Eugene planned to attend the Baltimore
Symphony's performance of *Messiah*. However, Charles Fensham, his friend from South Africa, had agreed to speak on apart-
heid for a student gathering at Central Presbyterian and asked
Eugene to help him navigate the bus line to the church. Eugene's
irritation over missing the concert evaporated the moment he saw
the same gorgeous brunette who'd taken his breath away the night
before.

During Charles's talk, Eugene watched Jan to make certain she
didn't slip away after the *amen*. Eugene introduced himself and in
a deft move arranged for a shared ride home. He dumped Charles
in the front so he and Jan could ride in the back. Here the stories

diverge—Jan told me that *she* finagled the ride. Both agree that those twenty minutes left them wanting more. But as Eugene stood on the sidewalk, watching the red taillights fade, he realized he never asked for Jan's phone number. Or even her last name.

Back in the dorm, Bob unleashed on his poor heartsick roommate. "You Christians! You are so stupid. You meet an attractive woman and you walk off without arranging for any way to see or talk to her again. How do you even manage to propagate your species? I've never encountered such idiocy."

Eugene called John, a classmate who went to Central Presbyterian, and described Jan to him. But neither he nor his wife, Anne, could place her. Eugene remembered that he'd grabbed a bulletin from Central Presbyterian's Sunday worship and that Jan had mentioned that she and her brother had been listed in the bulletin as students who would be attending the Urbana missions conference that year. Running his finger down the list, he found them: Janice and Buddy Stubbs.

"Bob," Eugene shouted. "I know her name—Stubbs. Jan Stubbs."

Bob grabbed Eugene's arm and pulled him out the dorm, across the street, and into a convenience store. Bob got change for a ten-dollar bill, then shoved Eugene into a phone booth, handing him a stack of dimes. "Start calling." Eugene opened the Baltimore white pages and flipped to *S*, only to discover there were sixty-two entries for Stubbs. With a sigh, he fed one dime at a time, alternating between a Stubbs from the top of the list and a Stubbs from the bottom. Each time, a ring or two, then a "Hello?"

"May I speak with Jan?"

"Who?" Eugene hung up and grabbed another dime.

Miraculously, he wasted only fifty cents. On the sixth try, Jan's dad answered and heard his future son-in-law's voice for the first time. "She's next door. Can I ask who's calling?"

"My name's Eugene," came the reply, "and I'm calling from a phone booth. I'll call her back."

Only Eugene never needed to call back. John called the next morning. "Anne and I figured out who you were describing! Jan Stubbs is coming to our house for dinner Friday night. Will you join us?"

Why yes, he most certainly would.

At home in Kalispell that Christmas, Eugene took Karen shopping downtown. He shocked his little sister when he walked into the Flowers by Hansen store and ordered a dozen roses for delivery to a girl in Baltimore.

When the florist rang the Stubbses' front door holding that massive red bouquet, Jan went weak. After the holidays, Jan and Eugene quickly became inseparable. Dates to museums, outings to bird refuges around the Chesapeake, spring picnics, long afternoons watching lacrosse—anything fun (that happened to be free, since Eugene was broke).

But there was a hurdle. Eugene planned to be a professor, not a pastor. Years earlier, Jan had asked God for a specific vocation— pastor's wife. She felt a deep calling to offer hospitality to neighbors and members of the parish. With this young man, head full of Hebrew and heart full of Greek, she had to make a decision: Did she want a pastor, or did she want Eugene?

Eugene knew what he wanted, though. Writing home, he gushed about what drew him to Jan so powerfully:

Her sensitivity to human situation[s], her feeling and passion, her depth of spirit that isn't quickly plumbed, her deep desire in the high reaches of the Spirit, her reckless abandon in learning, her capacity to love—all this and a lot more are what she is. I've not found many people with whom I've been able to talk freely of the things that are closest to me with no feeling of inhibition—but with Jan I can, and always there is that quick, warm, ingenuous response.

One Thursday evening in February (after only months of dating), Eugene knew that Jan would be at choir practice. So he called Jan's dad and asked if he could stop by. Sweat pouring, Eugene sat facing Mr. Stubbs; the room was spinning like the couch was fixed to a merry-go-round. Every creak of the floor echoed through the house, every tick of the clock a gunshot. Vincent offered mercy. "You don't have to do this. Let's go in the kitchen and get coffee."

A few nights later, Jan was recovering from a sinus infection and nursing an inflamed throat. Strangely undeterred, Eugene picked her up for dinner. They drove to Peerce's Plantation, a restaurant with a striking view of the Loch Raven Reservoir and famous for crab cakes, house-smoked salmon, and Chesapeake filet. Peerce's required men to wear a coat and tie, and the maître d' handed women menus without prices.

After a candlelit dinner—Shrimp a la Newburg for her, pork chops for him—Eugene insisted they drive by Fox Hollow Golf Course (a serene spot he'd scouted earlier). Jan protested, telling Eugene she didn't feel well and wanted to go home, but he persisted. Driving past a lush fairway, he suggested they go for a walk. A sprinkler shot blasts of water in a semicircle as misty steam rose from the ryegrass. The scene wasn't exactly working out the way Eugene had imagined, but he pressed forward. Jan, hoarse and incredulous, looked at Eugene. "Are you serious?" Finally, though, they made it to the bench with the view.

"Eugene was wondering how to get me in the right mood," Jan shared. "Well, he got me in the right mood by kissing me." He dropped to one knee and put a ring on her finger.

The lovers were eager to marry. But first Jan needed to graduate and Eugene needed to be ordained. Unfortunately, the date the council set for Eugene's ordination in June was the same day as Jan's graduation, meaning neither could be at the other's event.

At Eugene's ordination, pastors from the entire presbytery gathered and listened as the other five candidates read their statements of faith. With innocuous and predictable papers, most of the council yawned, passing them without a single question. Eugene, however, went for broke. A few minor theological fireworks flamed into a sharp debate, causing pastors to sit on the edge of the pews at what was typically a dull formality.

After I had finished, Eugene wrote home, *a man stood up and said "I move we extend a vote of gratitude to Mr. Peterson for provoking the first theological discussion that I've ever witnessed on the floor of this presbytery."* Eugene received encouraging nods to most of his answers, but one prickly pastor disapproved of one contentious interchange. (I so desperately wanted to know the heated issue, but Eugene could not recall.) When the moderator called for the vote, the group approved Eugene for ordination 147–1. So within hours of each other, Eugene received his ordination papers, and Jan received her diploma.

Soon the couple was picking out flowers and arranging for a reception space. The first time Jan met Eugene's parents was the day they arrived in Baltimore for the wedding. "That was intimidating," Jan recalled. But solely on the force of her son's love, Evelyn had already welcomed her.

For the bachelor party, Jan's dad planned a four-hour road trip to Monticello, Thomas Jefferson's iconic home. Ben Moring was Eugene's best man, and though they were driving into the heart of still-segregated Virginia, Vincent never considered the complications of having a black man with them. When the hungry crew entered a roadside café off Highway 29, heads turned. Locals watched as the owner stopped them at the door and explained that he would not serve Ben in his establishment. Vincent loaded everyone in the car and drove on. "Dad was so embarrassed," Jan remembered.

Thankfully, the following day yielded to joy. On August 2, 1958, Vincent walked Jan down the center aisle of Govans Presbyterian Church, her white long-sleeved gown gracefully brushing the floor. Jan watched Eugene through her sheer veil, her eyes moist. Her dad walked her under the buttress arch as sunlight poured from the single Gothic window behind the altar. Eugene, in a gray tux jacket, black bow tie, and black pants, stood at the front. His heart thumped wildly, right under his white boutonniere. Ben stood next to him with the rings in his pocket. Jan and Eugene said their vows, holding each other's gaze, and Pastor Lloyd Ice pronounced them husband and wife.

After a honeymoon at Deep Creek Lake in the Maryland Alleghenies, real life hit quickly. Eugene returned to his studies, and Jan began her first year of teaching at Govans Elementary. On the heels of *Brown v. Board of Education*, in which the segregation of public schools was ruled unconstitutional, Baltimore city schools were in upheaval. A flood of white families exited the suburbs, enrolling their children in private academies. Jan was hired to teach first grade, but two weeks into the school year, the desperate principal reassigned her to second grade. She found herself an overworked and undersupported first-year teacher in an overwhelmed school. She'd been moved to another grade, totally unprepared. And all this *after* the school year commenced.

It was a brutal introduction to the classroom. Eugene walked Jan to the streetcar every morning at seven. By the time she arrived home late in the afternoon, she crashed on the couch, wanting nothing but sleep. Unfortunately, often there was a stench that was anything but restful. The housing they could afford was a dank basement with little sunlight, and it reeked of waste and sulfur whenever the sewer overflowed.

Amid this stress, a miscarriage revealed that Jan was anemic. Her doctor instructed Eugene to nurse his wife back to health, telling him to "treat Jan like she's an athlete." The young husband took it to heart. Eugene went into overdrive, reading stacks of health books, purchasing yogurt cultures, cooking liver and black-strap molasses, and insisting Jan eat *everything*. At the next doctor's visit, in desperation, Jan asked the doctor, "How long do I have to eat this stuff?"

"What stuff?" the doc asked. Jan listed everything Eugene had shoveled onto her plate.

"Eugene," the doctor said, "I only meant no alcohol or smoking."

After completing his courses, Eugene and Albright agreed Eugene would write his dissertation on an ancient Palestinian sect with no documented history. At the same time, Biblical Seminary asked Eugene to return to New York to teach Greek and Hebrew and serve as what Eugene saw as "a kind of faculty utility infielder, each semester picking up a course vacated by a professor on sabbatical." Jan and Eugene left the sewer-cave and moved into a small New York City apartment.

But still, money was tight. The seminary could pay Eugene only a pittance. So the young professor couldn't believe his good fortune when, full of Semitic lore and poised on the threshold of a life of biblical scholarship, he received a call from a publisher. They presented the enviable assignment of writing a commentary on the Psalms.

Most scholars wait decades for an offer like this. "I had moved in a single day from a sandlot pickup game of baseball to the starting lineup in Yankee Stadium." Eugene went to work, studying the text, poring over the great commentators of the past, assembling notes and comments. "And then I wrote. I was well on my way when the project collapsed and my assignment was canceled. The only evidence remaining of that two years of immersion in the Psalms is a file drawer full of exegetical notes."

Still in need of income, Eugene jumped at the opportunity when White Plains Presbyterian asked him to serve as an assistant pastor. To top it off, the job included housing. It was entirely a financial decision, as he still had no interest in being a pastor long term. On Tuesdays and Thursdays, he boarded the train for a thirty-minute commute to teach, and the rest of the week he spent with parishioners, working from a small study in the eighteenth-century stone Gothic church.

The pastor of White Plains and Eugene made an odd couple. Eugene was athletic but thin and wiry. "[Bill] Wiseman was a big guy," Eugene remembered, "driving a big Chrysler car." Muscular and fierce, Wiseman had lettered in hockey, boxing, and football in high school in Ottawa. Wiseman took Eugene under his wing, taking him on pastoral visits—followed by regular racquetball matches. And with this relationship, a new image of healthy ministry entered Eugene's pastoral imagination.

Wiseman "took the whole business of being a pastor seriously. He wasn't a pulpit pastor. He was with the people, making hospital calls. This was legitimate work." Wiseman, who later became dean of the chapel at the University of Tulsa and in 1978 was named national Preacher of the Year, was no slouch behind the pulpit either. One newspaper described Wiseman as "renowned for his preaching and the eloquence of his pastoral prayers." Watching Wiseman, Eugene felt drawn deeper into the lives of these people who at first had mostly represented a paycheck. These people, he discovered, were the heart of pastoral work.

Eugene's heart was expanding in other ways too. On May 26, 1960, Jan and Eugene brought their first child home.

Karen, named for Eugene's beloved younger sister, woke before dawn most days. For much of her first year, Eugene carried her downstairs while Jan got a little much-needed rest. He strapped Karen into her booster seat and set her on the counter next to him as he brewed a pot of coffee in their little kitchen. She would coo and babble as Eugene counted scoops of beans for the grinder: *one, two, three, four*—the numbers that would become Karen's first words.

After coffee, Eugene carried her into his study. There, he would kneel with his Bible while Karen crawled across the floor, pulling dusty books from the shelves and chewing the edges. Decades later, Eugene would open his copy of Calvin's *Institutes*, and there they still were: Karen's scribbles. Eugene told me that many of his books were illustrated by Karen, and he explained how much it meant to him to find among his stacks those reminders of her first three years and their morning prayer routine. In his library, among vast volumes of trenchant theology, those Crayola squiggles carried just as much weight as Barth and Hildegard.

Amid everything new at the church and at home, Eugene was immersed in his Bible courses at Biblical Seminary. He found himself not merely studying these texts but *entering* them, inhabiting the land of Israelites and Philistines, the terrain of Mark and Mary. He walked inside these texts. He ate and drank them.

As I picked through Eugene's journals and letters, his vocabulary revealed how integrated he was into the Bible's reality; Scripture's language and imagery overlaid the narrative for his own story. He was "bogged down in Philistine stuff" or found himself "in the company of the Ephraimites." He needed to endure his "Moab" or wait for his "Shulamite's reward." As he taught a course on John's Revelation, the text pulled him in profound ways. He imagined himself in Revelation's apocalyptic world, taking on the identity of the pastor: John of Patmos, serving in the midst of the Babylonian Empire. On Tuesdays and Thursdays, Eugene delved into Revelation while being immersed in the affluence and poverty of New York's power-crazed metropolis— another kind of Babylon. The rest of the week, he waded into lives of despair and hope and sin and righteousness. This pastoral life that before seemed parochial and inconsequential suddenly seemed vast and substantial.

Eugene had assumed professors sat atop the hierarchy of religious professions. Professors were the maestros, the oracles of wisdom, while pastors were "shadowy, undefined figures in the background." And now he was a professor, "a bona fide player in the minor leagues of academia but on [his] way, [he] assumed, to the big leagues." However, as he walked around the world of Revelation and among the people of White Plains, he experienced a shift in his thinking:

> The classroom was too easy. The room was too small and orderly to do justice to the largeness of the subject matter— the extravagance of the beauty, the exuberance of the language. Too much was excluded from the classroom—too much life, too much of the world, too much of the students, the complexities of relationships, the intricacy of emotions. The classroom was too tidy. I missed the texture of the weather, the smell of cooking, the jostle of shoulders and elbows on a crowded sidewalk.

Around this time, he had another encounter, with his mom's older cousin Abraham Vereide, that further deepened his vision of pastoral work beyond what he had known. Abraham's parents died in Norway when he was only eight, and as a young man, he boarded a steamer to the United States. After reaching Montana, Abraham roamed the Great Falls area on horseback, an itinerant circuit-riding preacher with a rifle hung in a leather scabbard and a Bible tucked in his belt.

In Seattle, Abraham pulled together business and religious leaders to form a breakfast group. When Eugene's mom was just a young girl, Abraham once took her with him, and she was shocked to find "Democrats and Republicans, Lutherans and Methodists, Roman Catholics and Greek Orthodox, Jews and even an occasional Chinese Buddhist, Presbyterians and Pentecostals, churched and unchurched, sitting down together for a weekly breakfast of bacon and eggs, waffles and yogurt." In 1953, these breakfast groups evolved into the President's Prayer Breakfast, now known as the National Prayer Breakfast, held annually at the Washington Hilton.

Eugene attended the 1960 breakfast in DC, where he met Abraham. The following year, Abraham visited Jan and Eugene in White Plains. Abraham gave Eugene another picture of how a pastor moves out of "stifling sectarianism" into God's broad world with curiosity, generosity, and wide-open eyes.

These experiences, because of their richness, complicated Eugene's picture of his future.

That picture would only get hazier. Dr. Albright announced his retirement. He told Eugene not to worry, though, that he would recommend him to Brevard Childs at Yale. If Albright was a luminous fire fading into night, Childs was a fresh torch. Pioneering the field of canonical studies, Childs would become one of the most influential Old Testament scholars of the twentieth century, teaching at Yale for forty-one years. And now, as Albright resigned, Childs was actively looking for students for his growing program.

When Eugene visited Yale, Childs took an instant liking to this bright student, offering him a spot in the program along with a generous stipend of $7,000 per year. Eugene returned to New York, elated, seemingly with the key to his future in hand. Yet he felt unmoored. A dream in keeping with his whole direction up until that point had opened. And at one of the most prestigious institutions in the nation. So why was he wavering? Why didn't it sit right?

The answer was *Jan*. Eugene's love for Jan—and her love for him—had transformed him. From their early months together, Eugene had felt the power of her magnetism, how she drew him, with her playfulness and warmth, into the heart's unexpected terrain. "I was intoxicated with the life of the mind, the world of wonders opened up by these ancient languages—Akkadian and Aramaic, Ugaritic and Hebrew, Syriac and Arabic." But Jan, on the other hand, was "poised on the cusp of a world of relationships, anticipating learning the names and stories of the men and women, the children and elderly . . . just waiting to be met in conversations and meals, people to love and enjoy, people to sing and pray with."

Years later, Sister Constance (a Carmelite nun who became Eugene's spiritual director and a dear friend of both Jan and Eugene) reflected to Jan that her vocation was a bit like a Protestant version of Sister Constance's call to cloistered life. Jan *saw* people's wounds, and she wanted to help heal them. She faced injustice head-on, and she wanted to dismantle it. She saw isolation, and she instinctively pulled those lonely hearts into circles of belonging. Jan's passion, her unobtrusive, natural largeheartedness, drew Eugene into a life he had not known he wanted: a pastoral life.

In hindsight, Jan saved Eugene from the life he thought he wanted, a life that would have been a grave danger. He later reflected,

> Those years of graduate study could have marked the beginning of a slow withdrawal from a relational life into a world of books. She rescued me from that. I was in love with books and language and the life of learning. I never knew there was so much adrenaline in it. But I was also in love with Jan, the accessibility of her emotions, her immediacy to present things and people, her delight in the *hereness* and *nowness* of life. I had never met anyone quite like her. . . . Reading and writing books didn't seem a very attractive prospect without Jan.

Eugene went to Baltimore because of the languages and the books and the research. He had no idea he'd find something he didn't even know he needed or wanted. He had no idea he'd find Jan. He had no idea all the joy and the delight, as well as the sorrow, they would embrace together. Who could have known the love kindled in that first moment, catching each other's gaze across that Johns Hopkins lecture hall? Who could have known they would hold that intimate gaze for the next sixty years?

9

I Think I'm a Pastor

MINISTER

There are three basic views:

1. Ministers are Nice People. . . .
2. Ministers have their heads in the clouds. . . .
3. Ministers are as anachronistic as alchemists or chimney sweeps.

—Frederick Buechner, *Wishful Thinking*

It shouldn't be surprising to hear that Eugene's classroom had begun to feel claustrophobic. He'd always been drawn to untamed and gritty places: his dad's shop with its smells of beef and butcher paper, the light of long days disappearing over a lonely mountain, the sounds and songs of logging camps visited with his mom. In New York now, he sensed that familiar pull, to places where the lifeblood pulsed in the world. Eugene realized it was the church that felt most alive to him, most open and dangerous. Even though the opportunity to study with Brevard Childs at Yale had been once-in-a-lifetime stuff, the old scent was leading the young man on still, and the trail was winding behind a pulpit.

The revelation quietly clicked during a picnic. Eugene was shocked to realize that what really interested him was the parish, the people. In the church, the only set piece was eleven on Sunday mornings, but other than that, it was dealing with divorces and suicides and runaways. On a warm spring afternoon, he and Jan spread out their blanket in the park, with plates of sandwiches and cookies. "You know," Eugene said, surprising himself with the words, "I think I've always been a pastor—but I just didn't know what a pastor was."

That was it. That was enough. The next day, he telephoned Childs and thanked him for his generosity. But Eugene Peterson wasn't going to Yale. Eugene Peterson was going to be a pastor.

"Don't you think you've been an apprentice long enough?" Doug Bennett, an elder minister, asked. Eugene explained that he'd like to lead a new congregation but had no idea how to go about such a thing. Doug made a call to the denominational leader for new church development, and the next day, Eugene drove four hours to Baltimore. Within two months, Jan, Karen, and Eugene moved into a new white 1,400-square-foot ranch home plopped in the middle of a cornfield: 1321 Saratoga Drive. The brand-new subdivision was just two miles from the local village center.

Once upon a time, Bel Air, Maryland, had been a sleepy colonial hamlet. But as people poured out of Baltimore for the suburbs, Bel Air swelled. Eugene walked the town, neighborhood by neighborhood, introducing himself and the new church. He might as well have been back walking those lonely streets of Townsend, Montana, the way most everyone brushed him off. At one house on Ring Factory Road, a stylish woman in bright red pumps answered the door. She cut Eugene off, explaining that she was a member of the Church of Christ. "Do you get paid for doing this?" she asked, looking at him as if he might steal her purse. At Eugene's yes, she launched into a robust sermon explaining how the Bible forbids opportunistic swindlers like himself: people paid for ministry. When Eugene asked her to show him where the Scriptures said such things, she grabbed a Bible from the coffee table, fumbled, and hawed. Eugene asked if he could try, then turned to Matthew 10, where he read Jesus's instructions not to acquire gold or silver, nor to own a bag . . . or shoes.

"Is this what you're looking for?" he asked.

"That's it," she answered, punctuating with her index finger.

"Tell you what," Eugene said, glancing at her pumps. "I'll work for nothing, beginning right now, if you will get rid of those shoes and go barefoot." She slammed the door.

In truth, her concern was barely justified. *Paid* was a rather strong word for his church planter's salary. Money was a concern—and Eugene was on a ticking clock. The new church development (NCD) initiative would pay Eugene's salary and mortgage for three years, with their annual contributions reduced by a third each year. After that, the church would fly on its own. Or fall.

Richard Shreffler, the pastor of First Presbyterian, greeted Eugene with open arms. As the senior member of the town's clergy, most of his pastor friends referred to him as "His Holiness." Shreffler, a bachelor who was known for his excellent cooking, became a companion to Jan and Eugene. Shreffler's culinary gifts were genuine acts of friendship that had lasting impact. Once when I was staying with them at the lake, Eugene placed a salad on the table. Jan pulled a glass jar out of the fridge. "What we need is some of His Holiness's dressing." Half a century later, they still carried their friend's gift and generosity with them. Most of Shreffler's parishioners, however, knew him more for his bike than his kitchen. Folks referred to Shreffler as the "Pedaling Pastor," a title earned for his practice of making pastoral visits cycling around town. Shreffler encouraged members of First Presbyterian to join Eugene's new church in support of the young pastor, and thirty-one took him up on the offer.

After knocking on doors and receiving mostly yawns for weeks ("the most demeaning work in which I had ever engaged"), Eugene wrote a letter to every person who'd shown even an inkling of interest. He announced Christ Our King Presbyterian's inaugural worship service, which would meet in the Peterson basement on November 11, 1962. The weeks clicked by. On that first Sunday, forty-six people sat in metal folding chairs lined in neat rows between cinder block walls.

With those forty-six, something beautiful began. For two and a half years, the church met underground. To enter, parishioners descended eight steps down a little concrete stairwell into a room with a cement floor and six short oblong windows lined across the top of the exterior wall, allowing folks to peer out at grass during the service. The youth nicknamed the burgeoning fellowship "Catacombs Presbyterian."

Undaunted and adventurous, Jan gave birth to Eric in Christ Our King's first year. Having two young children added to the necessary home overhaul every Sunday, turning their living space into a sanctuary. Jan pulled down the clothesline, diapers stretching over the altar, and packed toys into closets. When Sparrows Point Presbyterian Church shuttered their doors, they donated a baptismal font, a communion table (with a chalice, paten, and linen), and three heavy oak pulpit chairs. Christ Our King's first baptism was Eric's (that font now sits in Eric's study). Eugene welcomed his son into the beloved community that was, slowly, taking shape around him.

But though the call to pastoral ministry was clear, the road from there was anything but. The young pastor quickly realized he was in strange territory. Eugene's supervisor, the NCD leader who'd brought him to Baltimore, handed Eugene an overstuffed red three-ring binder filled with instructions on *everything* one could possibly think of related to forming a new church. The promise of the binder was seductively simple—whatever problem Eugene might face as a pastor, he need only run his finger down the index and find appropriate instructions: how to organize a committee, how to lay out a church calendar, how to manage a budget, how to implement evangelistic strategies.

Small portions may have been helpful. But Eugene noticed how little *God* had to do with any of it. He sensed something elemental had shifted—from God, the Cross, the Resurrection, and the living Spirit, to finding out what people wanted. And then giving it to them. "The ink on my ordination papers wasn't even dry before I was being told by experts, so-called, in the field of church that my main task was to run a church after the manner of my brother and sister Christians who run service stations, grocery stores, corporations, banks, hospitals, and financial services." That first year at Christ Our King, Eugene attended a gathering for new church pastors led by a leadership guru who'd written a number of bestselling books on church growth. "The size of your congregation," the expert explained, "will be determined far more by the size of your parking lot than by any biblical text from which you will speak." Eugene eventually gathered the stack of books and tossed them in the dump.

Eugene felt alarmed. Not only because he sensed in his gut that this approach decentered God, but because so many of these perceived needs were actually destructive, dehumanizing. Even *antithetical* to the gospel of Jesus.

Eugene, though new to the pastorate, felt himself in the center of a great war. On the one side, the system of the world, invoking ancient sins and deadly temptations disguised in new raiment—advertising—comingled with the intoxication of American security. A soft Christianity using all the right words but missing the profound, revolutionary truth. And on the other, the community of Jesus. Small, slow, honest, stumbling forward. Suffering. Close to the Christ they sought to follow through the desert of modern life.

Nothing could have been more pastorally important than engaging this conflict. As families poured from Baltimore into the suburban comforts of Bel Air, an obsession with safety fueled isolation and a basic, compulsive self-centering. The response to fear or insecurity was not community solidarity or renewed peacemaking. It was to hunker—the least Christlike posture possible. The bunkers formed by this mentality were certainly metaphorical, but they sometimes became literal, physical extensions of the quiet fear pandemic. Eugene learned that in response to Sputnik and the panic over a nuclear attack from the USSR, a number of his neighbors had excavated bomb shelters in their backyards.

And yet in response to these real enemies in their midst, the red binder offered only vanity and emptiness. The community did not need a church to craft little programs to assuage their consciences or perceived needs for safety. It needed the church to invite people into a new reality ruled by the kingdom of God. Christ Our King needed to *worship*. With all this in mind, Eugene saw with a growing sense of both joy and desolation that what was most essential in all his work was the opening invitation he offered each Sunday— *Let us worship God*.

Those first years with their church literally underground (a bunker of a more hopeful kind) provided time for Eugene and the church to grow into who they were. Christ Our King had little to offer that was attractive or compelling for church shoppers. This unconventional setting allowed them to go deeper than common assumptions of what a church should look like. Instead, they began to focus on who they *were*. There in the little cinder block catacombs, with just fifty or sixty people gathering weekly, they could learn one another's stories. They could gradually find themselves caught up together in what God was doing in their corner of the world.

For any of this to be real, Eugene knew he had to get to know the people and their children and their stories. With the same energy he'd given to learning the names of the students he had represented at SPU years before, he dedicated himself to this quiet work. Every week, he wrote three names on a three-by-five-inch card and propped it on his desk. He kept those people in his sights as he prayed and studied that week's text. It was all very primal.

"I would immerse myself and our church-in-formation in the story of the first church-in-formation. Acts would give us a text for cleansing our perceptions from the blurring and distorting American stereotypes." Eugene preached forty-six sermons from Acts. Rather than disseminating information, he was trying to enter a larger world—and invite others to enter with him.

But even as God was gathering a congregation, that bloated red notebook whined for his attention. Eugene's gut told him the system it espoused was a dead end. His gut also told him he'd better get this right, and in quiet hours or moments of frustration, he often questioned if his instincts were correct. After all, what did he know?

Eugene was hung between two competing visions of what it meant to be a pastor. Preaching from Acts, he saw how clearly everything depended on God. But tossing in bed late at night or poring over endless financial forms whose figures made dark prophecies, it felt as though everything depended on *him*. And he was not sure he was up for the job.

Every month, Eugene had to complete a multipage report for the NCD. The first page held blanks for the details of Sunday attendance, giving, building plans, and the work of committees. The following pages offered space for the pastor to share how he felt things were progressing (How was his preaching? What insights or skills were emerging? Where was he struggling? Was God doing anything in the congregation?). After a year of writing these reports without any response, Eugene suspected the committee never made it past page 1. They surely thumbed through the statistics, but the rest likely landed in a dusty file. Feeling more alone than usual, he planned an experiment.

Eugene's next report offered a dark account of his (fictional) ever-deepening depression: "I had difficulty sleeping, I couldn't pray." He explained how his sermon preparation and parishioner meetings were robotic and his pastoral duties received only perfunctory attention with "no spirit, no zest." By the end of the report, Eugene had morbidly confessed that he sat on a razor's edge, even considering quitting ministry. He concluded by asking if they could recommend a counselor.

Dead silence. "I upped the ante. The next month I developed a drinking problem." His trumped-up addiction careened out of control. One Sunday, according to his report, he had stood behind the pulpit sloshed, slurring his words, incoherent. "Everybody was very understanding, but one of the elders had to complete the sermon. . . . I needed treatment. How should I go about getting it? Were there any funds available?"

Still no response! Eugene got even bolder. The time for the next report came, and now his alcoholism had pushed him into a four-alarm affair. Attempting to counsel a woman trapped in an abusive marriage, things went sideways. They "ended up in bed together, only it wasn't bed but one of the church pews, where we were discovered when the ladies arranging flowers for Sunday worship walked in on us." Eugene couldn't stop himself. His fictional ingenuity was hitting full steam. He added a masterful touch: "I thought it was all over for my ministry at that point, but it turned out that in this community swingers are very much admired. The next day, Sunday, attendance doubled."

Another month, Eugene reported on his recent inspiration, a

fresh liturgical tweak. Since this was the 1960s, "an era of liturgical reform and experimentation," his letter explained his attempt to energize their dull, melancholy worship: "I had read some scholarly guesses about a mushroom cult in Palestine in the first century in which Jesus might have been involved. I thought it was worth a try. I arranged with one of our college kids who was going to Mexico on spring break to purchase some psychedelic mushrooms." Eugene's imagination then went off the rails. He described how for the next Eucharist, Jan baked the mushrooms into the communion bread. "It was the most terrific experience anybody had ever had in worship, absolutely dazzling."

Months passed. The stories grew beyond the bounds of reason, more elaborate, more scandalous. Eugene began looking forward to concocting outrageous fictions and then sharing them with Jan. They'd sit in the kitchen, Eugene spinning ideas for the next installment of the tale, then Jan spicing it up by adding another provocative detail.

When the three years for the NCD's support of the church concluded, the committee asked Eugene to come to their headquarters to debrief. He sat before the committee as they quizzed him over his experience. Then he thanked them for the financial support and courteous posture. But he mentioned one disappointment: that they'd never read past the first page of statistics. The committee insisted they'd carefully digested everything. "How can that be?" Eugene questioned. "I asked for help with my drinking problem, and you didn't respond. . . . I got involved in a sexual adventure, and you didn't intervene. . . . I was using hallucinogens in the Eucharist, and you did nothing." The committee members' faces went ashy, followed by what he called a "splendid vaudeville slapstick of buck passing and excuse making." Eugene allowed the confusion and discomfort to go on for only a moment before confessing his fiction.

For Eugene, however, the experience was more sorrowful than humorous. He was alone. No one was looking out for him. "The people who ordained me and took responsibility for my work were interested in financial reports, attendance graphs, program planning. But they were not interested in *me*. They were interested in my job; they cared little for my vocation."

With worship in the catacombs under their house, the Petersons' homelife braided with the church's. One Sunday, Eugene ended his pastoral prayer with the standard *amen,* and Karen answered just like she did whenever her dad concluded his prayer around the dinner table, responding with "Amen." Her tinny voice filled the basement, as everyone else sat in silence. Laughter broke the quiet, and Karen turned red, covering her face. Seizing the moment, Eugene explained the family's mealtime practice: an *amen* answered with an *amen*. He practiced with them a time or two, and the next Sunday— and every Sunday that followed—a symphony of *amen*s echoed through the room.

Soon, Eugene created a weekly congregational letter, calling it *Amen!,* continuing the Sunday image of participatory prayer. He wanted to remind the church that they were in conversation, answering God together. Eugene wrote *Amen!* each week, including as many specific names and conversations as possible. This was a true *letter* to his church, half of an ongoing conversation, an act of pastoral formation. "I reflected on what I was doing when they didn't see me. I reflected on what they were doing when I didn't see them. I wrote it every Tuesday. The church secretaries mailed it out every Wednesday. A deliberate use of language to connect Sunday language with weekday language." He included notes like this: "Charlie Reiher's father died" and "Holly Christian was born." Then playful bits: "Kris Sherrock was discovered in the church early Sunday morning getting a hymnbook so she could master the hymn-of-the-month." Sometimes Eugene, likely thinking of his more fastidious and critical members, inserted a deliberate mistake or inaccuracy to see if people were reading.

"They were," he said.

Christ Our King followed no recipe. The people Eugene initially expected to show up—passionate, mature Christians eager for God—were few and far between. In the place of those idealized congregants was Gus Sakolis, a long-haul truck driver who dropped out of eighth grade and adored Elvis. There was Delores, a middle-aged woman living with her parents on their farm. She sang Sunday solos "with operatic zest but with all the higher notes flat . . . like fingernails scraping a chalkboard." There was the angry parishioner who always seemed to show up but for *twenty-seven years* just sat in the pew, mouth clamped through the hymns, the prayers, the creed. There was the biology teacher who critiqued Eugene's sermon every single Sunday. One week, it was grammar or pronunciation, another week exegesis, another week some hot issue Eugene had failed to address. There was the retired World War II colonel who could rarely make it to the first hymn before his eyelids drooped and his head slumped and who rarely woke before the benediction. A wife in a horrific marriage. A middle-aged man who knew only failure.

As far as "seasoned saints who know how to pray and listen and endure," only a handful attended, among a "considerable number of people who pretty much just showed up . . . the hot, the cold, and the lukewarm; Christians, half-Christians, almost-Christians; New Agers, angry ex-Catholics, sweet new converts." Eugene explained, "I didn't choose them. I didn't *get* to choose them." This was Eugene's church. And as he would continue to insist, this is *the* church.

When a psychiatrist with Johns Hopkins Phipps Clinic called Eugene with an invitation to join a small group of religious leaders (fifteen pastors and priests and one rabbi) to meet every Tuesday, he immediately said yes. The clinic formed the group to assist in the mushrooming mental health crisis (a result of societal upheaval: anxieties from the Vietnam War and the Kennedy and King assassinations, problems caused by the sexual revolution and drugs, the effects of disconnected suburbia). For two years, Eugene acquired tools to better understand trauma and enter the pain of those he pastored. Exhilarating for him, he learned unambiguous solutions for dealing with pastoral ambiguities, ways to motivate people and give them clear direction for their struggles.

"It was a time when pastors all over the country were abandoning their vocation to take up counseling. I could have ended up among them," he remembered long after. But his pastoral instincts led him to read deeply and widely in search of relevant perspectives for how to shepherd the whole human person. Eugene devoured the writings of Carl Jung, Bruno Bettelheim, Erik Erikson, and Viktor Frankl, among many others. But there were two sides to this. All this knowledge played into the temptation Eugene faced to be an expert, to be successful in his work. He began to notice "a latent messianic complex," where he was drawn to locate the emotional problems among those in his congregation and then *fix* them, efficiently. These experiences taught Eugene to value psychiatry and therapy (an appreciation he never lost), but he did have to wrestle, coming to the realization that he was a pastor, *not* a therapist. "Those two years of Tuesdays . . . clarified what I was not: I was not primarily dealing with people as problems. I was . . . calling them to worship God."

Worship was the call. *Worship* was the work.

After this quiet epiphany, Eugene visited a young woman in the hospital. Unable to diagnose her illness, doctors considered her problems psychosomatic. The therapeutic response would have been to ask if she wanted to talk about her troubles. However, Eugene felt on this occasion an invitation to silence. Driving home, he felt guilty, wondering if he should have done more to help. A month later, he visited again. "Is there anything you want me to do for you?" he asked. She thought for a moment, then innocently asked, "Would you teach me to pray?" Eugene tightened his grip on the pastoral plow.

However, there was other work to do. Years earlier, the presbytery had purchased land, and now the church needed to be built. They couldn't stay in the catacombs forever.

After Christ Our King's building committee had a disastrous meeting with a condescending expert from a large firm, they met Gerry Baxter, a young architect from the neighborhood. Gerry had never designed a church, but he had long dreamed of building a church that was a true expression of its place. He wanted to come worship with them and get to know them. As Gerry and Eugene became friends, they discovered they were both artists in their own way, committed to working with the materials and the place they were gifted with and resolutely determined to not impose anything artificial (or merely utilitarian) on their work.

So, what would this building be? They wanted a spacious sanctuary, filled with light. The design, with the roof sweeping dramatically skyward, reflected both a tent (like Israel used for their worship of God while wandering in the wilderness) and hands clasped in prayer. The worship space, built in a semicircle, would put everyone gathered around the communion table, the family table. They purchased green marble from a quarry twenty miles away to fashion the baptismal font, the communion table, and the face of the pulpit. One parishioner took burnished aluminum and formed Christ Our King's iconic image (a crown atop a cross, hung over a globe) to hang from the pulpit. A woodworker in the church took American black walnut timbers from his family farm in Ohio and crafted the large Celtic cross, suspended above the congregation. The sanctuary's massive arched beams were rich fir, the whole interior warm and expansive.

On July 12, 1964, Christ Our King broke ground. All parishioners received red metal shovels with their names hand-painted on them. Nine months later, on April 7, 1965, Jeager Construction pulled their last truck off the property and Christ Our King threw her doors wide. The sanctuary swelled with joy and gratitude. Eugene stood behind the pulpit and looked over the sea of faces, pausing at the wonder before he gave the great call that had become the central invitation of his life: "Let us worship God."

For Jan and Eugene, new life was bursting open in every way. Two months before the building project finished, Jan checked into the hospital with labor pains. She asked Eugene to stay home to help her mom with Karen, five, and Eric, three, rather than staying at the hospital. And he did. Eugene donned an apron, ran the vacuum, fixed meals, and corralled kids. Everyone was overjoyed when Jan came home from the hospital cradling Leif, swaddled in a blue blanket, like a little caterpillar inching from his cocoon.

Jan wrote a letter to Eugene's parents describing Karen's and Eric's reactions to Leif's arrival home:

> When Gene and I came home from the hospital with the baby I sat down on a chair with him to let Karen and Eric see him as I took his outer clothing off. What a priceless scene! I'll never forget little Eric's reaction as long as I live. "Ma-ma" he exclaimed as he pointed to five tiny little fingers on one hand and then cradled it in his own hand. "Mama" he squealed as two tiny little feet emerged from the bunting. "Ma-ma" again as he pointed to a perfect little ear and this continued as each tiny feature was discovered by him. . . . When I nurse the baby Karen refers to it as "milking the baby." Makes me sound like a cow, doesn't it? Ha!

Christ Our King's home was complete. And now so was the Petersons'.

10

Staying Put

> I am a man of little faith. In the dark night of the soul, I reach out to assure myself of things not seen. I must lay my hands on the side of the tree, must feel the prick of grass on my skin, must smell the dirt, must sing to myself a brave lullaby in order to sustain my hopes.
> —Scott Russell Sanders, *Staying Put*

Christ Our King poured their hope and sweat into constructing their outpost on that Maryland hill in the cornfield. It was a rigorous season of intensity yielding a pinnacle, a triumph. Within a month of moving into their new sanctuary, however, something shifted. Folks who had been so energized disappeared for weeks at a time, leaving more and more space in the pews. Disturbed, Eugene went to see his NCD supervisor. "What do I do?" Eugene asked. The answer was immediate: "Start another building program."

"We don't need another building program," Eugene replied, head spinning. "We need to mature as a congregation." His supervisor was adamant. "People need something tangible, something they can get their hands on, a challenge, a goal. Trust me. I've been through this before. It's the American way." Eugene returned to Bel Air confused and disturbed. "I could also feel the adrenaline drain out of my blood stream."

Eugene would describe the next six years with a telling phrase: "the badlands." After a grueling three years of pastoral work with little time off, Eugene craved wide spaces—the Swan Range, the Flathead Valley—and family he hadn't seen in far too long. So he and Jan made a decision. "We would drive to Montana and see if we could recover our breath."

Jan and Eugene loaded up the kids and pointed the car west. Five days on the road. At sunset, they'd pull into a state park, unpack their tents, and roll out their sleeping bags. A night at Indiana Dunes, a night at Loon Lake in Minnesota, a night in the Black Hills, a night at Missouri Headwaters State Park in Three Forks, Montana. Then, with a rush of feeling and an intoxicating breath of pine, Eugene found himself *home*.

This journey to Montana launched a tradition that would become an annual summer pilgrimage for the Petersons, returning home to ground that centered and nourished them. Lush farms and sprawling forests would give way to the Great Plains and then the towering Rockies. The landscape was part of the heart's secret healing—except for a long stretch through the South Dakota Badlands, "where nothing is green or growing. No trees, no water, no towns. The only sign of life was an occasional vulture cruising for carrion." Miles and miles of desolation, earth stripped of any visible sign of beauty. The only break in the monotony was signs for Wall Drug dotting the roadside for hundreds of miles. "Then suddenly, seemingly out of nowhere, a rambling, jerry-built structure spilling out with souvenirs and knickknacks." Eventually, they'd land in the Dakota forests, grateful for green again.

That trek through barren country spoke to something in Eugene. He'd spent so much energy getting Christ Our King on steady footing. They'd gathered a community. They'd built their church home. But he was exhausted. "I had just assumed that the energy would keep coming. Why wouldn't it? Isn't that what pastors are supposed to do? Stoke the fires? Prime the pump? Charge the batteries? Do the 'American' thing? After only three years was I already a failed pastor?"

For six years, Eugene stayed put and pastored in the badlands, with low energy and mediocre results, simply pushing forward for the next mile through lifeless country. Until now, he had lived from goal to goal: *Get good marks in school. Beat the time on the track. Gain your degrees. Get your professional qualifications. Work to move up the ladder.* But now he was trudging through miserable, monotonous conditions, with no relief in sight, with no goal he could identify to press toward. Submitting to the life he had been given didn't come easily.

In early 1968, Eugene interviewed with Summerville Presbyterian Church in Rochester, New York. The family traveled to Rochester, and the search committee visited Eugene and Jan in Bel Air. Eugene told Summerville he was prepared to make the move, but they chose another pastor. Eugene wrote his folks with the news:

> We heard from the church in Rochester that we had been talking with yesterday—and they have chosen someone else as their pastor. It was disappointing to us as we would have liked to go there. But we can't feel too badly about it either since we had great respect for the committee that talked to us on three different occasions. . . .
>
> But we are ready to leave here. We pray for guidance and help in what to do and where to go. At the moment we do not have conversations with anyone. It is a frustrating time—we feel that the impulse to leave is from the Lord; but at the same time He doesn't open up where we are to leave to.

Eugene described their experience in badland imagery:

It is a wonderful time for assessing lack of faith, and for exploring the feelings that expose our faithlessness. We have felt almost from the beginning that leaving Bel Air was primarily for our sakes, not the church's. And this is part of it—living through this time of emptiness. I notice now that the psalms are full of references to the rocks God split open to give them water during their wilderness wanderings. . . . Those wilderness years, the bare, hard, impenetrable rocks, became the very place that God refreshed them.

In another letter, Eugene revealed, a bit tongue in cheek, his bruised ego:

[Summerville's] choice narrowed down finally to us and one other person. . . .

There is always, I suppose, some curiosity about who the other person was. I have my share of ego—and was confident that I could do the job as well as any, and better than most! Who would they have chosen over me!

Then Eugene continued, describing the mercy he encountered:

Only a couple of weeks ago, I was in a committee meeting on Ministerial Relations, on which I serve in our presbytery. This committee has to approve all changes of pastoral relation. The chairman said, "We have a request to approve the call of the Summerville Church in Rochester to Converse Hunter." Converse is a neighboring pastor whom I know well! What a coincidence—what a surprise! Here was a church 800 miles away considering about fifty different pas-

tors and the two they end up with are only ten miles apart
in Maryland.

    *But the significant thing was the automatic response I
had. Within there was a kind of sudden joy, a leap of ap-
proval before I had a chance to think about it. The thought,
"Well of course—if they had to choose between me and
Converse they would obviously have to choose Converse;
he is the absolutely right pastor for that congregation."*

    *I could hardly sleep that night for excitement—it was
like I had been shown the inside movements of God's guidance. There are so many uncertainties in making pastoral
changes. I'm not always certain of my own motives—my
capacity for self-deception is enormous. . . . And when you
look around you there are so many instances of congregations calling the wrong pastor and of pastors responding to
calls for base reasons that you wonder if God is able to exercise his will in this system at all. . . .*

    *Ordinarily, you have to accept the results of such practice
blindly and without ever knowing reasons or consequences.
But in this case it was almost as if God said, "I don't very
often do this, and I may well never do it again for you, but
just for once I want to show you how I work. I want to dem-
onstrate to you that my will is determinative in all the vaga-
ries of the system and the conflict and ambiguity. . . . It was
no accident or chance or mistake that Converse was called
to that church and you weren't. And you can see that now.
But now that you have seen it, you must trust me to be doing
it in the future too, even if you don't see it."*

During these monotonous years, Eugene would have left Christ
Our King if any other church had offered him the job, but not a
single one did.

One afternoon, he saw Willi Ossa's grim portrait, and it sent a chill through him. Willi's prophecy didn't seem far-fetched now. This, Eugene knew, was who he would become if he entered "the American competition to be a pastor who 'gets things done' and who is 'going somewhere.' " Partly by choice but mostly by grace, Eugene remained in the badlands.

He would just have to keep walking.

Eugene felt adrift. He felt disconnected from the physical stuff of his life: the family he loved, the land he loved, the physical labor and exertion he loved. He felt he'd become a successful pastor but not a very good human.

Unnerved, Eugene knew he had to make concrete changes. He and Jan began a Monday Sabbath, a practice born out of desperation and as an antidote to Eugene's overly zealous pastoral energy. They also committed to spending at least a month every summer on the Flathead—and even more when the session (the church's leadership body) tacked on Eugene's study leave. Next, Eugene returned to two familiar joys: carpentry and running. Working with saws and a chisel and a block plane, fashioning something beautiful out of raw wood, he connected to both his sense of artistry and his craving to start something and see it actually accomplished. He built an elaborate workbench, followed by bunk beds. After bunk beds, he constructed a triangular picnic table, a project he was proud to unveil to the family. Over the years, he built desks for each of his kids, a small buffet table, end tables, a checkerboard, bookshelves, and his crowning achievement: a rocking bassinet that would cradle each of his grandchildren. In his final years, though his tools only hung on the wall, he still referred to his little corner of their one-car garage as his shop. The man loved to rub his fingers along the grain of a cut of wood, loved the smell of sawdust.

And running. After SPU, Eugene had boxed up his running shoes, but he felt that familiar ache for "the easy rhythms, the relaxed sense of being physically in touch with the earth under my feet, the texture of the weather, my body working almost effortlessly in long cross-country workouts." But there was also a more therapeutically complicated reason for Eugene's return to running: he possessed a competitive fire. Ambitious energy could be good, but as fuel for his life as a pastor, ambition wrecked his soul. Running—and eventually training for races— allowed him to burn that competitiveness. For years, Eugene came home in the late afternoons and ran five miles. He craved "the uninterrupted quiet, the metronomic repetitiveness, the sensual immersion in the fragrance of trees and flowering bushes and rain, the springiness of the soil on park trails, the Zenlike emptying of the mind that felt like a freedom to be simply present, not having to do or say anything." Some assume Eugene had an inbred revulsion for the modern addictions to success and winning, as though his loathing for these driven impulses were somehow simply part of his DNA. Quite the contrary. Eugene was so attuned to the temptations because they were such deep struggles in his own soul. He had to work out his demons on the pavement, as well as in his morning prayers.

And Eugene kept at it. Eventually he ran five marathons, including his pinnacle race: the 1984 Boston Marathon with his New Balance bib marking him runner 5543. The *Harford Sun* ran an article titled "He Preaches on Sunday, Runs in Marathon Monday." But all that was in the future. For now, Eugene was just trying to exercise those competitive juices. "Was I . . . running out of the badlands?" Eugene asked. "It felt like it."

As Eugene picked his way through the badlands desolation, several crucial encounters provided guidance that kept him inching forward. Iain Wilson was pastor of Baltimore's historic Brown Memorial Park Avenue Presbyterian Church. Born in the Scottish Highlands, Wilson studied Divinity at Edinburgh, then with Rudolf Bultmann at Marburg University. As World War II broke out, Wilson volunteered as a chaplain with the British army, participating in both the Dunkirk evacuation and D-Day landing in Normandy. After the war, he served a parish in Scotland before crossing the pond to serve a parish in Lynchburg, Virginia (the hometown of his wife, Madeline).

When Wilson, a sober preacher with precise sermons, stood behind the pulpit, his warm Scottish brogue enveloped listeners. Eugene noticed Wilson, who was new to the Baltimore presbytery, not only because of his elder status and prominent church but also because he spent summer holidays in the Montana Rockies, its craggy country offering familiar landscape to the Scotsman. After Eugene and Wilson both returned from a summer in Montana, Eugene saw Wilson, arm cradled in a blue sling. A coyote had spooked Wilson's horse while he was riding on the Bridger Range, and it had hurled him into a rocky ravine. "Those mountains are magnificent," he said, "but they have twenty different ways to kill you. Just like the church."

Eugene couldn't shake that line. Weeks later, he called Wilson and explained his vague sense of the kind of pastor he wanted to be: slow, personal, attuned to God and to the lives of those in his parish. Eugene wondered if it was possible to transform from a competitive pastor to a contemplative pastor—"a pastor who was able to be with people without having an agenda for them, a pastor who was able to accept people just as they were and guide them gently and patiently into a mature life in Christ but not get in the way."

Wilson offered no advice. But he invited him to come to Baltimore and talk. Every other week for two years, Eugene and Wilson met in an austere prayer chapel. Wilson knelt in a pew on one wall, Eugene on the opposite. Holding his Scottish prayer book, Wilson prayed while Eugene knelt in silence.

And then they talked. Leaving the chapel, they walked to a neighborhood diner. Over coffee and pie, Wilson shared his passion for bird-watching, from his boyhood days in the Highlands to the birding columns he wrote for the *Baltimore Sun*. They shared their love for the Montana wildness and their love, mixed with trepidation, for pastoring a church. As one of Barth's translators, Wilson encouraged Eugene to go deeper with Barth, seeing him as a "pastor's theologian"—encouragement that launched Eugene on a lifelong journey.

This experience of fixed prayers, in community, is similar to how many friends described evening prayers when they were staying with Jan and Eugene. They would sit in a circle, quiet before God, and then simply *pray*. And following the prayers, an easy, roaming conversation, often with mugs of tea in hand. An intimate connection between the ancient way of prayer in that silent, sacred space and the different form of prayer in free-flowing conversation that followed. Eugene first experienced this intimate, sacred act in that small chapel—and then the diner—with Wilson.

After two years, Wilson accepted a professor of philosophy post and stopped meeting with Eugene. In 1975, he contacted Eugene to gauge his interest in the professor of homiletics position at Pittsburgh Theological Seminary (a collision of worlds, as Eugene would have been replacing David Buttrick, the son of George Buttrick). However, Wilson's influence had taken root.

"By then, thanks to him, I was more than ever what I had been becoming for a long time—a contemplative pastor."

A second crucial badlands encounter was with Tom, a pastor friend. Tom introduced Eugene to Charles Williams, a British writer and member of the Inklings group (which included such writers as C. S. Lewis, Owen Barfield, and J. R. R. Tolkien). Eugene devoured *The Descent of the Dove,* Williams's key work on the Holy Spirit's presence in the church throughout history. Tom's most profound gift to Eugene, however, was a single comment spoken in exasperation over lunch at one of Tom's favorite diners.

Tom introduced Eugene to their waitress, Vanessa, a tired woman with sad eyes. As they rose to pay the check, Eugene stepped away to the bathroom. When he returned, he found Tom and Vanessa in an energetic discussion. Eugene grabbed a newspaper and a seat at the counter. As Tom and Eugene exited the diner, Tom exuded vigor. "Eugene, did you see us talking, the way *she* was talking—that intensity? I wish I could do that kind of thing all day long, every day. Every time I come in here and there are no customers, she wants to talk about prayer and her life."

"So, why don't you do it—have conversations like that?" Eugene asked.

"Because," Tom answered, with an edge, "I have to run this damn church."

Eugene shared Tom's story from the diner with his Tuesday pastors' group (after the psychiatrist concluded the two-year commitment, the group continued on their own). Most everyone immediately resonated with the suffocation of "running a damn church." Together, they determined that whatever else they might do, they would learn how to be pastors. Honoring the particularities of each of their personalities and their distinct congregations, they would share their mutual vocation. They would be a company of pastors.

Tuesdays were simple. Eugene brewed coffee, and everyone brought a brown bag lunch. They gathered in Eugene's study, opened a text, read, and pondered. The group rotated leadership, a different pastor guiding each week, picking one lectionary passage and introducing a few points of exegesis to discuss. Eugene sat in his chair, mostly silent. Every once in a while, he raised a question. Each of the pastors had their own areas of expertise (preaching, theology, pastoral care), but when there was a question of Hebrew or Greek translation, the group leaned on Eugene for clarification. But his primary role was providing his study and filling the carafe.

Whenever a new pastor arrived in town, they invited him or her to join the group. However, most came only once or twice. "When they realized we were not interested in debating doctrinal positions or moral 'stands' or comparing church statistics, they lost interest," Eugene explained.

At the end of each spring, they shared a silent retreat at the Bonham Wake Robin Wildlife Sanctuary. They concluded their time by sharing the Eucharist—a small band of friends gathered around bread and wine. Feasting on Jesus. This company sustained Eugene in the badlands. And it would keep sustaining him for decades beyond that inner wilderness.

The Scottish pastor and divine Alexander Whyte provided a third crucial badlands encounter, an introduction Iain Wilson surely made for Eugene. Whyte, a cobbler's apprentice, made his way to divinity school at the University of Edinburgh and eventually became the pastor of St. George's. In 1898, the assembly elected Whyte moderator of the Free Church of Scotland.

Rising before dawn each Sunday, Eugene sat in his study, a cup of coffee on the table as morning rays filtered through the window. He opened a book of Whyte's sermons. "I had already prepared the sermon I would preach that day—now I let him preach to me. . . . The quality that I wanted to absorb, and did, I think, was the fusion of scripture and prayer, prayer and scripture." In Whyte, Eugene discovered a pastor with "a truly biblical imagination. The entire biblical narrative came alive when he preached—not explicitly, but the tone and the allusions developed a storied coherence around every text. As I sat under my pastor's preaching, scripture ceased to be a sequence of texts and became a seamless story. And I was a participant in the story." For Whyte, Scripture was not a book to dissect but the widest realm possible in which one's entire life would be lived. Eugene entered this world with Whyte, offering a stunning— and revealing—observation: "The scriptures had become autobiographical to me."

For more than two decades, until he packed up his study and stepped down from Christ Our King's pulpit, Eugene sat in his study and read as Whyte, his Scottish pastor, preached to him. Whyte helped lead Eugene out of the badlands and then, for over twenty years, led him farther.

The badlands shaped, perhaps as much as any other voice or experience, Eugene's convictions about what it meant to be a pastor. He possessed a dogged commitment to his immediate place, to his holy charge to pastor this one (at times fledgling) community of ordinary people. And he exhibited a resolute determination to resist the siren songs insisting he must push to make something of himself and build something "significant" at Christ Our King. These convictions were forged in the long stretch of desert years when his commitments were severely tested. Through frustration and boredom and dark nights of the soul, Eugene determined he would be patient. He would plod forward. He would stay put. Even as he slogged farther into this barren country.

11

Pure Mercy

We are most deeply asleep at the switch when we fancy
we control any switches at all.
—Annie Dillard, *Holy the Firm*

Like most profound inner transitions, Eugene's growth into his vocation happened slowly, by means of human encounter and time spent in prayer and the long obedience of pastoral work, not through mighty revelations or rational argumentation. And, of course, Karen helped too—in one of the simple church episodes that would come to define his sense of call and what it meant to live it.

Eugene arrived at a crucial juncture midway through his bad-lands years. Though the sanctuary was completed and Christ Our King was financially viable, Eugene could not let off the throttle. "I formed committees. I made home visits. Longer hours. A longer workweek. . . . I had tried to slow down. I had tried to relax. But I was afraid of failing. I couldn't help myself."

After supper one evening, five-year-old Karen asked her dad to read her a story. "I'm sorry, Karen," he answered, "but I have a meeting tonight."

"This is the twenty-seventh night in a row you have had a meeting." Karen had been counting.

Convicted, Eugene explained how sorry he was and promised

to do better. On his walk to the church for his elders' meeting, Eugene's blood boiled, mercury surging. Before he hit Christ Our King's parking lot, he made a decision. When the elders sat down in his study, Eugene scrapped the docket. He recounted his conversation with Karen. "I've tried not to work so hard, but I can't do it. I resign." The elders leaned forward, eyes wide. "And it's not just Karen. It's you too. I haven't been a pastor to this congregation for six months. I pray in fits and starts. I feel like I'm in a hurry all the time. When I visit or have lunch with you, I'm not listening to you; I am thinking of ways I can get the momentum going again. My sermons are thrown together. I don't want to live like this, either with you or with my family." Then, Tom's line shot into the open, a piece of dynamite as punctuation: "I'm tired of running this damn church."

Craig responded first. "So what do you want to do?"

Words spilled, churning words Eugene didn't even know were there:

I want to be a pastor who prays. I want to be reflective and responsive and relaxed in the presence of God so that I can be reflective and responsive and relaxed in your presence. I can't do that on the run. It takes a lot of time. I started out doing that with you, but now I feel too crowded.

I want to be a pastor who reads and studies. This culture in which we live squeezes all the God sense out of us. I want to be observant and informed enough to help this congregation understand what we are up against, the temptations of the devil to get us thinking we can all be our own gods. This is subtle stuff. It demands some detachment and perspective. I can't do this just by trying harder.

I want to be a pastor who has the time to be with you in leisurely, unhurried conversations so that I can understand and be a companion with you as you grow in Christ—your

doubts and your difficulties, your desires and your delights.
I can't do that when I am running scared.

I want to be a pastor who leads you in worship, a pastor
who brings you before God in receptive obedience, a pastor
who preaches sermons that make scripture accessible and
present and alive, a pastor who is able to give you a language and imagination that restores in you a sense of dignity as a Christian in your homes and workplaces and gets
rid of these debilitating images of being a "mere" layperson.

I want to have the time to read a story to Karen.

I want to be an unbusy pastor.

The room went silent. Eugene's frustration surprised the elders. It surprised Eugene too.

After a few awkward moments, one elder, a retired colonel,
spoke up. "Why don't you just do it? What's stopping you?"

"Why don't you let us run the church?" Craig asked.

"Because you don't know how."

Mildred would have none of it. "It sounds to me like you aren't
doing such a good job yourself."

Before they left that evening, they'd revamped their organiza-
tional structure. Eugene would be the pastor, and the elders would
run the church. Other than the monthly elders' meeting, Eugene
would not attend meetings or be responsible for church administration. He had suddenly found himself freed from "running this
damn church."

Eugene stood up, slid his chair back in place, and walked out.

He stopped going to committee meetings, and he stopped
wearing three-piece suits to family dinners. Leif remembers the
unusual sight of his dad passing the potatoes in a simple cotton
collared shirt. In the early days, Eugene had always worn a suit to
dinner. "Even a watch and fob in the vest pocket," Leif recalled.

"He sat at the head of table, dressed as though he were heading for a vestry meeting—which he often was. It was very rare in those early days that he would not go back out after dinner to a meeting or something—he was building this church from nothing and it took a lot." The wardrobe reflected an inner change as well, an exchange of professionalized pastoral care for a style that was more intimate and natural.

One afternoon, Eugene came home from the department store with Dockers and polo shirts. "He dressed casually at work too. The change was just overnight, like he flipped a switch." Eugene wore a black Geneva gown and a clerical collar with preaching tabs when leading worship, but from that point forward, he dressed casually otherwise. "And I think this was around the time Dad started staying home more," Leif said.

Little by little, Eugene was becoming himself. He was finding where he fit.

The final badlands encounter involved a family of eight—the Rhoadses—who joined Christ Our King. Eugene noticed that each Sunday when the church recited the Apostles' Creed, David, the dad, said "I believe" and then went silent. After months of watching David out of the corner of his eye, Eugene noticed him tack on "In God the Father Almighty" before going mute. Every few months, David added another phrase, then another, until eventually he had joined in reciting the entire confession. The following week, he was baptized.

A couple of years later, David's wife, Janet, received a devastating cancer diagnosis. They buried her within six months. Soon after, David lost his job. Without asking Jan, Eugene loaded the three Rhoads brothers (Mike, Jimmy, and Jeff) and their sister (Darlene) into his car and drove them home. Eugene walked into the house, followed by a parade of children, explaining that they needed a place to stay. "There was no sorry about it," Jan explained. "My first reaction was overwhelmed, but then I felt flattered that Eugene trusted me and knew I could do that."

Eugene converted the basement into a bunkhouse for the boys, and Darlene roomed with Karen. Chaos ruled the house for the next three months. The septic tank overflowed ("Especially with those boys," Jan said, laughing), and every night for weeks, they transported all the kids, toothbrushes in tow, to the church for their bedtime ritual.

These were only the first of a long line of people who lived with Jan and Eugene. A fourteen-year-old girl, after jumping out of the car with her mom and running to the church to talk to Eugene, stayed with them while working on her relationship with her parents. Then an abused mother. A neighbor struggling with depression. Numerous others, some for a few nights and some for long stretches.

Prior to the Rhoads family, Eugene struggled to encourage the church to embrace their life together as a genuine community, to care for one another. His appeals evoked mostly yawns and blank stares. Eugene labored on the phone, drumming up meals for people coming home from the hospital or asking parishioners to take care of some tangible need for a neighbor. However, with the Rhoads children in need, something ignited. Deacons supplied funds for groceries. Others donated bunk beds, a cot, sheets, and blankets. One family donated a Renault so David could pick up his children and drive to church together. "The church couldn't believe that we would bring all these children into our home," Jan said. "After that, Gene didn't have to make one phone call for people who had needs in our church."

All of a sudden, with their home literally overflowing, life was flowing in the church too. Something about the encounter had pulled all the threads of their community tightly together. And

soon Eugene realized he wasn't in the badlands any longer. Eugene
and Jan had simply responded to the need, and the Rhoads children became part of their life. They had bonded. And when the
time came for their extended stay to end, he mourned.

We are a diminished family now, he wrote in a letter back to
Montana. *The Rhoads children left a week ago Saturday.*

As Eugene looked back after this time of struggle, the provi-
sion of God was obvious. It seemed pure mercy that Eugene
hadn't left for another parish. It was mercy that led him to Iain
Wilson. And Alexander Whyte. Mercy that worked amid sorrow
to bring the Rhoadses into their home. Christ Our King was becoming a church. Eugene was becoming a pastor. Together, they
found themselves submerged in "a way of worship that was non-
manipulative. A way of community that was nonprogrammatic."
One of the things Eugene "relished about being a pastor was
being immersed in these ambiguities, the *not* being in control that
allowed for the slow emergence of insights and resolve that developed into confessions of faith, and the unplanned, spontaneous
attentiveness . . . that over the years became a culture of hospitality."

Eugene had embarked on a path that cut against the grain of pastoral ambition and entrepreneurialism. And he recognized it. As a
sign of his deepening sense of self, he gathered his framed diplo-
mas touting his academic credentials and tossed them into boxes,
his external qualifications all set aside. Even after he retired from
the parish and moved back to Flathead Lake, if you were to go
into Eugene's study overlooking Hughes Bay, you'd find hardly a
single plaque, memento, or trinket signifying his many academic
or pastoral accomplishments. If you wanted to see his literary
awards or any of his international acknowledgments, you'd have

to find the small hallway closet, where they gathered dust next to forgotten papers and old cassette tapes.

In place of credentials, Eugene hung three pictures on his wall: Alexander Whyte, John Henry Newman, and Baron Friedrich von Hügel. These three became his longest and truest mentors in spirituality and pastoral work. Whyte, the Scottish pastor-theologian, had already cemented his place in Eugene's vision as an exemplary pastor who took God and the parish seriously, all with a glint in his eye.

Next to Whyte hung Newman, who modeled a great intellect content with the power of small things. He never considered the parish too small or confining, never thought his rich gifts required a grand stage or ivory tower. When Newman resigned his post at Oxford University to move to Birmingham, a working-class town dotted with mournful smokestacks pumping black soot, a friend chided him for exchanging Oxford's cultural epicenter for a place bereft of sophistication. Newman intended to create a small school for boys and would not be deterred. "The people of Birmingham also have souls," Newman answered. This story was poignant for Eugene, who resented suburban life and yearned to minister in a town abundant in culture, with intellectually curious people who wrestled with big ideas, people who were *interesting*.

"We grew up in a very suburban neighborhood, which my dad did not like," Leif explained. "He kind of considered it intellectual death." Yet here hung Newman, whose silent portrait insisted that each soul, whether a factory worker or college don, overflowed with wonder.

Then Baron Friedrich von Hügel. While noble von Hügel held no influential position, he had a brilliant mind, quietly editing old manuscripts of the great Christian mystics and writing about the spiritual life. Immersed in von Hügel's letters, Eugene discovered that they formed in him "a pastoral way of using language that was conversational—not condescending, not manipulative, but attentive and prayerful. Not instructional. . . . Not diagnostic, treating these unique souls [his parishioners] as problems to be fixed." Perhaps von Hügel's most profound influence appeared in Eugene's thousands of letters, written over decades. Attentive letters. Curious letters. Letters almost adamant in their refusal to give advice, to fix—often to the reader's frustration. Letters revealing an awareness of mysteries, a desire for genuine, holy conversation.

These three pictures symbolized three ways of being in the world, ways in which Eugene desired to live. They watched him as he studied and read. They watched as he labored over words to deliver, in prayer and from the pulpit. They watched as Eugene poured ink on the page for book after book. They watched as he met with person after person in his study, tending to souls.

They watched him live.

One of the souls Eugene tended was Lu Gerard, who saw how Eugene always honored people's questions and gave those who were weary and beleaguered generous space to roam and ponder and encounter grace. "Eugene never gave advice," Lu explained. "He only listened, prayed with you. Eugene always saw people as God saw them—as redeemed people, in light of the love of Christ, not as what they've done."

And then there were souls like Jim Dresher, who discovered that Eugene could be pointed, if the relationship called for it. For a decade, in which he built a prosperous business, Jim showed up sporadically on Sundays. Then a divorce kept him away for years more. Struggling through intense questions and reading M. Scott Peck's *People of the Lie,* Jim found himself in Eugene's study. "I need someone to talk to who's wise and Christ-centered but who won't be judgmental."

Eugene thought for a moment. "So, you're looking for some-body who's smart and kind?"

"Yes, that's it," Jim answered. And Jim poured out his life.

"Well, Jim, there's some chance here that the Lord is calling you, and that doesn't happen every day. You've been a dabbler, and I think God is asking you for a commitment. If I were you, I'd pay attention. This may be your last chance." Jim perked up. Eugene laid out four things to help him pay attention. First, he needed to pray the Psalms daily. Second, he needed to read an-other part of the Bible (Eugene recommended John). Third, he needed to set aside a half hour every day for quiet and for journal-ing about his life. And fourth: "Jim, no more dabbling. You've obviously got a problem with commitment. For at least the next six months, you need to be in worship every Sunday." From that point on, every Sunday Jim was in the pew, and every other week he was in Eugene's study.

Jim and Eugene talked about doubt and faith and about the connection between sexuality and spirituality. "Jim," Eugene ex-plained, "sexuality and spirituality are cousins. They're separated by a fine line." Jim once gave Eugene a pack of M. Scott Peck's tapes on the subject. Eugene listened but was unimpressed: "Our conversations are better than that."

"Eugene looked through biblical glasses," Jim remembered. "It was as if Eugene would say, *Here, look through my lens and see what I see.* He'd convert my story into a biblical story, into a more loving and forgiving perspective. I would sit in his study and say, 'This is the world and culture I live in.' And Eugene would say, 'That's actually not the world you live in. You live in a world of faith and Christ.' Eugene was a conduit between me and Christ. Eugene centered my life. He changed my life."

But the souls Eugene wanted to be most attuned to were those under his own roof. Even as he struggled with spending too many hours at church, and even as Jan and the kids struggled with how little they saw of him, Eugene's letters and journals reveal how he desired to be the kind of father he never had.

On one occasion, Jan and the boys dropped Eugene and Karen off at a bus stop, waving as the Greyhound motored away. Arriving in DC, Eugene hailed a taxi to deliver them to the Smithsonian, where they spent the entire day. *Karen is so excited with all the exhibits and displays—the dinosaurs and Indians and fossils. And it was completely leisurely. I could let her spend as much time wherever she wished without the boys getting restless and tired. We have been there before, of course, but never just the two of us.*

Once, he spent an afternoon alone with Eric, taking him to see the Orioles beat the Boston Red Sox. Eugene bought Eric an Orioles cap, which he refused to take off for days. On her ninth birthday, Eugene picked Karen up from school and took her to the bank to cash a five-dollar check from her Montana grandparents. *There followed a complicated explanation about how the money you put in the bank in Montana got to Bel Air—then we went to the dime store and she bought a little animaliddle kiddle—an animal miniature doll that is pinned to the dress. We celebrated by going to the drugstore and having a coke.*

Eugene introduced Leif and Eric to the woodshop, teaching his wide-eyed boys to handle keen tools and guiding them as they cut the frame for a birdhouse and feeder. (The boys continued in the succession of Peterson carpenters. Leif remodeled a farmhouse in Whitefish, Montana. Eric had a stint as a framer and later built the casket in which he laid his father before lowering him into the earth.)

The three children remember their dad plopped on the family

room floor, watching *The Rockford Files* with them as teenagers (during the short stretch when Jan and Eugene had a television, for the kids' benefit). Eric remembered an afternoon his senior year in high school when he came home and found his dad sprawled across the sofa, reading a volume of Barth's *Dogmatics*. "I sat down in a chair opposite him, and he just popped up and slammed down the book on the sofa and set it aside. And he leaned in. Engraved in my memory is that he didn't even mark the page. He was just killing time with a dead Swiss theologian, waiting for his son to show up."

And Eugene loved being in the backyard on warm Sunday afternoons. He stretched out in the chaise (one he'd built), reading until he began to catnap in the sun. As soon as young Leif spotted his dad, he'd snag ice from the freezer and sneak, catlike. "I'd put ice down his back, and he'd yelp. 'Woohooo! You got me, that's really cold'—no anger at all; he just played along. I would run away squalling, just thinking I was so smart, getting him."

However, these stories stand out in part because they were the exception. Karen's frustration over her dad's twenty-seven nights in a row revealed a struggle of presence that Eugene never completely overcame. He loved them, but he gave less of his time than they wanted and needed. Eric remembered this acutely. "It was a lack of *time*, primarily," he explained, "but when he was there, he was present. When I was younger, it was more play: chess, arm wrestling, Indian leg wrestling. He was actually quite playful. But I don't have any memory of my dad tucking me in. Mom would read Bible story books to us, and I'm grateful for that. But I missed my dad."

Eric recalled a crisp autumn evening when his dad walked in the front door wearing his trench coat. Before Eugene could even close the door, Eric buried his head in his dad, wrapping his arms around his legs. He remembers his father's smell and warmth enveloping him. Eugene picked Eric up and squeezed, hugging him as if he'd never let him go. This longing of Eric's never lessened. He always wanted more than his dad seemed able (or knew how) to give. Still, Eric never felt rejection, never doubted his father's love. "Whenever Dad was there," he said, "he was pleasant and affectionate." Only his dad wasn't there nearly enough.

The church was good work, holy work, but Eugene didn't always draw the boundaries he should have. He at times was more available to his parishioners than to his family. Years later, he would recognize—and regret—these failings. But it was hard for Eugene to see it clearly at the time. He actively resisted so many modern addictions and idolatries, but he didn't see them all. He didn't conquer them all.

The years passed, and Jan and Eugene's three little children grew into young adults.

Eric had a wild streak, but he kept it in check because he hated the idea of disappointing his dad. One afternoon, when he was thirteen, he gathered with buddies in the woods behind their house to smoke cigarettes. His dad, late for their confirmation class at church, called for him. Eric, startled, scrubbed the cigarette into the dirt and sprinted to the car. On the ride home after the class, Eugene said, "You reeked of cigarettes."

Eric froze. "Oh . . . really?"

His dad said nothing more.

"I don't think I ever smoked another cigarette after that. That was typical of his discipline. He didn't avoid things, but he didn't overdo them. That was also typical of his pastoral way. He wouldn't ignore things, but he was very patient with people. He'd pray and love and watch. He was gentle. And usually they'd come around. But he wasn't cowardly or avoidant."

Leif had a wild streak too. "But no more rebellious than any other kid," he insisted when I asked him how it was to be a Peterson boy in Bel Air. "There were normal shenanigans, but I never felt any pressure to be better or anything." This brought a welcome sense of freedom that, strangely enough, added weight to Leif's maturing understanding of how his choices mattered. "I went to school with a lot of pastors' kids at Whitworth. I think maybe I had a different experience than they did. My parents were very laissez-faire, so trusting, and they gave us so much freedom. I know that I always had in the back of my mind, *I damn well better respect that. I've been given all this freedom, and it would be a mistake to abuse it.* A lot of pastors aren't like that because they feel like their kid reflects directly on their job and their image in the community. I don't think my dad felt like that. I don't think my dad cared about that."

Leif caused the most trouble when he was his dad's running partner. In high school, Leif joined the cross-country team and then began registering for Saturday races with Eugene. They'd run 10K races multiple weekends in a row. "He always beat me," Leif said with a grimace. Eugene, however, didn't think the wins came easily. In one letter home, he mentioned an upcoming race. *Leif and I have a race on Saturday that we will run together. This is a 6.2 mile (10 kilometer) at Johns Hopkins. Leif has a track meet on Wednesday, so he might be tired enough that I will be able to beat him.*

But Leif kept losing. "At the end of one cross-country season," he explained, "I was determined to beat him. I was in great shape, but I kept training. He ran downhill better than me, but I ran uphill better than him." They registered for a race in Lancaster County, Pennsylvania, and several of Leif's friends clued Eugene in to how Leif was pounding the pavement, training with renewed ferocity. Eugene didn't say a word, but he added on extra miles too. A duel, a friendly death match between son and father.

For the first mile, they ran a steady clip, side by side through

Amish country. However, when they hit the first of ten hills, things turned serious. Leif, a stronger climber, pulled ahead. Downhill, Eugene made time and inched ahead. Ten hills—and they swapped the lead ten times. The finish line was at the local college stadium, and Eugene knew that to hold Leif off, he needed a stronger lead. Eugene went for broke. He stretched the final strides, sprinting with his absolute last burst of energy to the stadium entrance, leaning for the tape. Only there was no tape. The finish line was another quarter mile away, a full lap inside around the stadium track. Eugene sputtered like an old lawn mower missing spark plugs. As Leif cruised past his gasping dad, Jan yelled, "Leif, you better not beat your daddy!" Leif never broke stride. "It was probably the most satisfying loss of my life," Eugene wrote to a friend. "And he was completely modest in victory. He didn't crow."

Karen, however, took advantage of her parents' openhanded parenting when she graduated from high school, itching to move west and work on a ranch. "My goal in life was to be a hermit," Karen explained. Jan and Eugene hated the idea, but Eugene lined up a job for Karen in eastern Montana anyway, tending sheep on a twenty-four-thousand-acre ranch. "Horses, cows, pigs, chickens, rabbits, gophers, and rattlesnakes," Karen recounted. "The wind blew every day. I loved it. I worked twelve-hour days, seven days a week. Working outside was wonderful. My love of nature is deep in my bones." As a graduation present, Eugene and Jan bought Karen's bus ticket and waved goodbye.

Growth brings change, and change brings new revelations. "When I was fourteen, I *finally* beat him in arm wrestling," Eric remembered. "That was one of those amazing, awful moments when I realized I could beat my dad. Realizing I was becoming a man, and that Dad did not put the moon in the sky."

The summer before Eric's junior year, a road trip to Spokane marked a significant shift in their relationship. In Montana for their summer pilgrimage, Eric and Eugene took a day to visit Whitworth University, where both Leif and Eric would eventually attend. As they drove the ten hours round trip across I-90, watching the beauty of the Coeur d'Alene National Forest out the window, their conversation unfolded with the miles, ranging easily from geology and the Ice Age to love, romance, and relationships. Eric asked his dad, "Do you know who my favorite person in the Bible is?"

"No," Eugene answered.

"Jeremiah."

"Why Jeremiah?"

"Because," Eric said, "he was also the son of a priest." Eugene melted. That was the day he determined to write a book on Jeremiah (what became *Run with the Horses*, which contains this dedication: "For Eric, also the son of a priest").

The next day, they were swimming in Flathead Lake, and Eric said, "I really enjoyed that time with you. I wonder if we could continue that after we get home." And they did.

Back in Bel Air, every Tuesday, Eric rode his bike to his dad's study. They read 1 Timothy, discussed ministry, and prayed. "We called them our Timothy conversations," Eugene said. Decades later, Eugene and Eric shared letters, continuing this intentional conversation between father and son. They called them the Timothy letters. And for Eric's ordination, Eugene preached a sermon from Jeremiah.

It was these flashes of intimacy that made a certain ache worse somehow. Years later, as a grown man with a child of his own, Eric's longing for intimacy with his dad was still unfulfilled, still a source of melancholy. At the encouragement of his therapist— and though he wrote it for himself and didn't know if he'd ever give it to his dad—Eric penned a letter, trying to make sense of his sorrow:

It seems that I resent [Dad] putting so much energy into birthing Christ Our King Church rather than parenting me. The church and I were "born" the same year, and there was sibling rivalry at work, each fighting for parental affection. It seems ironic to me that I would, twenty-seven years later, embrace the church with vows of ordination, that same church which for so long got to take cuts to the front of the line.

Yes, of course there were joy and wonder and affection. Eric went on to reminisce about a litany of wonderful experiences (road trips, summers in Montana, the Whitworth trip, Timothy conversations). And then continued,

But something's not right. Why can't I recall such good memories without wanting to cry? Was it because it happened so late in our relationship? Was it because I was scheduled on his appointment calendar? . . . Or does it have something to do with the timing and circumstances of how and when our friendship really blossomed? Because when I met him on his turf (ministry and faith issues) we suddenly became very close. At no other time in my life was he as involved with me. . . .

I love my dad. I'm proud of him: proud of who he is, what he's done, and proud to be his son. But that's not the point. The point is that I am missing something in my life because he didn't give it to me. And I need to learn how to recover it, or at least how to resolve the conflict that I am experiencing.

The following day, Eric arrived at clarity:

[I've realized] what the issue is: Sorrow. I'm sad because of the gaps in the early years of our relationship. There are big holes there. I long to be able to recover those lost moments, but know that it is now impossible, it's too late. But what can be done is for the pattern of absentee-ism to be broken. He has before him the opportunity to do things differently with his grandchildren. A second chance.

Several months later, Eric wrote his dad a letter, outlining his hurt. During a hike, Eugene and Eric sat atop a mountain, and Eric nervously unfolded the paper. Through tears, and having to pause often to regain composure, Eric read the hard words. When he finished, Eugene looked at his son, eyes moist. "I'm so sorry, Eric. I didn't realize how much I've done to you what my dad did to me. I'm so sorry."

Over the years, the sinews of Eric and Eugene's relationship would pull and fray and ultimately strengthen. A son coming to terms with this father he loved—a father who was flawed, human. "My dad learned how to be a dad from his dad. And he did better than his dad did. We all have father wounds. My dad has always been a bigger-than-life figure. In recent years, the word that I have is *hero*. This is because there is no one I have more respect for or anyone I would more want to emulate."

The 4,800-mile pilgrimage every summer to Montana and back continued to shape the family. In the early years, the kids bedded down in the back of their green Rambler station wagon. "We'd drive all night, all day, all night," Eric recounted. Eugene had a six-pack of Coke and chocolate bars to keep him caffeinated. They never stayed in hotels. At night, they'd pull out their sleeping bags and fire up the camp stove. Under the stars and feeling the breeze rustle the flaps of their tent, they were slowly entering another geography, another cadence.

"The time in Montana was terribly important," Eric explained. "I daydreamed about it during school. I loved being in Montana— on the lake or in Glacier Park or with my grandfather. I *lived* for those weeks."

They spent those Flathead days in the woods, climbing peaks, on the water, from dawn to dark. They crisscrossed the mountains. Once when Karen was little, Eugene took her solo for an alpine hike. Sighting a grizzly, this "immense animal of clumsy grace and elegance," they crouched quietly, watching the bear lumber through the vegetation, munching. They grew nervous, and Eugene decided they should turn around and make their descent. After a mile or so, Karen piped up: "I got two prayers answered today. I saw a grizzly; he didn't see me."

The boys became their grandfather's companions, running errands and going into town to see their grandpa's friends. Don strapped a utility belt on his grandsons so they could help build a deck and a shed. It was a strange thing, all these hours Leif and Eric spent with their grandfather, when this intimate time was exactly what Eugene had wanted his entire boyhood yet had so rarely received. "My grandfather was not very close with my dad," Leif explained, "but he loved my brother and me. He would spend every moment with us he could." Don spread out the paper every morning and clipped coupons, sorting them by store. "Grandpa would drive us into town, and we'd go to one store for toilet paper because they had a big sale, another store for something else because they had a sale, another place for something else. Then the big treat was we'd go to McDonald's for lunch." Don drove a French-made Simca. Rolling down the highway, he would lay on the horn and say, "Listen here, boys. We have a French horn."

After their trip in the summer of 1974, Jan jotted a note back to Montana: "Eric and I had a tear in our eyes as we boarded the airplane at Missoula, Dad. It has meant a great deal to your grandsons, especially Eric, to be able to spend so much time with you this summer. He prayed last night that you would both stay well through the winter."

Once, Leif remembered his grandfather dropping them off at the airport. "I started cruising down the Jetway, and my dad says 'Hey' and grabs me by the shoulder and turns me around. My grandfather was there crying." Eugene told Leif to go back and say a proper goodbye.

Reflecting on this story, I wonder what Eugene felt at that moment, seeing his father's genuine affection for his grandsons. Grateful, I'm sure, but also there must have been an ache.

Did Eugene's dad ache too? Maybe Don Peterson was trying to reach for something that had long been lost to the past, reach for it the only way he knew how. Reach for Eugene.

While Eugene was riddled with regret over his relationship with his dad, he abounded in gratitude for his relationship with his mom. He once wrote to his mother, describing how when leading couples through premarital counseling, he often found himself asking questions about each one's mother:

> *"What kind of woman was she? . . . Would you like to be like her? . . . etc." And [I] inevitably get a picture of a woman who is much less than adequate as a mother. All the time I cannot refrain from silently—almost unconsciously—making comparisons with my own mother, and being grateful for the strengths, the virtues, the genuine righteousness that nurtured me through the years of growth and development.*
>
> *This kind of almost automatic comparison, and grateful*

remembrance, is a daily part of my work now. You are much more with me these last 2 or 3 years than you ever were before. It is surprising to me how vividly you permeate my life—much more than you did 10 years ago.

I don't think I have ever said this to you, Mother, (and it is a fairly recent development) but it is a kind of presence which is strong and good—and which makes it possible to be a minister of the gospel with a special kind of freedom and confidence.

I had always supposed that the crucial years of motherhood were during the years of child-rearing—but these present years of separation seem to me to be almost equally influential. What you are now, not what you have been, is enormously important to me and feeds into the kind of person I am and the ministry I share. There is an operation of our Lord's grace here that I do not understand but feel as if I have some faint, glimmering apprehension at the edge. Prayer is without doubt a major factor. But there must also be some special energy attached to the office of motherhood (at least your motherhood) that our Lord uses for his glory.

This is being said badly—clumsily—but I hardly know what I am talking about, except that you are extremely important to me today, that my love for you has been strangely magnified recently, that you seem to be a vital part of the ministry I share with others, that God uses you in an unusual way with me.

Eugene would insist that his entire life, even the failures, even the treacherous places, was lived under the mercy of God, led by his strong and generous hand. This was most evident with those dearest to him. From his boyhood home, he received immense grace, even as, over the years, he also had to work through pain. And with Jan and Karen and Eric and Leif, though he'd reflect on his regrets (the things he'd missed, the fatherly work he'd left undone), he still felt, more than anything else, a river of gratitude.

12

Words Made Flesh

The idea that the writer is a wise person . . . I tend to shrug my shoulders about that. A writer's responsibility isn't to be wise. There are wisdom keepers in all societies, and they aren't necessarily storytellers. The storyteller's responsibility is to remember what we are all prone to forget, and to say it memorably.

—Barry Lopez, "The World We Still Have"

As Eugene grew into his life as a pastor, a twin vocation crystallized. "I saw that alongside and intertwined with being a pastor I was also a writer. My vocation was bipolar." He understood his writing to be an act of worship as well as work honoring the God who from "in the beginning" has always pulsed with creative energy. Writing, like pastoring, was knit into his life of prayer. Eugene even wrote several pieces he labeled "Prayers at the Writing Desk," one of which reads,

Lord Jesus Christ
Word from the beginning
Word made flesh
Shape words also into speech
and bring them to print
that tell the truth
and speak your glory. Amen.

But this instinctive tug toward writing was nothing new. Since he was a boy, Eugene always dreamed of writing fiction. And now, an encounter with Chaim Potok, the astounding novelist and Jewish rabbi, served as a cattle prod. After Potok released his groundbreaking novel *The Chosen* (sitting on the *New York Times* bestseller list for thirty-nine weeks and selling more than 3.5 million copies), Eugene heard that he was scheduled to speak at Shriver Hall on the Johns Hopkins campus. During his talk, Potok shared how his mom worked tirelessly to dissuade him from being an impoverished writer, wanting him to be a brain surgeon instead. His mom badgered him, pushed him, told him he had a responsibility to keep people from dying. Finally, Potok exploded: "Mama, I don't want to keep people from dying; I want to show them how to live!" Eugene recognized the fervor.

Unfortunately, he kept running into brick walls. Once, in need of money, Eugene interviewed when Chuck Colson was considering potential ghost writers. Colson chose someone else, and Eugene immediately felt relief. What was he doing? Eugene needed help. He needed a guide in his life as a writer the way Whyte, Newman, and von Hügel had guided him in his life as a pastor. After several failed attempts to connect with writing mentors, Eugene happened upon the novelist Fyodor Dostoevsky. Eugene had never read Dostoevsky, and he had no hint of what made him first pick up *The Idiot*. However, the impact was so immediate and intense that Eugene threw himself into Dostoevsky's corpus. He penciled *FD* into his calendar three times a week (Tuesdays, Thursdays, and Fridays) from 3:00 to 5:00 p.m. Eugene closed his study door, nursed a steaming cup of tea, and pored over Penguin paperbacks: *Crime and Punishment, Notes from Underground, A Raw Youth, Devils, The Brothers Karamazov.*

In Prince Myshkin, Dostoevsky's idiot, Eugene found a man who befriended everyone but stood detached from the consuming passions: position, image, influence. And from *Crime and Punishment*'s Raskolnikov, the poor law student who murdered a corrupt pawnbroker while trying to convince himself he had noble reasons for the violence, Eugene learned how easy it is for good people to do evil things for supposedly good reasons.

At Christ Our King, Eugene felt pressure to gather a crowd quickly. With his writing, he felt pressure to get published. "Crisis. Decision time. I wanted to be published; I wanted to have a large congregation. But I couldn't be a writer and be published. And I couldn't be a pastor and get a large congregation. Not on the terms that were being offered to me at that time." Eugene put the question in stark terms: Would he be true and live a life of fidelity to God, or would he become a prostitute pastor, a prostitute writer? "I saw myself as Raskolnikov. Not murdering exactly, but experimenting with words on paper and parishioners in the congregation, manipulating them in godlike ways to see what I could make happen." It was as though he were watching his future, a man disintegrating, play out on these sprawling pages.

Over the decades, poets and novelists proved to be among Eugene's most trusted teachers. Once, Eugene asked himself in his journal, *Who are my novelists? Who are my poets?* On the list, which included Gerard Manley Hopkins, William Faulkner, Wendell Berry, Luci Shaw, William Stafford, and more, Dostoevsky sat at the top.

Reflecting on his ministry and Dostoevsky's influence, Eugene concluded,

In terms of my pastoral and writing life, the first writer who really started shaping my imagination was Dostoyevsky. He wrote about the whole of human experience with such seriousness. There's no moralizing in Dostoyevsky, no preaching. He really does understand how faith works, how prayer works, how deceit works, how sin works. Perhaps the best thing about him is that he doesn't make it easy. You have to enter his imagination. In the world of spirituality and religion, reduction and oversimplification are just endemic, and the minute that happens, we lose our participation. We stand off at a distance and criticize and evaluate the options. Dostoyevsky doesn't much do that. He's not an analyzer.

Eugene's early writing mostly resulted in piles of rejection letters. One article was rejected by three periodicals in quick succession. In 1972, a Presbyterian group commissioned him to write a book describing new expressions of evangelism. (He wrote the book, but they never found a publisher.) The executive editor of *Eternity* magazine answered one 1975 query with a bit of free advice: "This could stand a good bit of thinning out to be more readable. E.g. . . . omit the Hebrew and Greek word studies, and conclude with some pointed applications." And Harold Lindsell, editor of *Christianity Today,* responded to another query a couple of months later: "The editors have taken a look at your manuscript. I read the article myself after the other editors had looked at it. I found some problems that trouble me. . . . You might be interested to take another hard look at your essay."

In 1976, Eugene collected the parenting articles he had written for Russ Reid (a friend from SPU days who had worked in publishing before building a prosperous and booming marketing business) and added new content to publish *Growing Up with Your Teenager.* The book caught no one's interest.

After a 1979 volume, *A Year with the Psalms,* barely registered, Eugene's third book, *Five Smooth Stones for Pastoral Work,* emerged from imagery Eugene gleaned from the resident rabbi in his Tuesday pastors' group. Published in 1980, *Smooth Stones* cut much closer to the bone. It was Eugene's first attempt at exploring his convictions about being a pastor in America.

But this book (in many ways his real writing debut) had a rocky start. The editor was unimpressed with Eugene's writing and blasé about the book's prospects. When *Smooth Stones* released to a lackluster response, the relationship soured even further. It all felt wrong. One night Eugene had a dream that he sighted *Smooth Stones* on a newsstand at the grocery store—only the cover had been updated to a glossy photo of a nude woman. "What have you done to my book?" he asked the editor in his dream. He responded, "Well, Eugene, you can write the book, but I've got to sell it."

Given his poor sales, when Eugene finished his fourth book, *A Long Obedience in the Same Direction* (mining themes of discipleship from the psalms of ascent), no one would touch it. His brother, Ken, encouraged him to just keep sending it—to every publisher he could find. So Eugene stuffed the manuscript into manila envelopes and started mailing. Twenty-three publishing houses. Twenty-three rejections—getting a letter back if he was lucky. Jim Hoover, a first-year editor at IVP, was assigned to read from that day's collection of unsolicited manuscripts. After the first couple of pages, he thought, *This won't work; it's just reworked sermons.* But Jim kept reading. And he found himself engrossed. This was a writer who obviously loved words, coupling artfulness with keen biblical insight and spiritual depth. After eight chapters, he was hooked. Jim laid the manuscript on the senior editor's desk with a note: "Send contract immediately!" "That was a brash move on my part," he admitted.

Eugene culled the title from Nietzsche's *Beyond Good and Evil* and considered the line poetry, both for how it rolled off the tongue and for how it turned Nietzsche's faithless words inside out. "I mean," Eugene said, with a Cheshire grin, "you can't get better than Nietzsche for a book about discipleship, can you?" Those words—*a long obedience in the same direction*—have become shorthand for faithfulness and a life of devotion to Jesus, even among people who've never actually read the book. "It's a witness," Jim observed, "to how many people have read Eugene and to his influence."

"Eugene was an excellent writer and serious about the craft," Jim explained. "In the early days, Eugene's only problem was too many adverbs. So I cut them out. Eugene never pushed back." InterVarsity published three more of his books in short succession: *Traveling Light, Run with the Horses,* and *Earth and Altar.* Eugene felt the thrill of momentum.

But it was a mixed bag, and his early sense that publishing could hold him back from being an actual *writer* returned. For the first time, he had to reckon with the impediments of success.

I hate messing with these details—I can't be a different person in marketing my book than I am in writing it, but am ill-equipped it seems to insist on what I think is important. . . . Is it too much to hope that the Spirit will do for me what I can't seem to do for myself? At any rate, I think I have arrived at a new position of detachment from any emotional relation with publishers; will be able, now, I think to more objectively ask for the publisher I want and take charge. I have been so pleased to be wanted that I feel like a puppy dog wagging its tail, flattered to be noticed!

Months passed, then a couple of years. At times it felt as if nothing were happening. But unseen to Eugene, as he called Christ Our King to Sunday worship and as he and Jan practiced their Monday Sabbaths, amid all the other days with their large and small moments, people around the country were picking up books with his name on them—picking them up and sensing they'd found a voice that spoke their true language. Vast numbers of readers recognized in Eugene's words a hunger they'd forgotten, a craving for an authentic encounter with God. They were hungry for a vision calling them into the wondrous expanse of a life that honored what it meant to be a beloved (though finite) human living under the mercy of a magnificent, generous, infinite God. They found all this in the words of a pastor from Maryland, and they couldn't get enough.

Speaking at a writers' conference in Chicago, Eugene encountered one of the first audiences of readers who took him seriously as a literary figure.

What extraordinary encouragement to continue writing. Tim Hansel ranks me with Henri Nouwen and Frederick Buechner. Am I that good? I hope to be, but doubt it. But I am going to keep at it—and keep at it pursuing excellence. All those 50 retreatants had read nearly everything that I have written—much of it several times. But I feel quite detached from the compliments and praise—something that is apart from me—a gift, not an achievement.

Even as all these doors opened for Eugene, he suffered the nagging fear that he was an impostor. In the fall of 1984, with both Leif and Eric at Whitworth, the college invited Eugene to speak at the school's annual weekend at Camp Spalding. In his journal, Eugene worked through that fatherly desire for his sons to be proud of him, comingled with self-doubt.

> *Eric is in charge and Leif is program director. At Forum yesterday I was more nervous than I thought I should be: I wanted to do well and be well received for their sake—didn't want to embarrass them! But it went well—some said it was [the] best Forum in memory!—but I wish I could escape or grow out of my self-consciousness: anxious about whether I am doing a good job or not, and just be here in ministry. It was better this morning, but still not entirely free.*

Seeing his sons in their element delighted him.

> *Reflecting on the weekend. Incredibly proud of Eric and Leif—their leadership, their unselfish ways, the kind of friends they choose, their spiritual maturity. And continually surprised by their pride in me. I keep expecting them to discover my clay feet and become impatient and critical of my shortcomings. But if they do they don't let on to me.*

This Whitworth weekend revealed inner tensions. Eugene sensed there was work he needed to do—ways he needed to offer himself—that remained unfulfilled. He felt his impact was marginal (particularly as he compared himself to the prestigious headline speaker). From his journal:

> *I have the deep sense that I have something to do that is better and deeper than what he is doing and saying. I'm very*

aware—maybe too much—of his prominence and my obscurity—and that what I do has to take place in the obscurity: working in the darkness of the mines.

I affirmed this in a slight way last evening when I turned down the invitation to go to [a faculty member's] home . . . to meet [a prominent speaker] and visit in favor of going out for nachos and beer with Eric and Leif. They are the raw material of my life that I need to contemplate and be with and love and understand and respond to.

And prayer. Matins this morning in my room instead of rushing to the library and stuffing myself with ideas and information.

Relationship with his boys and prayer—for that day, this was where he needed to put his attention. The real call.

Eugene concluded with a fine point.

Contrast: my pervasive sense of inadequacy and inferiority (with Leif and Eric quite confident and self-assured), along with [the] conviction of something quite extraordinary to do (. . . if only because I am embracing the life of the mystic and prayer so much more deliberately).

Months later, Eugene circled back to this feeling, which surely was a deep and honest one: *My overwhelming and recurring sense: I am ready to do far more than I am getting an opportunity to do: to engage people and words at a far deeper level than anybody around me is interested in. And so I read Barth! And play my banjo.*

A year before this inner wrestling match began in earnest, Eugene had answered the phone and heard his brother's broken voice: "If you want to see Dad before he dies, you better come quickly."

Don had fought colon cancer for years, but it had spread to his liver. Eugene and Jan flew to Montana. The first day they were back, a nurse plopped an orange on the table and taught Eugene, with a needle piercing its aromatic peel, how to give his dad injections. For ten days, Eugene cared for his father. He pumped the dying man with morphine, scooped him in his arms and carried him to the bathroom, fed him. "We had never been very close," Eugene stated years later in his memoir. "He gave most of his attention to his meat-cutting business. I was covetous of his attention but never got what I wanted. But in these ten final days of his life, I received a full measure of the intimacy that I had missed growing up. It was more than enough."

Don passed, and though Eugene's mom had brief stretches of lucidity, she suffered from Alzheimer's disease. In spite of his own advancing sickness, Don had cared for his wife the past couple of years. When they carried his body out of the house, Evelyn asked, "Who is that man?" But there was mysterious grace here. "Dad's dealing with cancer was redemptive to him," Eugene's brother, Ken, explained. "And his care of Mother was redemptive. He had ignored her most of his life, and she had to marry herself to her ministry work. But Dad became very attentive, loving, and caring in those later years. Dad was sweet in the end, and we felt our relationships were healed."

The season of goodbye was not yet over, though, and Evelyn's illness advanced quickly. Eight months after burying his dad, Eugene traveled back home to say goodbye to his mom. "That was the hardest funeral I've ever done," he said. "I barely made it through." As Eugene sat with his daughter, Karen, after the service, a well-meaning pastor approached, offered a few vacuous words, and quoted a few scriptures. When the pastor mercifully left, Eugene turned to Karen. "Oh, Karen, I hope I have never done that to anyone."

Karen looked at her dad with love. "You'd never do that, Dad. You'd never make someone even lonelier by handing out words like that."

But Eugene was lonely. His mother, the one who shaped him in so many ways, was gone.

But there would be healing too. In 1989 at the age of fifty-six, Eugene recounted a dream in his journal, a dream that gave him a redemptive picture of his troubled relationship with his dad.

> *Dreamt of my father last night. We were working together on some vast and disorganized construction—he was going about it confidently and knowledgeably, and I was helping—following orders when he gave them. But also feeling left out because he didn't converse. And in the midst of it noticed that he was singing or praying (not sure which) and thinking, "He is a Christian"—the feeling/understanding that "he is a Christian even though I am not experiencing any of the side-effects from it in love or intimacy from him; but it is enough that I can work alongside him." A good dream an integrating dream.*

Though never fully resolving the impact of his father's failings, he grew to honor what his father had been for him. In his later years, Eugene felt genuine gratitude for what his father did provide. "My father," Eugene wrote, "working those long and hard hours, determined to put bread on the table and meat in the pot, [laid] foundations that would undergird my eventual vocation as a pastor."

On June 21, 1993, what would have been his dad's eighty-third birthday, Eugene wrote, *Today is my father's birthday. Remembering him with gratitude and asking forgiveness for dismissing his gifts and his love in the way he expressed them.*

Grief, vocational restlessness, and sheer exhaustion threatened to bury Eugene. On Sundays, he wanted nothing more than to be at Christ Our King, leading worship. However, by Wednesdays, he wasn't so sure. *Everything takes too much effort,* he wrote. *I feel crowded, uncreative.* A couple of months later, he confessed more.

I am again at the place of feeling the lack of fit between all the stuff inside me—vocational/spiritual energies—and the work I do here as pastor of Christ Our King. The critical question: is the "lack of fit" because I am out-of-proportion, my life is losing a base in humility—in letting go? Or is it because there is something else or more that God is wanting me to do?

Eugene needed a break. He'd been in ministry for well over two decades and had never had a sabbatical. And he didn't think a few months would do. He needed a year. The session was willing to work on this with Eugene, but there were a couple of barriers. The first was how to pay for it.

Eugene had never done anything like this in his life, but he called up his friend Russ Reid. Russ had moved on from publishing and built an astoundingly successful marketing agency. An *LA Times* obituary credited Reid with helping World Vision grow "from a modest organization with 60 workers to a billion-dollar network with 45,000 employees in nearly 100 countries." Russ had made a lot of money, and he regularly asked Eugene if there was anything he could do for him. Eugene always said no, but now he had a big ask. Russ didn't blink; he'd provide Eugene's salary for the year.

The second barrier was finding a pastor to fill Eugene's shoes for twelve months. Steve Trotter, a student at Fuller Seminary, had been reading articles Eugene had written and regularly quoting lines to a friend. Finally, the friend, tired of constantly hearing about Eugene, said, "Why don't you write him and ask for a job?" And that's what Steve did. A week later, Eugene dialed Steve's number. Steve, always the prankster, picked up the receiver and said, "Joe's Bar and Grill." Remarkably, Eugene hired him, and in early 1985, Steve moved to Bel Air. He would have a few months with Eugene to get oriented, and then he'd fill in during Eugene's sabbatical.

Those first months, Steve saw a side of Eugene few people experienced. "Eugene could get pissed off. He didn't suffer fools gladly. There was a denominational exec who was nice—but a clown and name dropper." Once, Eugene got off the phone with this executive and unleashed: "This guy's an idiot. Why doesn't he get a job and stop wasting my time!" Once, Steve remembered, "we were driving down a thoroughfare and noticed a butt-ugly church building. And Eugene said, 'Have you ever noticed the worse the theology, the worse the architecture?'" What struck Steve most of all, though, was Eugene's authenticity. "His humility is real."

The admiration was mutual. Eugene appreciated having someone with whom to share pastoral intimacies.

Steve, yesterday, told me [about the view of ministry] and what he experienced here, where I am not trying to do very much, but am looking for what the Spirit is doing. Well, I'm glad he sees that and wants it. I think he knows, at least a little anyway, of how difficult it is—but more of the difficulty is inward, the struggle to be here, stay out of the way, and to pray without forcing anything—or running out and contradicting by action what I enter into by prayer.

With funding and Steve both in place, sabbatical plans were set.

13

Living at the Margins

He walks with the effort of a man burdened, a man carrying a great bale or a barrel, who has carried it too far
but has not yet found a place convenient to set it down.
Once he could carry twice this weight. Now half would
be too much.
—Wendell Berry, *The Memory of Old Jack*

Before the sabbatical commenced, Russ wanted Jan and Eugene
to join him and his wife, Cathie, on a trip to Israel. Eugene had
visited once before, and Russ wanted him to explain the biblical
history and serve as Russ's spiritual director for the trip. For
Eugene, this experience pulled together the two things that were
essential: spirituality and physicality.

*What do I want from Israel: I want to be there—at the begin-
ning, source-places. I want a sense of first-handedness. . . . I
want to engage in pilgrimage: feel some of the difficulty, testing and arduousness of living the faith in physical conditions:
rock and sun, sand and rain. The conjunction of holiness and
weather—working out the integration of worlds.*

In Tel Aviv, Eugene and Jan took the Reids to a Hungarian
restaurant they'd enjoyed four years earlier. They visited Cae-

sarea, and Eugene walked among Herod's impressive ruins, images that would resurface when he wrote *The Jesus Way* decades later. They visited Mount Carmel and Capernaum. They swam in the Sea of Galilee and walked the streets of Nazareth and stood atop Mount Tabor. Jerusalem and Bethlehem, Jericho and Beersheba. The Valley of Elah and the Mount of Olives and Masada—all the tastes and smells, the dust and the cool sea. On their return, they visited Athens and Rome, where they heard Pope John Paul II speak in St. Peter's Square.

Unfortunately, as soon as they arrived at the Baltimore airport, the rest dissipated. A session member picked them up and barely got past the greeting before informing them that trouble was brewing. "Eugene, you've got weeds in your garden, and they need to be pulled." In Eugene's absence, several session members had voiced criticisms: he wrote too many books (and the church didn't pay him to write books); he traveled too often; he planned to use the sabbatical as cover to leave the church.

Eugene was reeling. This personal criticism hurt and angered him. A journal entry gives a fly-on-the-wall perspective of his frustration and spiritual catharsis:

> *I was furious after Tuesday night's session meeting. . . . On Wednesday I got through my visits a little early and stopped at the church: from 5:30 to 6 o'clock I locked myself in the sanctuary and yelled/shouted/prayed for a half an hour. Got all the tensions out of my stomach. Got rid of the sense that I was just passive and now was shouting down the devil: used Psalms 24, 114, tongues, Yahweh Elohim, chant. Haven't done this for a long time, but it was wonderful, even though temporary.*

During this tumultuous season, he wrote the introduction for *Working the Angles*. No wonder those pages level some of the sharpest words Eugene ever wrote about the conflict between people's expectations and the work of a pastor.

> We can impersonate a pastor without being a pastor. . . . Being the kind of pastor that satisfies a congregation is one of the easiest jobs on the face of the earth—*if* we are satisfied with satisfying congregations. . . .
>
> It is very difficult to do one thing when most of the people around us are asking us to do something quite different.

Around this time, we find the first journal entry where Eugene worries that he may rely on alcohol more than he should. *Slept late this morning—8:50! Didn't feel like getting up. Head foggy. Do I drink too much at night? But I like that hour of reflective unwinding—but maybe there is a better way. I don't want to ruin my liver and brain both!*

Eugene, while a man of immense discipline, was not immune to weakness or the temptation that a bottle might offer as a coping mechanism. His grandfather and several uncles had succumbed to the bottle, and for years, Eugene wrestled with how to enjoy drink without overindulging. And in times like this, when stress was high and the need to loosen his clerical collar intense, bourbon seems to have moved from gift to burden.

Several weeks after his congregation's withering criticisms, Eugene's heart settled. He experienced fresh lightness and grace as the conflict faded. The "weeds in the garden" had turned out to be only a small (but disruptive) minority. After several frank discussions with the session, he was ready for his sabbatical. And it couldn't come fast enough—he was exhausted. *I keep reflecting on what is going on/not going on with me,* he journaled. *Why is every day so difficult? Why am I so tired! Is this something the*

Sabbatical will cure, or is there something else? How can every-thing seem to be working so well and I not feel better about it?

As his sabbatical neared, distractions abounded. He said no to multiple speaking engagements that would threaten to interrupt his sabbatical. In one week alone, he turned down a Lutheran pastors' conference in Wisconsin, a church retreat, and a World Vision staff retreat.

Then the offer of an exit from Christ Our King arrived. Louis-ville Presbyterian Theological Seminary approached him about joining their faculty as a professor of homiletics and worship. However, the seminary world offered no allure. His conviction solidified after he joined the editorial board for Princeton Semi-nary's *Theology Today* journal. The board included luminaries: Walter Brueggemann, George Lindbeck, Thomas Long, Susan Thistlethwaite, Richard Neuhaus, Cornel West, and Stanley Hau-erwas. Eugene considered Hauerwas "the best ethicist in the country" and was also astounded at how Hauerwas could work a particular expletive so colorfully and effortlessly and so many times into a single conversation. "I have never seen so many inven-tive variations on the word in all my days." One piece Eugene wrote for *Theology Today* titled "Annie Dillard: With Her Eyes Open" introduced Dillard to a wide Christian audience—and she once told a PhD student researching her that Eugene understood what she was up to as much as anyone did.

Though the conversations and personalities at Princeton were stimulating, he was always eager to get home. He was a *pastor,* not an academic. And at the moment he was an exhausted pastor, questioning how long he could keep at it, marking days off his calendar, dragging himself toward his sabbatical.

The second week of October 1985, Jan and Eugene loaded

their car and began their familiar trek west. But this time they wouldn't return for twelve months.

The year was glorious. They hiked and cross-country skied and spent long evenings by the fireside, books in hand. Months before, Eugene had read his first Wendell Berry novel, *The Memory of Old Jack*. Hooked, he bought every Berry title, hauled them to Montana, and devoured them, sitting on the deck in the morning light and by the fireside as the moon hung over the lake. A friend took Jan and Eugene flying over the mountain range, dipping in and out of valleys, giving them a view of their home from a hawk's vantage point. That Christmas, the entire family joined them. The bay was completely frozen. Everyone skated and then gathered around a massive bonfire on the ice under the stars. All was well.

For the first time, Eugene had the luxury of living the life of a writer, a rhythm of mornings writing in his study. On New Year's Eve 1985, before the ball lit up Times Square on the other side of the country, Eugene typed the final sentences for his tour de force on the essential elements of pastoral integrity. *Finished* Working the Angles *last evening. Looks pretty messy, but the* writing *is done. I hope it is a good book— and I hope it brings a few pastors back to obedience.* Jan worked her magic to clean up Eugene's self-confessed mess, typing the completed manuscript into the first form of what would become a modern classic.

In a groove, Eugene immediately began writing *Reversed Thunder*, unfolding the praying imagination by exploring Saint John's apocalyptic vision. He found this work to be heavy slogging, the work that, other than *The Message*, took him the longest to write. *Revelation is agonizingly difficult—midway through ch. 10—Judgment. Can't seem to keep my pastoral focus. The concentration seems so shaky. I would leave this and go to something else—but feel if I once abandon it I will never get back. So I will sit here until I get it right.* He finished late March but awoke a week later with a pit in his stomach. He knew it was shoddy work—too many footnotes and quotes, dry, no heart. He needed to rewrite the whole thing.

So he did. Back to work, shredding sentences, crafting new pages from the debris. When he finished, he pulled out fresh paper and started a third volume in that same fertile year—*Answering God: The Psalms as Tools for Prayer.* The sabbatical was generative: words poured as though a deep well had finally broken open in the man.

But the year ended, and they left Montana for the return to Maryland. On the trip home, they camped in Yellowstone. *[We drove] through these gigantic mountain ranges festooned with blazes of yellow aspens and cottonwoods and willows.* The drive, grand visions at every turn, baptized them in beauty and grace. But with each mile east, they steeled themselves. As a final preparation before reentry, they spent several nights at the Nada Hermitage, a Carmelite community in Moffat, Colorado. *Jan and I have been talking a lot about our return to Christ Our King. We both know how difficult it is going to be—but feel we are ready—prepared to do the incredibly difficult work of living as Christians in the middle of a parish.* Jan wasn't so sure *she* was ready. Dread. Apprehension. "The sabbatical had been so great because I had my husband all to myself. I wasn't ready to step back into the chaos and having Eugene pulled in multiple directions."

Nada Hermitage provided the perfect atmosphere for their sabbatical's coda. Eugene felt entirely at home with the Carmelites: the rhythmic hours of prayer, the quiet and reflection, all surrounded by a stark and rugged landscape. After meeting with Sister Constance (Connie, as he and Jan called her) for years, he felt at home in this familiar environment. And he recognized anew the richness of Sister Constance's gifts. *When I am in conversation with her I am at my best—her presence/life are so true that I am true. I hope I have that effect on people—at least a few of them.*

Eugene hoped to exit his sabbatical and, as he put it, never hurry again. He returned rejuvenated to Christ Our King. "I felt like I could go another twenty-five years," he said. But the glow didn't last. Before too long, his emotions swung wildly. After hours meeting with parishioners, immersed in difficult stories, he prayed a desperate prayer: *God, I don't want to be a pastor anymore. I can't take this.* Then, only hours later, as he reflected on the people he loved and this true, alive work, his prayer made an about-face: *God, I'm so glad I'm a pastor.*

One of the revelations of the sabbatical year was Eugene's recognition of how often he held back the full weight of who he was. He often felt misunderstood and dreaded the rejection that might come if Christ Our King encountered the depths of his convictions or the full brunt of his sideways vision of the church.

There was truth to this. Not everyone loved Eugene. As an introvert and contemplative, some thought of him as a "cold fish." More than a few people heard Eugene preach and said, "His books are great, but in person, not so much." In the pulpit, Eugene was slow, methodical, talking about deep things. And with his raspy, whispery voice, you had to work hard to hear. If a man ever needed a mic, it was Eugene.

Whatever else you might say, though, Eugene was a pastor *with the people.* He sat with members for hours in his study or in their living room, in extended stretches of unhurried silence, looking at them with that huge smile that warms the bones. His journals are filled with names, particular people, particular stories, littered with his desires to be with more people, to use the phone more often and check on more parishioners.

After Jan and Eugene attended a Pete Seeger concert, Eugene was so mesmerized by Seeger's banjo that he bought a five-string Aria for twenty-five dollars at a pawnshop. The banjo became part of his pastoral tool kit as he carried it with him to visit elderly homebound members. During preschool chapels at Christ Our King, you could often find Pastor Pete down on the floor, picking a tune for the children. Leigh and Joe Phipps wanted a touch of Emmylou Harris at their wedding, so Eugene pulled out his banjo and strummed "Farther Along" as he and Jan sang.

Eugene believed in the uniqueness of each person in the parish, and he believed pastoring was slow, individualized work. One summer when he and Jan were traveling, Jack Craft, a young member of the company of pastors, agreed to fill the pulpit and house-sit. Jack was disappointed when he moved in and discovered that the Petersons had no television. In a Sunday sermon, Jack shared how he had to visit a friend on Thursday evenings so he didn't miss an episode of *Hill Street Blues*. Eugene later pulled Jack aside and gently chided him: "You're giving away my secrets." Rather than Eugene broadcasting a discipline for everyone else to follow (a move that would also have brandished his reputation as a spiritual ascetic), most folks in the church had no idea Eugene and Jan didn't own a television. Eugene preferred to help others discover God's unique invitation for their own life.

Living at the margins posed difficulties, and 1987 was gloomy. Though he had written several books and was being looked to by some as a leading voice on pastoral vision, he often woke with a sense of disappointment, feeling more effective in his books than in person. He felt he was doing a poor job leading the church. He was able to see only an accumulation of failures. And his preaching wasn't clicking well either. Eugene typically wrote his sermons, but sometimes feeling enlivened and free, he'd go for a stretch without notes. After one especially disjointed Sunday, Jan suggested he start writing his sermons again.

No wonder, then, that in August 1988, we hear the first inkling of Eugene considering retirement. *[The Flathead carries] a deep sense of sacred ground, a holy place of enormous energy, spiritual empowerment. I want to spend more and more time here—and to retire here. There is no place where I feel more at home than here.*

Eugene's most profound wrestling, however, was for his soul to be authentically surrendered to God, for his outward persona to be congruent with his interior. While speaking at a conference in North Carolina, a rousing sermon from a prominent speaker troubled him. *Slight uneasiness—is this preaching or religious drama? I guess what I am mostly interested in these days is holiness. I am on the watch for saints.* And then Eugene scribbled the line he would repeat many times over the coming years, a line he would voice only in the solitude of his journal: *I want to be a saint.*

Perhaps out of context, such a line would strike a grandiose chord. But scrawled in the forty-nine-cent black-and-white comp book Eugene used for his journal—the private thoughts of a man naming his deepest longings before his God—the words echo a holy haunting. And this desire was not for hyperspirituality. Rather, Eugene longed to be more and fully *human*, following in the way of Jesus. *Why not be a saint? Why this minimalist spirituality? Why stop with getting rescued from hell? Why not start exploring heaven? "Saint" doesn't mean* nice. *Polite in the presence of God. Not a stained glass voice and . . . angel wings. Not whispering in church. Censoring your vocabulary.*

As Eugene's notoriety grew (with his books gaining attention and speaking requests flooding his mailbox), these tensions tightened. His truest longing was to be holy, to be a saint—and yet this desire often stood at odds with the seductions of the public stage. He was impressed not by preachers who traveled the circuit drawing large crowds but rather by preachers who carried a fire, an integrity, a seriousness about their task. Preachers like Desmond Tutu, whom he heard speak at Hopkins. *Tutu was a preacher— passionate and simple. A moral life is very impressive when you see it in action.* And yet Eugene still wrestled with all the temptations. He journaled about his struggle with his ego, his awareness that his writing, though warmly received, was mostly discounted in light of bigger names, more dynamic voices. He desired to offer something substantial, to be a respected voice on matters of prayer and spirituality—and yet he feared these desires would destroy him. He feared he did not have the spiritual resources to step into greater prominence without surrendering what was most essential: humility, communion with God, holiness, his longing to be a saint.

Perhaps what he needed was Bel Air's obscurity, this out-of-the-way spot.

I reflect on this strange position I find myself in—well-known away from home, unknown at home. What does it mean to stay in Bel Air? Do I stay out of fear of entering a larger challenge and failing at it? Possibility. But I don't think that is true. Maybe I need to explore and examine exactly what this Bel Air "exile" means: the cultural deprivation, the absence of friends, the separation from mountains and wilderness, the constant fight/struggle for pastor/ writer identity (nobody asking me to do what I do best— and what at least a few people across the country affirm is my best). Does this add up to suffering? I feel that it does— but also that it is my calling, to carry this out, to find out

how to be a pastor and then just do it where I am, not look-
ing for a place or church that will appreciate my gifts, a
place where I can shine. Embrace the isness *of Christ Our*
King.

Make me a saint. I am so far from it—such a long journey.
I think I am on the right road. . . . That is what I want to be
as a pastor. "There is only one sadness, not to be a saint." . . .
Nothing else matters. And nothing else will make any dif-
ference. And now I regret all the posing I have done from
time to time to appear competent and worldly-wise—
competing. . . . But I was never able to keep up this postur-
ing for very long.

This exile imagery went deep. Living at the margins—even if it
was only something he felt internally—was a solitary path. *I miss*
companions. With my books and my wife and my congregation I
have my companions—and I must be content. Blessed. And I am
mostly. But why do I end up with these gaping wounds of loneli-
ness?

Of course, Eugene struggled with the same worries every pastor
has: Where are the people? Where's the money? During one season, he prayed for three hundred in worship and $4,500 in the of-
fering plate, but the numbers stayed low and the money short.
And he felt the sting of lackluster commitment.

And now I reflect back on yesterday—the bittersweetness
of each Sunday—the energy and sense of reality; and the
hurt of so many absences. Why isn't everyone there? Why

*isn't that sanctuary full on Sunday morning? If worship is
as good as people say it is, if I preach this well, if the community is flourishing—why aren't more people pulled in,
more people faithful? This is a deepening hurt and sorrow. I
feel the personal rejection, but also the God-rejection—it is
not me they are being so feckless with, but God. Do they
have any idea of what they are missing? What a poor trade
they are making?*

It's important to hear that Eugene prayed specific prayers for
actual people in the pews. This gives nuance to his conviction regarding the danger of church growth. In his later years, as Christ
Our King's size inched upward, Eugene's feelings about these
things strengthened.

*I'm about to be dogmatic on one detail in this: good, au-
thentic, pastoral work—the working out of vocational
holiness—cannot be done in a large congregation. It requires a small community. "Big" introduces dynamics and
perceptions that destroy intimacies. I am willing to concede
occasional exceptions—but only in exceptions—never as
models. We must repudiate the desirability of the large congregation and the so-called professional staff. 500 is top
number.*

Eugene's conviction solidified not because he was a stodgy
pastor who didn't understand modern ministry but rather because he believed pastoring could not be done en masse. Pastoring
was a personal, relational art. And Eugene, whatever his struggles
or weariness, loved being a pastor. He loved the people.

But he was not able to sustain the energy. Something was shift-
ing. March 1989 offered ominous lines: *I keep saying that I will
stay here as pastor until retirement—9 more years. And some-*

times I really believe that. But today I wonder—I don't know if I want to—or even if I can. The sheer, unrelenting effort seems at times like this—overwhelming. Eugene aimed for nine more years. He'd make it a little over two.

And disruption was imminent not only in the life of Christ Our King. Jan and Eugene's marriage was about to enter a swirling tempest as well.

14

The Long Obedience

It is something—it can be everything—to have found a fellow bird with whom you can sit among the rafters while the drinking and boasting and reciting and fighting go on below; a fellow bird whom you can look after and find bugs and seeds for; one who will patch your bruises and straighten your ruffled feathers and mourn over your hurts when you accidentally fly into something you can't handle.

—Wallace Stegner, *The Spectator Bird*

Jan and Eugene had become a true team at Christ Our King. A regular refrain I heard from the people there: "Church ministry isn't Eugene's ministry. It is Jan and Eugene's ministry." Eugene was the force, but Jan was the glue. People came alive when they encountered her hospitality and effervescent warmth. She wooed people's stories out of them. And Jan poked holes in Eugene's seriousness, loved to say outrageous things. Once when they were skiing with a pastoral friend, Jan pointed at Eugene. "Doesn't my husband have the cutest little hind end you've ever seen?" Eugene turned every shade of red.

With Jan's increased freedom after the kids left home, Eugene asked her to travel with him when she could. *Jan with me this time. What a difference. Feel so much more* whole. . . . *I am in the* way *of marriage and it is as much a part of my spirituality as celibacy is for the monk. I need to keep this at the fore and not go off on any speaking expeditions solo unless it is deliberately decided.* His journals in this period reveal his resonance with the monk's way, his desire to be a saint consumed with God, though for Eugene, this was intertwined with his life with Jan. Marriage provided a mystical spiritual encounter. Teresa of Ávila had her flaming visions; Eugene had Jan. *The spirituality of marriage is far more complex than its sexuality. Today I want to simply be attentive and obedient and* believing *in Jan—my icon spouse.* While Jan was away with Karen on an extended road trip, Eugene pondered further.

> *Marriage [is] a way of holiness. Holiness develops in a context of love—a love defined by covenant and faithfulness, a love that matures in family and hospitality. As I look back over the 3 decades, I think I have not so much been fulfilled in marriage as deepened, chastened, honed and simplified. Marriage has kept my attention on the "long obedience." There has certainly been plenty of sexual activity—but that erotic content is not what stands out as prominent: rather the returning to daily obedience, discovering obscure sanctities. . . . I want holiness—but nothing tame or domesticated. Jan has nurtured and prayed that in us, in me.*

For their thirtieth anniversary, Eugene whisked Jan away to Berkeley Springs, West Virginia, known as the "Country's First Spa." A bouquet of flowers awaited Jan in their room. And an intimate poem from Eugene:

> *We've been peacemaking now for three decades*
> *and having a lot of marriage fun,*

and though we've not yet set world records,
I've been lucky to live in the sun-

Shine of your lovemaking body and love-
making heart. Mornings and nights
past number the moon above
smiled beatitude on the sights

Of Jan and Eugene's thirty blessings,
each year a deeper drink of joy,
a longer look of love, of caressings
and kisses: Marriage is heaven's envoy.

Marriage—heaven's envoy. Marriage—the particular place (the "actual conditions," to borrow Eugene's phrase) where Eugene would discover God, be transformed by God. Marriage provided ground zero for Eugene's desire to be a saint.

But like all marriages, there was friction. Eugene withdrew—to books and silence. Jan wanted to debrief every encounter, verbally sift through every interior thought. Eugene wanted to retreat from the press of people, while Jan sometimes felt overshadowed, as though she didn't have her own voice. Once, when a pastor leaned past Eugene to continue an intense conversation with Jan, she was shocked. "That never happens," she said. "People ignore me all the time, but no one ever ignores Eugene." Eugene was serene with an almost metrical evenness, while Jan exhibited immense energy—joy and zest but also anxieties about relationships and quotidian details, about all the moving parts of their life. One marital spat landed amid a Baltimore heat wave.

Hot. Hot. Hot. A real sizzler. Didn't sleep very well. Jan
went downstairs—we had a minor quarrel—last evening—
she's irritated with my impatience over her fussiness about

the upcoming drive across the country. Thinks I should be more understanding of her anxieties and insecurities—and I think she shouldn't be so indulgent of them.

Sitting in the upstairs office, with Eugene in his rocker, I posed a question that led to something far starker and more ominous than general marital discord, a conversation that reopened an excruciatingly dark patch in their marriage. "Do you have any regrets about your life?" I asked.

He paused only a moment. "There were two women who fell in love with me . . . but I didn't handle that the way I wish I had." Further conversation with him and Jan, along with reading their journals, revealed how Eugene's complicated relationships with these two women created a deep crevice of pain. Jan felt compassion for the first woman. "She was a good person with a horrible husband. It's no surprise that she responded to a good man." However, when I mentioned the second woman, she took a breath and her eyes narrowed. "She was *trouble*. She was after Eugene."

Getting a handle on the layers of this second pastoral relationship is knotty, especially in our voyeuristic culture, where everything between women and men is immediately framed by questions of sexual intimacies. We have little space for relational layers and complexities, the many-angled dimensions related to being in proximity and relationship with another human. Either we run roughshod over propriety and boundaries or we become prudish and act as if emotions, and even attractions, are something to deny with puritanical terror. When this particular woman, vibrant and earnest, came to Eugene for spiritual direction, he responded to her with genuine delight. He found her warmth, vibrancy, and spiritual hunger a gift. Over an extended season, this woman met with Eugene, enjoying lunch around the kitchen table with him and Jan. Eugene admired her spiritual vitality, her unsullied faith, her passion and willingness to risk. In so much of his pastoral life, he felt as though he were slogging through mud alongside resistant people, and here was someone brimming with energy and hunger for God. *[In contrast to all the] spiritual indolence and sloth . . . [to now encounter someone who is] passionate—vulnerable to God, to love, ecstatic and radiant. . . . I catch this wild wind of beauty and grace coming off her and then get very discontent with the stagnant, fetid swamp waters of parish life.* And yet Eugene (fifty-seven at the time) wondered if, in his buoyant response to this woman, there was anything else at play, any red flags indicating he should proceed with extra caution. *[But] is this what is going on? Am I telling the truth about myself, to myself?*

It was a vital question. Later, Jan recognized how her own twin struggles (her "lack of grace and . . . negativism") contributed to the accumulating tension. She felt that Eugene, with his soaring ideals and his intense spiritual pursuits, could get ungrounded, and this cued her anxious response: "dragging my feet and digging my heels in so he didn't lose his tether in outer space with his enthusiasms." Jan longed for Eugene to enter her struggles with her. He was so good at entering others' pain, giving others immense space to be wherever they were without judgment—and Jan needed more of this grace and presence herself. So, in a season when Eugene was hungry for vibrant affirmation and partnership, Jan resisted. And in a season when Jan needed more of Eugene's tender presence, he was absent. They were missing each other.

One afternoon, Jan discovered on Eugene's desk a letter from this woman. All of Jan's bells rang five-alarm fire. The woman displayed a familiarity with Eugene—and she expressed her love for him. This initiated an intense crossroads.

Through distressing conversations with Jan, Eugene explained that his relationship with this woman was uniquely invigorating.

And in an immensely painful moment, he shared that there was even a sense in which he could say he loved her—though there had never been any physical impropriety. Eugene explained how he encountered a spiritual energy in their conversations that he believed was holy and not in any way sordid or crossing lines.

It's difficult to parse all the emotional layers to this relationship, and Eugene's journal reveals a reticence as he tried to process these complexities on those white lined pages. He did not shy away from the very human reality of feeling levels of attraction to another woman, but he sought to channel that energy in a holy direction, always adamant in his commitment to never betray his marriage. *I'm not a good journal keeper. I always think someone may read this and misunderstand, misinterpret—and so I am inhibited—self-censoring.*

Jan understood, to a degree, these ambiguities. She knew our emotions are never as tidy or siloed as we'd like to pretend. But she also reached a boiling point. "I am tired of spiritualizing," she journaled. "Eugene *has* siphoned marriage energy off. . . . I have to face that. I would hope he could also. I can no longer hide behind a spirituality of justifying that something is going on here that is beyond. . . . Why does Gene need to dangle the marriage relationship over the cliff?"

Resolution came, and realization with it. Eugene heard Jan's concerns and stopped meeting with the woman. Not long after, she sent Eugene a letter chiding him for his aloofness. The exchange, in which this woman expressed powerful emotions, alarmed him. He did not answer her letter.

This episode inflicted grief in Jan and Eugene's marriage for several years. In intimate conversations, the whole encounter would reemerge. Eugene would at times sift through interior terrain to understand what exactly had transpired, once tracing his story to a point of illumination: *[there is a] deep fear in my psyche*

that makes me vulnerable to such ventures onto thin ice. When
Jan and Eugene read Stegner's *Spectator Bird* aloud to each other,
they found parallels in Joe and Astrid's story, parallels that led to
fresh conversations that opened old wounds. *[Jan] is still capable
of feeling the terror, the outsider-ness, of those days. The possibility of rejection—of divorce.* Jan felt that Eugene had not cherished her. Even if he had not transgressed clear boundaries, he
had not pursued Jan and thought of her needs above the other
woman's. Jan wrote,

> We've always subordinated our marriage needs for others
> because our marriage is so solid and good. But . . . it's a
> wonder more pastors and their wives don't end up in the
> divorce courts. This is dangerous business. And if I had
> been working outside the home around men and had to deal
> with temptation when there were times that Gene was so
> preoccupied, who knows what might have occurred?

Fifteen years later, Eugene felt the pain with added acuteness—
saw the whole terrain as even more serious—than he had at the
time. *The perilous time that could have destroyed [our] marriage,
family, vocation . . . and the gracious rescue.*

In the years to follow, Jan wrote in numerous ways about how
rich her marriage was, how connected she felt to Eugene. "All
Gene wants to do is write and love me," she once wrote. And that
afternoon when I asked Eugene if he had any regrets about his life
and he led me into a story I was not prepared to hear, he leaned
back in his rocker, smiled, and sighed, as if he'd just tasted pure
satisfaction. "What I love most about my life now, since I'm done
with pastoring and writing, is that I can show Jan how she's the
most important person in the world to me. I haven't always done
that. But I am now."

Another woman brought both Eugene and Jan only joy. Other than Steve Trotter, who was mentored by Eugene and filled in for the sabbatical year, there'd been only a few part-time assistants and parish associates at Christ Our King. For several years, Eugene had prayed for an associate to lead the youth and deacon ministries. When Tracie Bullis (at that time, Cloninger) arrived, Eugene was ecstatic.

Immediately, Eugene and Jan welcomed Tracie into their family. She joined them on their Monday sabbatical walks. When they stopped for lunch, Eugene was thrilled to have someone else unwrapping a tuna and onion sandwich, someone else to rebuff Jan's upturned nose.

Tracie watched Eugene, observed how intimate and relational he was, how often he was in people's homes. He had a regular night when he'd make phone calls to parishioners. Anyone in need could always get an appointment with him within a week. After Eugene left Christ Our King, the question Tracie heard multiple times was "Who is going to marry our kids?" The congregation couldn't imagine these significant life events without Eugene's presence. He was the pastoral mentor you'd choose if you could. "He communicated well," Tracie recalled, "always honoring my ideas, genuinely listening to me when we brainstormed." He always signed his notes to her with "Partners in the Faith." "All this—and I was his kids' age." Tracie discovered that for years, Christ Our King had not paid Eugene the presbytery's minimum salary, but he had said nothing. For years, Jan scrimped and saved, made their clothes, grew vegetables. Eugene didn't think much about money, and he overturned Presbyterian sensibilities by refusing to lead a giving pledge. Even after Eugene's departure, Tracie and her family visited the Petersons for an annual summer vacation on the Flathead.

The whole Peterson family was growing, changing. Karen worked her art—her glasswork hangs in the Flathead house, and her eight-foot Celtic cross stands sentinel next to the driveway—and carved her quiet life out of the Montana wild. Leif threw himself into his writing and then published an upstart literary magazine, *Kinesis,* which he eventually sold.

After a summer climb of Reynolds Mountain with Leif in Glacier Park, Eugene reveled in the maturing depth of their relationship. Eric, aware his dad had tried at least twice to get accepted to Princeton Seminary, couldn't wait to call him with his news. "Dad, I just got my acceptance to Princeton," Eric said. "Let me read it to you: 'Dear Mr. Peterson, thirty years ago we refused admission to your father, much to our chagrin now. But we are hoping to make some penance for that by accepting you.'"

Eugene and his son broke into laughter.

Seminary was fruitful in many ways for the younger Peterson, and when Jan and Eugene got the happy news that Eric and his wife, Lynn, were expecting their first baby, Eugene spent weeks in the woodshop building a cradle for his first grandchild. He journaled, *The cradle is a physical reminder of our hopes and expectations.* Drew Peterson arrived with gusto, the first of a string of grandchildren to enjoy Eugene's handmade gift—and what it symbolized.

Eric, true to his lineage, loved the carpentry craft. And even through seminary, he always held on to the possibility that he might build houses when he was done with school. However, at Princeton, Eric found the clarity of his call to the parish and set his sights on ministry. Eugene was honored when the seminary asked him to deliver the commencement address for Eric's graduation. He felt the nerves far more a few months later when Eric returned home so he could finish his ordination through Christ

Our King and Eugene preached the ordination sermon. Eugene opened his Bible to Jeremiah, Eric's old biblical patron. When Eugene laid hands on his son, it marked a beginning for Eric. But for Eugene, an overwhelming sense of completion overcame him. He felt that something passed from father to son. Eugene held this revelation close to the vest, but later he would recognize it as the day he knew his time as a parish pastor was near its end.

Amid all that was changing in life and ministry, a tectonic shift began to appear in Eugene's journals.

> *My holy vocation of writing/pastoring. I dare now, with all the affirmation of the past year, to call myself a writer, as well as a pastor. Pastor-writer, writer-pastor. The holiness of words, the holiness of people—both at the same time, neither sacrificed for the other. Not many have attempted this, protecting the integrity of these two ways of holiness.*

He saw the call to the page as a spiritual discipline, one expression of his hope for a saintly life. But it wasn't quite idyllic. He found it increasingly difficult to find the time necessary to write, and the deprivation felt like a slow bleed.

> *I must write. Writing is my vocation now. Just stop whatever I am doing and write—anxiety is a call inwards—a sign that I have left myself. A warning signal, to stop my action and write myself into being. . . . My anchor to my soul and my God is in this pen.*

> *I feel that to keep my sanity—my spiritual sanity—I must simply walk away from the demands and duties and create.*

Work at my own stuff. I am willing enough to return after a few hours to the responsible and the routine—but if I cannot pray and run and read and write I cannot live.

Eugene hungered to hone his craft, to honor the holiness of words with work that was not only true but also beautiful. Reading Anne Tyler's Pulitzer Prize–winning *Breathing Lessons* stoked the burning in his bones. *I want to write a spirituality with the same literacy as she brings to fiction. Why is it so common that people think when they write about God and Bible and Spirit, they are somehow exempted from writing* well? At breakfast, as Jan read from the paper names of writing luminaries presenting at the American Booksellers Association, his question spilled out: *Can I write an evangelical American spirituality, that is as well-written as anything* they *are writing? That is what I hope. Too ambitious? Prideful?*

As Eugene's attachment to Christ Our King diminished, he noticed the growing ease at home. *Marriage with Jan is deepening in insight and tenderness—a freedom and delight that is quite overwhelming. I seem to have so much leisure with her. As my attention is withdrawn from the congregation, there is so much more for her. I realize how very much energy goes into the parish.*

In these later years, several churches, including Madison Avenue Presbyterian, where Eugene had sat under George Buttrick, contacted him about being a pastoral candidate, but he never considered their offers for long. He wasn't looking for a new pastoral charge. He wanted space, freedom. He wanted to write and teach. The pastoral duties that once signaled commitment for Eugene had begun to signal confinement.

With all this building beneath the surface, it took only a simple invitation to set large gears turning in the Peterson home. Pittsburgh Theological Seminary invited Eugene to join them as a writer in residence. The arrangement was appealing—the seminary would provide an apartment, and they could take any meals they wanted in the commissary with students. Eugene would teach one class, and the rest of the time, he could hole up and *write*. A dream. A call too.

On Sunday, April 7, 1991, Eugene announced his resignation. He and Jan felt jumpy the week before but were relieved when they encountered people's blessing as they processed the announcement, rather than waves of anxiety and hurt feelings. Those last months were a blur. So many meals, so many goodbyes.

Eugene told Jan he wished he could pull a Frodo, slipping on a ring of invisibility for a discreet exit. That playful conversation evolved into a local jeweler crafting them two sets of three thin interlocked rings. One silver ring represented their life at Christ Our King. Another silver ring represented their future work. The gold ring in the center represented their marriage. The symbolism multiplied: three decades at Christ Our King, three kids, the Trinity. Eugene and Jan called them their Frodo rings, and they never came off their fingers.

But the leaving—even with all the relief and anticipation—was *hard*. This had been his home, his patch of earth to tend. These had been his people. Powerful emotions overcame Eugene those final weeks. He fought tears as he stood before the church and spoke for the last time those words that lay brightly at the heart of everything he'd been and become as a pastor, as a man: *Let us worship*.

Though never doubting his decision, Eugene carried an aching sadness. A beautiful portion of his life was finished, like a well drained of water. He had been faithful with what he had been given in Bel Air, Maryland. But now the old familiar scent, the bright pull of the spirit, was leading him onward.

Eugene wrote his final *Amen!* letter, thanking the church for their last Sunday together. It paints the picture better than a photograph:

> You could not have done it better, said goodbye to us, blessed us with your gifts and prayers, more appropriately. Jan and I were, and continue to be, moved by your thoughtful and tasteful generosity. Just showing up was gift enough, filling the sanctuary to overflow, gathering with us in the presence of our Lord, listening to God's words, bringing offerings, singing and praying.
>
> We had a story that gave a biblical shape to our experience—Moses and the congregation of Israel taking leave of each other at the Plains of Moab. They had become a congregation at the base of Mt. Sinai, and now they were getting ready for their next venture in the shadow of Mt. Nebo. Mountains provide landmarks in our pilgrimage, inviting us to the Beyond. We lift up our eyes, but we work it all out in the Plains of Moab, the place where we listen to the word of God and each other, where we sing and pray our responses, where we bless one another name by name by name. At the Plains of Moab, we gather up all we have experienced and learned in the years of worshiping together, and get ready to move into the new land under the leadership of Joshua, whose name in Greek is Jesus.
>
> And then the Great Hall luncheon and farewells. Children and youth sang their songs, witnesses from each decade captured first one and then another aspect of our life together, you presented going-away gifts. Led by Jim, Rand and the Elders, you commissioned Jan and me to our new

work of writing, we served one another the Eucharist around the tables, and then sang "Sometimes a Light Surprises" together. With her narrative, Tracie stitched the diverse voices and perspectives into a colorful quilt. The actual quilt that you made for us will keep it fresh in our memories.

The embraces and tears, laughter and anecdotes all fuse together now into a blessing that pulsates memory and anticipation, looking back and looking ahead, making us feel so very deeply connected with you and confident that "he who began a good thing in us will complete it in the day of Jesus Christ."

As his final pastoral act, Eugene served the Eucharist at Christ Our King's intimate Wednesday communion service. He broke the bread and passed the wine to the people he had loved and served for three decades. *I guess I don't want to miss anything. Don't want to miss any of the meaning and fruition as things are completed here. "This happened that the scripture might be fulfilled . . ."—that my vocation might be fulfilled.*

On their last afternoon in Bel Air, Eugene walked the church grounds, pondering three decades.

[I] felt all the old difficulties of accommodating myself to these conditions—entering into the smallness, the sluggish ways and doing good pastorwork. How hard that was. . . . And how good it feels to leave all that complete and appreciated and go on to something so much easier, but no less demanding of spirit and mind and body.

With that, Eugene Peterson left his beloved parish and stepped forward with tears and a smile into the final great season of his life.

PART THREE

15

So Lucky

Dear God, I want to be a writer to your glory—I want to shape sentences and words out of my soul, not just my mind. . . . Fresh, alive, prayerful sentences. So The Message is true. I offer myself as [a] servant to this text—and accept the ascetic appropriate to it. Please, dear Lord, help me to be moderate and submissive to your yoke. And serve you and marriage/Jan in this way.
—Eugene Peterson, journaled prayer

Over the next two decades, Eugene's writing would thrust him onto a prominent national stage, but the words he put on the page grew out of Christ Our King soil. Every verse, every sentence and chapter would have been impossible without his parish ministry.

In the early eighties, Eugene grew alarmed at the anxiety that was overwhelming suburbia. With the economy gripped by a recession, (mostly white) people exited Baltimore in waves. Even more disturbing was the racism, which was often veiled as a desire for "security" but transformed to paranoia. In the aftermath of the 1980 Miami riots—with the unrest extending to other cities—many people, including parishioners of Christ Our King, bought .38 Specials, installed home security systems, and stocked canned food in bunkers. Worse, slurs and biases aimed at African Americans were rife.

Eugene knew his church was being absorbed by a fear-laden American story, not Scripture's story. Radical individualism undercut the Bible's foundational themes, and racism slashed at the heart of the Bible's basic teaching. But the pews at Christ Our King were filled with people who couldn't hear the Bible's clear word. Long vexed over America's racial sin, Eugene once told Jonathan Wilson-Hartgrove that he'd been drawn to march with Dr. King (particularly in Selma in 1965) but had kept sensing the Spirit telling him his job was to fight racism in the suburbs. And here he was, fifteen years later. This was his time. Eugene would fight back quietly: Eugene told his Sunday school class that they would spend the next few months in Galatians.

This book about freedom in Christ would be their antidote to the rampant individualism, fearmongering, and white superiority that had shadowed so much of the American mentality. For months, Eugene brewed coffee, pulled chairs around the fellowship hall table, and opened the text. But their conversation flatlined. Galatians was electric, but the class had all the inspiration of a wet marshmallow.

Struggling for any spark, Eugene decided he'd personally translate the Scripture text for each week, putting Greek into the language of Harford County, Maryland. Maybe that would get their attention. The first Sunday that he passed out his rendering, people leaned in. Discussion ignited. They were onto something.

Similarly, when people asked Eugene for help learning to pray (a primary task for a pastor, he insisted), Eugene guided them to the Psalms, the Bible's prayerful songbook. The Psalms were brutally honest—almost irreverent in their audacity—yet many heard the common versions of these prayers, often translated in highbrow Elizabethan or a cleaned-up American vernacular, as sanitized. Polite. Cautious. A tragic mistake. "In Hebrew, the Psalms are earthy and rough," Eugene insisted with real passion. "They are not genteel. They are not the prayers of nice people." He wanted to help people at Christ Our King *hear* these gritty prayers, *really* hear them, past the religious language, past the habit of old sentences. So, like Galatians, he started translating them himself to pass out on those Sundays in the fellowship hall.

In 1982, Eugene wrote *Traveling Light,* based on Galatians, placing the texts he'd written for his Sunday school class along-side each chapter. An editor from NavPress, Jon Stine, loved the translation so much that he cut out the Scripture portions and pasted them together in a single document he could carry with him. In 1990, Jon called Eugene, proposing he translate the entire New Testament. The conversation struck a match. *I can't quit thinking about it, doodling at it. . . . Did Matthew, ch. 1, yester-day morning when I should have been doing something else. I would love to do this—is God bringing another piece of my life into harvest?*

Eugene wrote to Bruce Nygren, editorial director at NavPress, sending him pages of translation.

> *I didn't expect to be sending this off to you this soon, but I couldn't quit doing it. Every spare minute I found myself digging into this, trying out different modes, voices. And while this is not finished copy, I think I have found my "voice" and so am giving a fair sample of what I am capa-ble [of] in this, this rendering into "koine American."*

Then in 1991, Eugene wrote an article for *Christianity Today* titled "Listen, Yahweh," unfolding the gut honesty of the Psalms. As a supplement to the piece, he included several of his psalm renderings. Readers were euphoric. Where could they find more?

When literary agent Rick Christian opened his issue of *Chris-tianity Today,* he didn't get past the psalms in the sidebar—never even read the article—before tracking down Eugene's number.

"The psalms are extraordinary," Rick effused, followed by a pitch for Eugene to do this with the entire Bible. Eugene listened, with Rick at times wondering if he was still on the call.

Finally, Eugene asked one question: "Who have you worked with?"

"I don't know who you read, but one of our novelists is Walter Wangerin."

"Yes, Walter and I are friends," Eugene answered.

"And another is novelist Virginia Stem Owens."

"Ginger and I have been friends for years."

"Oh," Rick said. "Another is the poet Luci Shaw."

"Yes, Luci and I are friends."

The line went silent.

Rick scrambled, explaining what an agent does, how the relationship works, and what the role adds to the publishing process. Rick assumed Eugene was still on the phone. "It felt like I was trying to sell him Amway," Rick recalled. "I thought this was going nowhere fast. I would say something, and he would respond with three words."

Eventually, Rick ran out of things to say and hung up.

Three days later, Eugene called. Walter and Ginger and Luci had all vouched for Rick. "Let me pull back the curtain," Eugene said. Eugene then explained he'd translated Galatians, a slice of the Gospels, and a chunk of Psalms. Eugene shoved everything he'd written through his Xerox and mailed a stack to Rick. "Rick, I know nothing about publishing. I don't have a marketing bone in my body. All I know is I want to undertake this, but I need someone who can oversee the business side of things if you'd be willing."

"I'd love to," Rick said, and he went to work, crafting a proposal for every major Christian publishing house. Then Rick waited for the phone to ring. Nothing. Not a peep. So he packed his suit and suitcase ("I felt like the Fuller Brush salesman") for the Christian Booksellers Association meeting in Orlando, where eleven thousand publishers and retailers convened. Rick met with Zondervan, at the time the eight-hundred-pound gorilla in Christian publishing. "I met with the entire brain trust," Rick said. "I felt like I was being cooked."

Zondervan asked who the audience for the translation would be. "Pastors are the driest tinder," Rick explained. "They'll listen to what Eugene says, but then they'll pass it along. I think it'll penetrate churches across denominations. Men, women, high schoolers, collegians, eventually the church wholesale. It's for everybody." The room went silent, a few half smiles. They explained to Rick how the market worked and the fierceness of the competition among Bible translations. They explained the naivete of expecting such a wide audience. "It's not realistic. You need to come up with a better answer."

Still, Zondervan left the door *slightly* ajar. They sent samples to their top retail accounts, high-volume bookstores. Because Eugene was unknown to the average churchgoer (unlike big names such as Chuck Swindoll or James Dobson), Rick was afraid people would discount the whole thing as stupid without ever actually reading. So he asked Zondervan to send blind samples. The results were worse than Rick or Zondervan could have anticipated. Not a single retailer thought the translation was any good. Worse, they feared it would kill their business. One response was apocalyptic: "If we sold this stuff, they'd burn down our bookstore."

The only real fish on the line was NavPress, who'd never published a Bible. Eugene inked the contract, and the Petersons packed for Pittsburgh, where they set up shop in a small seminary apartment while Eugene began to till the ground for one of his great legacies: *The Message.*

Joe worked for Allied Van Lines, and he helped Jan and Eugene during their last days in their home, packing boxes and loading the truck headed for Montana, where they'd keep most of their things, transporting only essentials back to Pittsburgh. Joe's eyes went wide at the stacks of books—Eugene's library made up a *full third* of the weight on the truck. As they worked, Joe shared about his family and his years on the road, hauling people's lives from one coast to the other. And he became the audience. As Eugene translated, he frequently had Joe the Mover on his mind, aiming for a translation he would want to read and would readily understand.

Translation is both a science and an art. It drew upon every part of Eugene—scholar, poet, pastor, wordsmith. Grammar was not enough. The text had to breathe, to move from one way of being into a fresh one, and faithfully. It was *relational*. The goal was a fresh spiritual encounter, similar to what early listeners and readers would have experienced.

Eugene's translation required interpretation (the basis of much later critique), but this was true of all translations—and more, this was the *point* of it. The freshness and sense of pastoral invitation were a direct result of that dynamic. Languages are not mathematical equations; they are complex and expansive modes of thinking and communicating. Eugene never presumed his method, or his purpose, exhibited the only (or best) way to translate. But this was the best way he knew to help the people he had in mind hear Jesus's voice blazing in the old texts. Eugene believed translation is a kind of "*lectio divina*—more than only getting the words right, there is spirit, the vibrancy of the text, the livingness of the message." The Bible was not a dead book. It was vibrantly alive.

But Eugene understood the minefield. He was aware of how in the 1940s English critics hammered J. B. Phillips for taking "liberties" with the biblical text, how in the 1950s, literalist fundamentalists skewered Kenneth Taylor for similar work. *Taylor got death threats. I hated to think what I'd get, knowing how mean the literalists could be in the name of Jesus.* Still, he dove into the daunting work.

> The task is not to get back to [the] original (careful and cautious) but to re-create in the present—take risks. The risks mean that you can fall flat on your face—but it's the only thing worth doing here.

> Am I doing good work? I keep feeling that at some critical point someone is going to say it's bad work—presumptuous. All the same, I have to do it for now—and know some of it is good. I fantasize (remotely) being classed with Phillips and Tyndale, Luther and Jerome. Hearty company!

Eugene kept at it, day after day. He finished the Beatitudes, and the editor loved what he read. (And so did Jan. Eugene began reading them to her while she was folding clothes. "Stop," she said. "I've got to sit down and really hear this.") There was only one problem. Rather than using *blessed,* Eugene inserted *lucky—* not a bad translation of the Greek word *makarios,* whose meaning carries "fortunate" as well as "blessed." Eugene kept thinking about folks at Christ Our King: "Pastor Pete, I got a clean cancer report. I feel so lucky." Or the elated dad: "I got really lucky. I landed the job." *Lucky* was their word to describe abundant, unearned goodness, grace. So *lucky* it was.

"You can't use *lucky,*" the editor explained. "There's a whole world of Texans out there who think *lucky* is the code name for Lucifer. And a whole other group who think *lucky* is an evil word denying God's providence. We'd lose a chunk of our audience." Eugene picked up the phone. "Rick, they're taking away my *lucky.* You got to get it back in there." Ultimately, Eugene surrendered, though he smuggled *lucky* in a few places elsewhere. Eventually he got his way with his volume of poetry based on the Beatitudes: *Holy Luck*.

Months passed. The work continued. *Finished Romans 8 yesterday,* he recorded at the end of March 1992.

> *This is going slower than I expected—and sometimes I know I'm doing excellent work, but sometimes it is pretty pedestrian. Jon Stine thinks I have my "voice" back. I finally have it figured out—they want a "Peterson-rendition"—the distinctive writing voice/style that I have developed. . . . Working myself into more freedom and spontaneity—hope I have internalized this text sufficiently to be trusted with this.*

On Easter Sunday of that year, it didn't feel like resurrection. Eugene felt buried.

> *Feeling very subdued this morning—the weight of the translation on me—feeling so inadequate. What I am writing is just not that good—what I come up against several times each day is that I am mediocre in this. I wonder what NavPress sees in this—and I hope they don't lose their shirts.*

In September, he limped across the finish line, completing the New Testament. Over the past year, he'd poured himself into the pages. Jan endured hundreds of hours typing revisions. However, rather than elation, Eugene mostly felt fatigue, paired with apprehension and resolve.

The translation continues to reinforce my feelings of inadequacy—and pushes me to prayer—trust—ego-less work. Willing to be vilified for this work? Yes—it's the work God gave me to do—not the Presbyterians, not NavPress, certainly not my ambition. Keep working in the "corner."

As Eugene honed his writing and plodded through the grueling translation that would become *The Message,* a community of writers formed a unique circle of kinship for Jan and Eugene.

In 1986, Richard Foster convened a cohort of luminaries: Madeleine L'Engle, Calvin Miller, Emilie and William Griffin, Luci Shaw, Walter Wangerin, Philip Yancey, Robert Siegel, Stephen Lawhead, Harold Fickett, and Karen Burton Mains. Among them they had *New York Times* bestsellers, Pushcart Prize nominations, National Humanities Medals, National Endowment for the Arts awards, and ALAN awards. "It was like inviting a bunch of anarchists to form a democracy," Foster recalled. But there was synergy, and the Chrysostom Society was born. Two years later, Eugene and Jan joined the circle.

The society eventually landed at Laity Lodge in the Texas Hill Country for their annual gathering. They would read their work, share meals, and commiserate about the publishing industry or current events. After Salman Rushdie's work incited assassination threats, Virginia Owens told the group, "I wish someone took my writing seriously enough to want to kill me." That comment stuck with Eugene. What writer doesn't want his work to carry gravity? Eugene typically said little at Chrysostom gatherings but listened intently, offering encouraging words to his friends. They would often tap Eugene to lead in worship or communion on Sundays. Always the pastor.

The Chrysostom Society, perhaps unlike any other community,

offered a place of belonging for Eugene. While he still felt distinctly other, he also forged profound bonds. He and Luci and Walter (who sometimes referred to Jan as his "sweet sister" and Eugene as his "elder brother") passed regular letters. During one gathering, his gratitude spilled into his journal: *Appreciating friends—relationships . . . the rich texture of love/friendships that grow and mature and bear fruit.*

After he finished the New Testament portion of *The Message,* Eugene and Jan looked over an open frontier—and felt the call to teach more strongly than ever. When the Presbyterian flagship Princeton Seminary offered him a job (surely bringing more chuckles when he thought about how they'd rejected his application as a student), he traveled to New Jersey for the interview. Eugene met with the president and several faculty members in the lounge of the Nassau Inn, "a bit of an old-boys club where influencers meet." Seated in red leather chairs, all those in attendance crossed their legs, and Eugene noticed he was the only one wearing short socks, the only one with his calves exposed. In that brief encounter, he realized he didn't fit in at Princeton. He didn't know the Ivy League code and couldn't be himself. He'd been considering an offer from Regent College and had felt drawn to Vancouver, and that moment in red leather chairs, pasty white calves bare in the cigar parlor, sealed the deal. Canada it was.

Regent had a stable of powerhouse theologians: the systematic theology of J. I. Packer, the biblical exegesis of Bruce Waltke and Gordon Fee (Eugene's old track mate), the spiritual theology of

James Houston, the creation theology of Loren Wilkinson (who became Eugene's closest friend at Regent), and a pioneer in marketplace theology, Paul Stevens. Eventually Regent made an offer, which Eugene accepted. As he considered the faculty's stellar reputations, he feared he would be found out as an intellectual neophyte, that he would disappoint his colleagues and that his scholarship would not prove up to their level. Jeffrey Wilson, a younger pastor who spent years with Eugene as his spiritual director and became like a member of the family, counseled Eugene away from the move, fearing the prominence he was sure Eugene would gain. *[Jeffrey] is strongly against my going to Regent— thinks I am vulnerable to guru-itis.* What Eugene felt, however, was inferiority.

When Eugene arrived in Vancouver a week before Christmas, his vigor renewed.

> *Our first morning, waking up in our own place—our Vancouver apartment. . . . Hard to believe that all the transitional moves have been negotiated and we are here at last, ready to begin this last (or next to last?) lap of the journey. I've been sitting here, drinking coffee and praying for the last 1 ½ hours, watching the dawn come and the mountains emerge into visibility. And thinking about our new life— our marriage and vocation.*

A fresh season, but the same old, deep longing:

> *All I want to do is become a saint—but secretly, so no one knows it—a saint without any trappings. . . . Every detail of routine and imagination, every letter I write, phone call made, gesture and encounter—gathered and placed on the altar and* bound—*every day another trek to Moriah.*

For the first time in their lives, Eugene and Jan needed to find a church. They visited a small parish close to their apartment (always his recommended way to find a church: whatever was in your neighborhood). *50 or 60 people at most, spare surroundings—simple. That's all I want in worship: a place and time to attend to God, and no pastor or priest getting in the way. Will we be able to find that?* What Eugene wanted from Regent was simple too: intensity of purpose and a community for relationships. Before stepping onto campus, he read every professor's books. And he strolled to his lectures thirty minutes early so he could walk through the atrium and talk to students.

Just as he had at Christ Our King, Eugene moved toward those at the margins. Regent was the unlikeliest place to find Cuba Odneal, a single mom who knew almost nothing about Regent but thought it would be a good place to get reintroduced to her childhood faith. "I was an odd person at Regent," Cuba remembered in a conversation with me. "I shouldn't have been there." Overwhelmed and considering withdrawing from school, she attended a luncheon for new students, "feeling very much the outsider." She was sitting alone with her bowl of soup when a bubbly woman, "quite chatty," sat beside her. Next, a balding, gray-haired man sat across the table. It was several minutes before Cuba realized they were together, introducing themselves as Jan and Eugene.

"Their quiet presence immediately set me at ease, and over the course of that meal, I decided to stay at Regent." Over lunch, Cuba asked Eugene what courses she should take, and after some prodding, he eventually named a few options. None of them were his courses. "But I didn't want to study any of those things. I wanted to study *him*." For the next two years, Cuba was in the classroom every time Eugene taught. "I supplemented his classes with others, but there wasn't a heck of a lot that was meaningful to me that I learned outside of Eugene's courses." Cuba found echoes of what so many of Eugene's students and parishioners remember: "Eugene saw that God-part of people. He saw that and defined me in that way—the other stuff didn't define me. That was astounding."

Gisela Kreglinger met with Eugene every other week at Regent for spiritual direction. "In our first meeting, he just sat with me for an hour as we both looked out the window. He knew I needed him to just sit with me. That was profound." Gisela grew up in Germany, living in a seventeenth-century grain storage house later converted into a family home. The house boasted a massive cellar with four additional levels. She suffered nightmares for years, running up and down the stairs trying to escape an evil presence.

Before she left Regent, the nightmare came again. The same house, the same terror. Only Eugene appeared in this dream. And the evil shadow that had long haunted her disappeared. "I could have been weighed down with the dark specters for my whole life, as the wounds were so deep and severe," Gisela recounted, "but Eugene's faithful presence and insistence to wait with me before God brought about deliverance that only comes when someone really moves into the neighborhood of one's soul and decides to stay, to love and care. Too many Christian ministers get impatient with slow learners and profoundly broken people like me. But Eugene didn't. He stayed around, confident that God would heal and restore and mend." And he did.

It was the simple faithfulness of who Eugene *was*, this way that the world shifted in his company. The rhythm, the silence, the holiness—all were transformative. "I learned just from his presence, solidly grounded in being there and in God," Cuba recalled, "grounded to an anchor, a polestar. He was *fastened* in God. You could go wherever you wanted in conversation, but it always came back there." Few people emphasize the biblical knowledge they gained from Eugene, though there was much of that. People speak of his presence.

David Taylor, a student of Eugene's who is now an Anglican priest and professor at Fuller Seminary, remembered the sound and the feel of that altered reality as Eugene rocked gently in his chair, gazing out the window. Sometimes David would wonder, *Does he remember I'm here? Is a timer going to go off? Should I say something?* It's not enough to simply describe the space as *silent*, however. "His *body* was quiet," David recalled, searching for the right words. "He moved slowly. He talked slowly. He responded slowly. Comfortable but not casual. Occasionally he would ask a personal question. A sweet, kindly demeanor." And Eugene would sometimes pull books off the shelves. "Try this one," he'd say, or "Have you considered this?" And there would always be prayer, a quiet, slow, personal prayer. And on rare moments, a word that seared the soul. "Eugene defined my future," David explained, "because he named me as no one had before. He saw who I was. He saw that I was both a pastor *and* an academic. He named me as no one ever had, and now I find myself living into that name."

Desperately wanting to meet Eugene, Pete Santucci made a fifteen-minute appointment during his office hours. Nervous, Pete jotted down three questions, to which Eugene gave concise replies. Then he just sat and smiled. "He was so fine with silence. He felt absolutely no responsibility to carry a conversation." In later meetings, if there was nothing to talk about, Eugene and Pete would enjoy the quiet. That first meeting, Eugene called Pete by the wrong name—Steve—the entire time, but Pete was hooked. He signed up for Eugene's Soulcraft class and was immediately struck by his humanity.

Pete actually found Eugene's teaching boring at first, "a plane circling a few times before it lands." He even considered dropping that first course, but he missed the deadline by two days. So he stuck around. More than a few students dropped Eugene's classes. One female student approached him after the second day of class, agitated. "Dr. Peterson, three times in that lecture you didn't say anything for thirty seconds—I timed you." Another student, after a week, complained, "I didn't sign up for a class on prayer. I wanted to study the Psalms." Students often told Eugene it was midsemester before they got what he was up to. "I had to become Eugene's TA before I understood what he was doing," Pete admitted. "Eugene wasn't interested in most things everyone else was talking about." He approached things sideways, teaching novels (*Middlemarch, The Power and the Glory, The Book of the Dun Cow, The Brothers Karamazov*) right alongside Scripture. Students started paying attention.

Jan flourished at Regent too. Once when she spoke in chapel, Eugene was aglow. Numerous students, like Toni Kim, sought out Jan. Toni and Jan met for three years, always over a hot pot of tea. And many of these friendships dug deep. In the years to come, waves of students would visit Jan and Eugene at Flathead Lake. Once, when Gisela and the Santuccis visited, Gisela talked the girls into skinny-dipping. "Well, we won't tell anybody we did this," Jan said. The next morning, however, she was on the phone with a prestigious theologian, telling him all about their bare plunge. It was good fun with good people—and in their older years, Eugene and Jan found themselves, strangely enough, in college again.

It was a special time, in part because their new home was a special place. "It was an entire ecosystem at Regent," Walter Kim explained. "There was something about the environment, ethos, and physical location, the *beauty*, that made it what it was. It all allowed Eugene to be heard the way he was." Eugene offered a unique pastoral voice within that spiritual and relational ecology. One student compared him to James Houston, the iconic theologian and principal at the college. "Houston was the exact opposite of Eugene," Walter remembered. "If you went into Houston's office, he would type you via the Enneagram and talk away rapid fire. With Eugene, however, if you walked into his office and sat down, he'd just smile and wait for you to talk." And some preferred Houston's way. Unlike most academics, Eugene was slow to offer opinions and frustrated students with his reticence to give advice. In all the years they met, Gisela said Eugene made only three concrete requests of her: (1) not to get email, (2) not to pursue a PhD, and (3) never to take a personality test.

Apparently, the third request revealed a particular grievance of Eugene's. Once, he asked another Regent student, Kristen Johnson, if she knew her Myers–Briggs type. "No," Kristen said.

"I knew I liked you," Eugene answered.

"He rarely gave us advice," David Taylor said, "and while he seemed constitutionally allergic to doling out practical counsel, he did pray for us. He prayed for us because he believed that that is what we needed most as seminary students: to pray and to be prayed for." Eugene prayed, and Eugene sang. At the beginning of each class for his Biblical Spirituality course, he passed out lyrics and had everyone sing the hymn "I Bind unto Myself Today," the text from Saint Patrick's Breastplate. The song has seven verses and a refrain. "It's truly one of the most complicated melodic pieces of music human beings will ever sing," David explained, chuckling at the memory. "It's a gorgeous text, but goodness . . ." The song was a train wreck, over and over again. But every class, Eugene had everyone stand, and David would groan. "It was so off-putting. So many words, so hard to sing, took so long." But after four or five weeks, David realized what Eugene was doing.

By having them sing this laborious hymn, he was not merely teaching them truths but was drawing them into a life of faith. "Eugene was helping us understand that we do theology by praying our theology—and by *singing* our theology. And he wanted to show us how certain practices of prayer demand something from us. This hymn demanded something from us. Certain things— like prayer and God—cannot be mastered in any quick, immediate way."

Julie Canlis had her own brush with Eugene's resistance to mastery and quick answers. Julie and Matt Canlis were Regent students who became dear friends, and Julie came to Eugene during a personally dark season. God seemed to have suddenly disappeared, and Julie couldn't find her way. Before, she had always maneuvered difficult situations by reading her Bible more. As questions mounted, she simply added more chapters, more study. But her reliable tactic failed her now. She signed up for her first office hour with Eugene. Surely the professor who had translated so much of the Bible could invigorate her Bible reading. But instead, after hearing her struggles, Eugene gently leaned over and took her Bible out of her hands, then placed it on the shelf. He looked over his stacks of books, as if he were working through rows in his garden. Eugene pulled down ten novels, including Dostoevsky, Kingsolver, and Eliot. "Come back and talk to me after you've read these," he said. Julie left, books in her arms and holding a new thread of hope.

Though Eugene felt his early days in the classroom were disastrous, students eventually flocked to his courses. He always invited the students to open the class by praying with him. "But then he'd wait an interminably long time before he actually said any words," David recalled. "It was likely only a minute or two of silence. But in the moment it felt like the silence would never end; it engulfed us, weighed down on us, discomfited us and was utterly ambivalent to our feelings. Our feelings never came into the picture." And then Eugene stood at the lectern, in boots and denim shirt, teaching with his raspy voice, often pausing for even more great gaps of silence. Awkward at first, this rhythmic silence eventually formed a liturgical cadence. Though two hundred students packed into the lecture hall, the room was stone silent before class began. Light streamed through the windows, the hall a cathedral for these holy hours. "There was a sense of gravity and richness to his teaching because you knew he really believed what he was saying," Walter Kim remembered. "Even if you never took a class with Eugene, there was still something of his presence and way and ethos that pervaded Regent."

"Eugene was never a needy professor," David said. "He was simply himself. He had things to say that of course he hoped we might hear, but he never indulged us, never sought to impress us, never kept himself aloof." Eugene was himself, offering his presence and pointing toward God.

Jan and Eugene loved life in Vancouver. Walking Stanley Park, with its grand forest. Wandering funky Granville Island. Dining in Queen Elizabeth Park. Strolling the Spanish Banks. Exploring the anthropological museum at the University of British Columbia. Taking the ferry from Tsawwassen to Sidney on Vancouver Island to stroll Butchart Gardens. Eugene especially enjoyed his solitary walks in the woods, his "afternoon vespers." And in the long, happy evenings, he pulled out his banjo.

One monumental adventure was Eugene's attempt to climb Mount Rainier with Leif and Eric. Unfortunately, Eugene overestimated his vigor, and the only real training he'd done was to take the stairs a bit more. Then the weather turned, never to be under-estimated in the wild Northwest.

As a furious storm ravaged the mountain, the three bivouacked while white rage pounded them for hours, ruining any attempt at the summit. "Dad wouldn't have made it even with clear skies," Eric said. "He was exhausted." Still, Eugene was elated, reveling in their harrowing effort and feeling a new kinship that perhaps only an aging father in the presence of his sons can know.

> *It was a wonderful hike. . . . Both of them were so good to me, took care of me—didn't mind my slowness. The cama-raderie on the mountain is simply incomparable. Even though we didn't make the summit (we couldn't have, given the weather conditions) every detail in retrospect seems perfect—weather, vistas, mountains, Rainier itself, banter, physical exertion, pushing ourselves to limits. And being there with my 2 sons! It was a rich experience—the scenery, the comradeship, the bivouac, the danger.*

But in keeping with the theme that ran throughout his life, he never was wholly at home at the university. A letter from 2001 reveals a dissonance of this time, an unsettledness that underlay the joys.

> *I hesitate to write this, because Regent was very good to me and I was surrounded by generous people and the interna-tional company was very stimulating and congenial. But I am so glad to be away from academia. There is too much noise and paper and hurry and information. The classroom has to be the most uncongenial, unpromising environment ever devised to shape minds and spirits, to cultivate wis-dom, to nurture love and relationship. It is just fine for in-*

formation and accreditations. But it sure does wipe out the imagination.

But students abounded at Regent. As did the writing. The academy didn't wipe out his imagination. During those years, Eugene wrote *Under the Unpredictable Plant* and the Praying With . . . series, among other titles.

But it was *The Message* that turned Eugene's world topsy-turvy. In April of his first semester, Rick Christian called with news that NavPress was "electric with excitement." They'd already sold thirty thousand copies of *The Message* New Testament. And it wasn't even typeset. Rather than elation, though, Eugene felt a gnawing dread. *All this makes me feel very nervous—scared. I want to retreat a little, pull back into obscurity and non-recognition.*

Then in July, a box arrived.

The Message *came on Saturday—finally! And as I hold it and read it I find I am pleased. Have a hard time seeing my name on it—it seems so much* more *than I am. I have never felt like I was doing anything special or important or significant—just doing my daily work. And now, lo and be-hold!, it is the talk of the town.*

In 1993, he mapped out his next decade of work. He aimed to complete the Old Testament, envisioning years of happily cloistered obscurity plodding through the Hebrew texts. That anonymity was a dream. Within months of *The Message* New Testament's release, Eugene became a national figure. In addition to crammed classrooms, six hundred people packed the auditorium for his public lectures. He received as many as fifty requests a week for speaking engagements. He declined requests in droves, but the sheer volume was suffocating. Eventually,

Eugene let his office voice mail fill up so that he could no longer receive new messages. In his journal, he revealed an increasing detachment, then alarm, in response to the notoriety. *The longer I'm here and the more I'm celebrated the more uncomfortable I am—I don't fit; I'm not a scholar; I feel that I'm going to be found out any minute. . . . I'm a pastor here, not a professor.* The more people sought after him, the more he feared for his soul. This insidious pedestal. The seduction of celebrity. *I fear a huge discrepancy between who I am and who people think I am—the prominence, the applause—there is a depersonalizing aspect to it.*

Thrust into this new reality, Eugene was unsettled. *I want—need!—an interior adequate to my exterior. Everyone thinks I'm so wonderful—but . . . I know so much more than I live.* Teaching his course on prayer, with over two hundred in class, evoked dismay. *Makes me very uncomfortable—what is going on in their heads anyway? Who do they think I am? Here I am, having the hardest time ever in my prayers, and all these people showing up to hear me teach on it.* Eugene loathed the notoriety. *I skimmed through the latest* Christianity Today—*and saw the celebrity appearances—I once wondered if I would ever get noticed. And now all I want to do is stay hidden, hide out in Montana obscurity, keep my name out of circulation.*

Amid all the public attention, behind the curtain, Eugene's health was struggling. In December 1995, his doctor diagnosed prostate cancer.

Eugene postponed the surgery until after Leif and Amy's February wedding, using the time to finish *Leap over a Wall.* He had a contract with NavPress, but when he submitted the manuscript, they asked him to rewrite it, to make it simpler. That didn't sit well. "No, this is the book I intended to write. You can publish it or not." They passed, and HarperOne snatched it up. *Leap over a Wall* was a smashing success, even making its way into the Oval Office when Gordon MacDonald, a spiritual adviser to President Clinton, gave a copy to the president and told Eugene he was reading it.

Immediately after the nuptials, Eugene went under the knife. The surgery removed the cancer, but concern grew when months past the expected recovery, his incontinence continued. *I have no plumbing capacity,* he wrote. And he missed intimacy with Jan. *I feel like a Eunuch.* Eugene was never whole again, acutely aware of his weakness and mortality. For years, he'd insisted that spirituality must be lived, integrated into the full human experience, into bodies. Now his conviction carried deeper meaning.

What does the Trinity mean in my life? How does it give shape and structure and content to me right now? If theology/dogma means anything, it must mean something now. . . . That's why saints are of so much interest and concern. If it doesn't have to do with my sphincter somehow or other—I'm not sure I'm interested.

In addition to the notoriety and health troubles, Eugene also struggled with an old nemesis, wondering afresh whether bourbon interfered with the intentional life he desired with God. Was whiskey working against his yearning to be a saint? He enjoyed, as the psalmist did, the blessing and cheer of his evening beverage, but did he *depend* on it too much? In 1992, taking cues from his old friend Barth's rigorous discipline, Eugene struggled with implementing serious boundaries.

*Through the night and waking—a distinct, gathering will
to cut out the bourbon at night. Not drinking, as such, but
those mind-dulling doubles that interfere with morning
prayers—and perhaps night prayers. I've had these thoughts/
feelings before and nothing came of them, but this feels
more like the Barth-decision, out of something deeper. Call
this the Beam-decision.*

Just before Eugene's arrival at Regent, he had renewed his resolve.

*And now I must test the necessity/validity of my tentative
Beam-decision. Alertness at night securing alertness in the
morning. Fish or cut bait then—do I really want to be a
saint? There is an element of withdrawal/retreat in the
bourbon—a pseudo-spirituality. And it may have served
an excellent purpose until now. But this translation, [work,
and] marriage intensity requires something more of me.
And I do want to do this well. These next ten years of
writing/loving/teaching. And there's this Beam-decision.
I'll tell Jan this morning in the car. Drive a nail into the
vow!*

A month later: disappointment. *My Beam-decision hasn't
amounted to much—still going along the same pattern. Is absti-
nence the only solution?*
Eugene referred to his struggle (at one point, he said the low-
grade struggle with alcohol lasted thirty years) as his "Ephraim's
bow," another example of how he saw his life *within* the Bible's
world. Like the Ephraimite men who ran from battle, rather than
employing their skill as archers, Eugene considered his dalliance
with bourbon the battleground where he must choose whether to

run or engage. Would he galvanize his desire for discipline, for asceticism, for deeper intensity and God-awareness—or would he yield to ease and comfort? Would he move further into his longing to be a saint? When one friend shared with Eugene his lifelong battle with alcoholism, Eugene recognized the danger: *I could end up that way too.* However, the real disquiet centered on the loss of his spiritual edge, his awareness that at times he was *blurry of spirit—not ascetically sharp or taut.*

Two journal entries reveal his conflict:

> *A gathering accumulating dictate for the unfocused, dithering sloth that I slip into via the evening bourbon. And every morning I feel the effects of an undisciplined spirit. And I've been doing this for a long time—decades! But surely it is time to stop: to enter these final years—10, 20?—as athletic in spirit as I ever was in body.*

> *I pray—but my prayers are not seeping out of my life comprehensively. I work each morning with resolve to abstinence. But it fades away by evening. And I use bourbon instead of prayer to commit myself to the keeping of the angels and the night's rest.*

Eugene was a man of remarkable discipline. His marathon training, his daily regimen, his hours poring over Scripture in the original languages, his memorization of vast tracts of the Psalter, the intricate care he took with words, the ways he exhibited immense self-control (over his writing, his diet, his schedule, his prayers)—all these venerable traits might tempt us to put him on precisely the sort of pedestal he loathed. Eugene lived with an intensity of desire for God and holiness—a consuming desire to be holy—but this desire always loomed in front of him, always beckoned him further.

Eugene also struggled with the evangelical subculture. Though the nomenclature was not Eugene's, most considered Christ Our King an evangelical church, and his affiliations and inclinations meant most people assumed him a member of the tribe (and his theological commitments certainly placed him within the older, broader evangelical stream). However, he'd always existed at the fringes, never cared to join any broad movement. Eugene certainly never felt sympathy with any of the clamoring energy, with the quest for political power, with culture wars, with any fusion of God and country. His parish—Christ Our King—had been local. And now he felt more comfortable at home in the pew at Eidsvold Lutheran in Montana than in a Regent faculty meeting.

Though there were numerous Regent faculty Eugene enjoyed and admired (and he found the president, Walter Wright, refreshing, with his *lack of pretense and no concern for image*), Regent exuded an institutional environment that didn't suit him. He thought some people took themselves too seriously and were too certain of *what God is doing.* Eugene sensed unhealthy irritants swirling around the dominant Christian subculture. *There are fleas in the evangelical ethos,* he wrote.

After one article landed in the flagship magazine for evangelicals, a periodical he wrote for often, he reflected on his misgivings.

My article on spirituality has just appeared in Christianity Today. . . . *It reads well, I think. But I am uneasy with [the] term "evangelical" as it is being used so much. Doesn't it foster sectarianism? Pride? Immaturity? Why do we need an adjective—at least one so prominently used? . . . I find that I am a little irritated at the compulsive self-identification that goes on . . . under that label. I don't mind the positive meanings that are represented, but rather the implicit (maybe explicit) criticism of others who don't share the label. Too much wall-building takes place in an over-use of the term.*

Over a year later, he wrote with more clarity.

I am not a truly card-carrying evangelical—there is a sense in which I am most comfortable as an "outsider evangelical" within the halls of tradition. Regent is too comfortable for me—and there is no sense of larger context: the reality of church complexity. Evangelicalism is too combative and clear-cut for me.

Once, when a pastor asked him what he would say to evangelical pastors, Eugene's discomfort surfaced:

I think the primary thing that I want them to hear is that they simply must quit taking themselves so seriously. Not taking the Lord seriously, and not taking their vocations seriously, but themselves. Evangelical pastors take themselves seriously, but they don't by and large take theology seriously, they don't take the Bible seriously, they don't take congregations seriously: theology is a means to an end, the Bible is a tool for teaching/preaching, congregation is a raw material for programs and causes. But all of that destroys growth in the Spirit, growing up in Christ. We keep trying to do the work of the Trinity ourselves. And we are not the Trinity. I would want to tell pastors to quit being so busy and learn quiet, to quit talking so much and learn silence, to quit treating the congregation as customers and treat them with dignity as souls-in-formation. The primary thing that we are dealing with as pastors is the Word of God. And the primary stance we must learn both as pastors and congregations is to listen. *There can be no language that works at all if someone is not listening. And since God is the primary voice in this gospel world, we pastors have to lead the way in listening, doing it ourselves and encouraging others to do it.*

By and large evangelical pastors are not deficient in energy or motivation or knowledge. But they are not conspicuously attentive, reverently listening to the voice/word of God and in being totally and personally present with the people we meet and serve. "Holy" requires reverence, the "fear of the Lord" is the biblical phrase. A holy Bible *requires reverent listening; and a* holy *church/congregation requires a reverent being present.*

At Regent, Eugene did not settle into the ease of sunset years. He encountered the holy voice anew, the ancient voice speaking very old words into his soul, as if he were a young Montana boy again, awakening to fresh wonder. His life narrowed in years even as it deepened in intensity. *Ready to make a fresh saint start. There is a growing realization that I am starting over in this gospel business—learning how to be a Christian as a dying person.* The vistas thinned and the vigor dimmed; but the holy fire burned hot.

16

Monastery in Montana

We shall not cease from exploration
And the end of all our exploring
Will be to arrive where we started
And know the place for the first time.
—T. S. Eliot, "Little Gidding"

As Eugene's five-year commitment at Regent neared its end, he planned his departure. He felt immensely grateful for the relationships, the congeniality, the opportunity to work with so many keen thinkers. However, he feared a growing tension in his soul. Dangers had arrived via his notoriety and the constant attention on him.

So, another chapter was closing. The years narrowed. This final step would be a homecoming that surely seemed inevitable from the beginning of his story. He felt that he required solitude in order to ward off the poison of recognition. The isolation of Montana would be the cure.

It wasn't a clean-cut inner transition, though. After his departure, it surprised him how much he missed the deference he'd had at Regent. Hardly anyone in Kalispell knew of his accomplishments—and no one cared. It alarmed him how much he craved the attention he no longer had. By his own accounting

later, it would take him three years to be "at ease again in anonymity." The Regent years had been a danger zone.

In one of his last courses, Eugene recounted, with his raspy
voice, the sad contours of David's final years, how this man with
such desire and fervor, such promise and intention, squandered
the last part of his life. Eugene paused often. "He would just be
very quiet," Cuba remembered. And then, after one long stillness,
Eugene offered a single line: "We don't always finish so well."

Eugene longed to finish well, to live a faithful life. To be consumed, to the end, by God's fiery love. To become a saint. And to
finish the final miles, he would need to return to his quiet home.
Eugene needed Montana.

His main project was completing the Old Testament for *The Message,* an undertaking that had required him to hole away every
spare minute during his teaching schedule and for great tracts of
every summer. A decade of translation, a laborious slog he feared
he'd never finish. Ezekiel proved especially tedious since he felt
Ezekiel had no sense of humor. He broke out in goose bumps,
however, working in Exodus. "Those old writers, to say nothing
of the Holy Spirit, sure knew how to write a good story." Working with a large cadre of Hebrew scholars and exegetical special-
ists was often a joy (like Prescott Williams, his old Johns Hopkins
classmate, and Luci Shaw, who edited the Psalms). Other times,
though, editorial comments had him pounding his head on the
desk, like the "schoolmarmish edits" of one editor with a "tin
ear."

More consuming, Eugene had to answer a constant barrage of
charges concerning the validity of his translation philosophy
from critics concerned that his work veered from literal render-

ings. He insisted that many of the critics misunderstood what he was doing.

> *So I went outside the Bible and got the three or four most respected translations of the Iliad and the Odyssey. What both surprised and encouraged me was that none of them are at all literal, and the best ones were praised by Greek scholars as "literary" not literal. That literal is almost always a bad translation—you can't get one language into another by being literal. Interpretation is always involved. The task is to get the tone and meaning of the original into something equivalent in English. That gave me courage and I went ahead. I couldn't believe that "inspired" meant that it couldn't be translated into . . . colloquial and vernacular American.*

Yet it wasn't that Eugene felt free to insert his fanciful speculations. *Translation is a kind of dogged obedience to the text; the less of me that gets into it the better.*

Then there were tussles with his publisher. Eugene had always fought verse numbers, insisting they were a modern nuisance that created a barrier to the reader's encountering the text as a whole, integrated story. Verse numbers weren't in the original text, and they imposed too much editorial force. However, resounding feedback from readers insisted it was too difficult for groups to read and study together without them. And contrary to Eugene's intentions, pastors were using *The Message* in pulpits, and it was impossible for congregations to follow along. Eugene protested as long as he could but eventually compromised, agreeing to have verses grouped in paragraphs, with numbers indicated quietly.

On June 5, 2001, Eugene scratched out the final sentence of Judges: "At that time there was no king in Israel. People did whatever they felt like doing." A despairing note from a mostly despairing book. He couldn't believe he'd saved a text with such violence, misery, and hopelessness for the end. He thought he'd never dig his way out. But he did, barely.

Now Eugene was in his peaceful Montana home, with *The Message* completed. Now he could write his books and spend time with Jan and family and dear friends in quiet. He had no idea he had boarded a runaway train.

After a massive first run with Christian booksellers, *The Message* went mainstream, flying off the shelves of every major bookstore. At Sam's Club alone, alongside tires and large-screen televisions and five-pound bags of peanuts, one thousand copies of *The Message* sold each week. By 2003, sales of *The Message* topped seven million copies. Cover stories splashed across magazines around the country. Eventually, Alex Trebek even referred to *The Message* in a *Jeopardy!* question. However, what truly tickled Eugene was the coverage in Kalispell's *Daily Inter Lake.* "I'd rather be featured there than the *New York Times,*" he said.

Letters overflowed the Petersons' PO Box. There was a fair share of kooks, like the woman who asked Eugene to translate *The Message* into a long-dead language based on the Coptic alphabet and insisted all Christians move to the North Pole, the location for Jesus's return. One man asked for details on the malignant fungus in Leviticus 14:44. But most readers from every walk of life, every denomination—and even lots of inmates—wrote with profound gratitude. Readers mailed Eugene art and music inspired by *The Message,* letters written in calligraphy, letters attached to intricate drawings.

Eugene especially appreciated letters from children, like this one:

Dear Mr. Peterson,

  Hello, my name is Brianna. I live in . . . Canada and I
am 9 years old. During family devotions we were reading
"The Message" from Samuel One about David and Goli-
ath. Me and my brother pointed out that you quoted Goli-
ath as around seven feet tall. After devotions I looked in
the New International Version of the Holy Bible and saw
they quoted him as over nine feet tall. Nothing to worry
about though. I just wanted to tell you. I like "The Message." It is much easier to understand. Have a good day.
Bye.

Most critics were not nearly so generous, however. *The Mes-*
sage roused fierce detractors. At the invitation of his friend Arthur
Boers, Eugene visited Tyndale Seminary to lecture. Outside the
seminary, the reception was harsh. As protestors gathered with
placards, chanting allegiance to the King James Version, Arthur's
wife, Lorna, walked out on the street carrying a plate of cookies.
"We are brothers and sisters; we are Christians. I'd like to pray for
you." As she began to pray, the rabble went quiet. But at her *amen,*
they recommenced their heckling and chants.

  A surprising number of letters accused Eugene of inserting
witchcraft or New Age spirituality into *The Message.* He offered
an exasperated reply: *I know nothing at all about "new age"—I*
mean nothing. I have never known . . . witches, etc.

  It stung, of course, for a man who longed for quiet and to be
at peace with all. But the condemnation that most deeply af-
fected him was from Hank Hanegraaff, the Christian apologist,
author, and radio host known as the "Bible Answer Man."
Hanegraaff dismissed Eugene's work as untrustworthy and, in
Eugene's opinion, skewered him in blistering fashion. *I have*
been attacked by people I thought were on my side: I don't quite

know what to make of that—a little disorienting—to find that you are "the enemy" to people you thought were on your side.

One repeated criticism was that Eugene did not use the word *homosexual*. He walked through each case, giving textual reasons for his choices (such as the ambiguity of a rarely used—and hard to understand—Greek term, a myriad of interpretive concerns, and the cases where his translation was actually more explicit). However, he avoided the term even more for pastoral reasons:

> *Something has happened to the word "homosexual" in our time: the word has become polemicized; it has become a depersonalizing label, with consequent dehumanizing attitudes. "Homosexual" is taken out of the context of Paul's list (idolaters, adulterers, thieves, greedy, drunks, slanderers, swindlers) and treated no longer in terms of an immoral behavior but as an immoral identity which is then attacked as an enemy. The term has been used so frequently in mean, dehumanizing ways, that it is difficult to use it in the spirit of Paul and Jesus in our culture.*

There were numerous questions about grammatical issues. Sometimes readers had a point, and Eugene would say, "I goofed there. Thank you." He responded graciously to anyone who disagreed with him but wrote with goodwill. However, the firebrands who made loony or arrogant judgments annoyed him to no end.

After one such searing letter, Eugene had enough and offered no quarter.

> *I translated the text that is in* The Message *directly from the original Hebrew and Greek texts. I have taught both of these languages in evangelical Christian seminaries for years. . . . When people have addressed me as you have with*

questions and asking for clarification, I have always an-
swered them as best I could, and have never had a single
person respond to me whether thanking me or condemning
me. And so finally I quit. What I do now is suggest that my
critics learn Hebrew and Greek and we can discuss the word
or sentence in question. But I find it nearly useless to discuss
something totally out of context—if you are not willing to
deal with the language from which I was translating I don't
think we can do much. I have never had any takers. Three or
four years on each language should equip you to discuss my
translation. But I am 82 years old now and so will probably
be dead by the time you are ready.

Alongside insufferable critics, the business of publishing—the
marketing and the acclaim—disturbed him. He'd left Regent to
remove himself from center stage, but the spotlight had only
grown brighter. The whole thing was impersonal, dangerous.
After one gaudy interview with a Christian radio station in Dallas, he felt violated. "I felt cheap and dirty the rest of the day," he
said. "No more interviews like that."

While *The Message* may be how most came to know the name
Eugene Peterson, he never considered it truly his own work. He'd
been keenly aware of his limitations, how he always fell short of
the text. And yet in another sense, the translation was profoundly
personal, an encounter with God. *No one notices or remarks on*
what it is that I have done in the translation—read and listened to
the text with my heart, not just with my head—kept the stories in
my imagination alive and present all the time. And even as he finished, he felt that few people understood what he'd actually done,
the particularity. *Every word translated in* The Message, *arrived*
on the page in the context of rhythms and syntax and diction

learned on the roads of Harford County . . . with considerable composting in the humous of Montana.

The intentionality Jan and Eugene desired for their remaining years centered on their home on Flathead Lake. A trip to Iona Abbey in Scotland revealed the depths of this vision. After Eugene delivered lectures at Lichfield Cathedral, Regent friend Gisela joined the Petersons at Iona, and their immersion in this luminous space offered clarity. They wanted to bring this Celtic spirituality to their Flathead home, so they christened it Selah House. This would be their own version of a "monastery in Montana." They would ask Karen to craft the Celtic cross for their driveway entrance, and they scribbled a list of first guests to invite.

Another sacred pilgrimage held profound meaning for Eugene. On a trip to Israel with Western Theological Seminary (Holland, MI), guided by Ray Vander Laan (whom he absolutely loved), Eugene met Trygve Johnson—who became one of his fondest sons in faith. Ray introduced Trygve and Eugene to the Jewish ritual cleansing bath (*miqvah*), and Eugene was so taken by it that he began to wash himself every morning in the lake.

Eugene and Jan determined to carve out a quiet life of love and simplicity, writing and hospitality. They welcomed friends and weary sojourners into their two guest rooms on the second floor. Jan pulled people into the kitchen to knead bread or cut vegetables. Eugene welcomed friends into his study for conversation, watching the lake through the tall windows, keeping an eye out for ospreys. Pilgrims joined their rhythms of prayer, walks in the woods, meals, and laughter. The number of guests they welcomed was astounding. Combing through their calendar and journals, you'd think they were proprietors of an inn. They loved the people, but the number grew so that often they couldn't catch their breath between visits. One (fairly typical) year, they counted 152 guests. Even Jan, the consummate mother, a woman who lived and breathed to open her door and spread her table for friends, journaled about her exhaustion, the feeling that she couldn't keep up.

Even as they struggled to find equilibrium with their monastery in Montana, the land renewed them with infinite delights. They took guests on walks around their property, explaining the name of every tree and flower. For years, the Flathead Lutheran Bible Camp just down the road asked Jan and Eugene to guide their summer counselors on walks during orientation, providing an education of local flora. And they did.

They loved every living, growing thing. Once Eugene described the animals he'd sighted in a single day: *a grizzly in a meadow, a mountain goat with her kids, three marsh hawks, a hoary marmot, a Columbian ground squirrel, a mule deer, a couple of horse flies, five mosquitoes (newly arrived from Canada), and a stray dog.* Cross-country skiing on Blacktail Mountain, they watched for fowl and beasts. After one hike, Eugene noted how *the birds were in full voice: Western Tanager and solitary Vireo prominent among them.* Another afternoon, they crossed a pile of guts, twenty feet of fresh intestine strung across their path. Pungent bear scat scattered around a grassy area soaked in blood—but no carcass. *We figured a cougar had a field day. A gentle stroll through the apocalypse.*

Eugene experienced a lifetime coming full circle. *I love the smell of the woods in the rain—and the dancing light off the water. Old memories of this place going back 45 years reverberate in my head as I walk and remember and pray. I hope I can become all that I have experienced—all that childhood and adolescent* stuff—*and praying it into a mature holiness now.* They bought two kayaks and enjoyed brisk mornings paddling out to the edge of the bay through the fog, which rose like ghosts from the water. Eugene often stood at his kitchen window, hands in his pockets, staring out as the sun's light melted into the expanse of blue water stretching all the way to white-capped mountains. "I love the sensuality of this place," he said.

Eugene relished this quotidian life, a spirituality fully imbedded in the particulars of their place.

> *I get up at 5:50, go to the kitchen and prepare the morning coffee for Jan and me. I turn on the radio to the NPR station to orient myself to the world's idea of what is going on: I grind African grown coffee beans—either from Kenya or Zimbabwe. While they are brewing in a French press, I walk down to the lake shore and perform my morning* miqvah—*a purificatory prayer . . . in anticipation of following Jesus for the next 18 or so hours. The so-called news is fairly predictable: the death of some world leader or celebrity; war casualties; political scandal or infighting—conspicuously deficient in person, in beauty, in goodness, in truth. There is no sign of transcendence.*
>
> *The coffee is done in 6 minutes. I pour 2 mugs into an aluminum coffee flask and take it to Jan. I pour myself a mug and take it to a bench overlooking our mountain lake. I sip it, pray the Psalms, meditate the presence and word of God, pray . . .*

Eugene felt a growing urge, a deep necessity, for his focus and hospitality to be directed toward Jan. "The greatest gift of these final years," Eugene told me, "has been how I've been able to show

Jan, in ways I realize I failed to do before, that she is the most important thing in the world to me." Eugene called marriage his "school of holy love." *If I am ever to be a saint, it is a saint of the basics: love Jan, be faithful at my prayers, write well and abundantly, prepare to die.*

However, Jan and Eugene had always wrestled to calibrate their needs. Eugene's native language was silence, inhabiting a deep, interior world, a vast reality where his mind and soul brimmed with rich contemplation. Jan needed more words, more interaction, more feedback. "I just wish the boy would talk more," Jan would often say, patting Eugene on the knee.

Three journal entries, written around the time of the Vancouver years, reveal a lifetime navigating this tension:

> *Yesterday was a good Easter Sunday: worship, lunch, a walk to the Spanish Banks, lovemaking, dinner, conversation. The dinner conversation got a little bumpy—Jan wants "more"—more intimacy, more access to my inner life, more accommodation to her pace. I keep trying—I know I'm not good at this, and I want to be—want to be the best friend/ lover/husband possible to her. Sometimes I have this overwhelming need to withdraw—to incubate ideas and prayer and feelings—and then she, quite naturally, feels left out. Is there any way I can still be* myself *and provide the intimacy that she needs to be* herself?

> *The complexity of marriage: wanting the most extensive intimacy with Jan, wanting to serve her with my self—give myself to her; and at the same time wanting to nurture solitude and prayer and creative space. And I felt that yesterday keenly—the [intersection] of husband/father/ writer/prayer.*

Along with my Barth-decision and Beam-decision there is also my Jan decision—the decision, quite deliberate, to turn my erotic energies fully towards Jan, cherish and nurture her. . . . All those years of pastoral sacrifice—loving so self-lessly and deeply. But from now Jan gets all of it: and that feeds into the singlemindedness and concentration for these next years.

This marital tension never completely dissipated. In their final decade, they discussed seeing a marriage counselor. Eugene journaled about a difficult evening: *Somehow she doesn't trust me—I am still, as she says, Number One. I tried to stay with her in a long listening: 2 ½ hours it was. We seemed to come into a clearing about 11 p.m. Is this a turning point—or just one more of the same old thing?* But he kept growing. Though household chores were never Eugene's strength, at seventy-eight, he decided it was time for him to start doing the laundry. Once, after dinner, Jan prodded Eugene to dry and put away the dishes. "If you don't, you can't sleep with me tonight," she said, chuckling. She looked at me with a mischievous grin. "I know how to get him to do what I want. Sex is a very important part of our life."

Yet their love was sturdy. Since their first week of marriage, they practiced an evening ritual: an hour reading aloud. They'd as soon miss a meal as their evening routine. Eugene stoked the woodstove and Jan poured glasses of wine, and with the sun dipping behind the mountains, they read memoirs and novels. They even added an afternoon ritual (what they called cliff time) of sitting on the bench overlooking the water, talking about their lives, their hopes and sorrows.

For their forty-seventh anniversary in August 2005, they backpacked into the Jewel Basin, their final camping trip. At trail's end, they pitched their tent in an "Edenic valley" flanked by Picnic

Lakes "with a towering white-capped peak as the backdrop," talking and reading Leif's novel *Catherine Wheels* into the wee hours.

> *Spectacular beauty brimming with memories of hikes with our children over the years—wildlife sightings, prayers—our marriage and its much giving and forgiving. We sat on a log before we left yesterday and prayed our memories and gratitude in that sanctuary of sub-alpine fir spires—and the freshly risen sun haloed on Mt. Aeneas and Great Northern. . . .*
>
> *But we have never been so tired physically—our bodies stretched to the absolute limit. Carried 30 pounds, each of us, in our packs. Staggered along the final mile both coming in and going out. . . .*
>
> *A great sense of accomplishment and fulfillment. We wonder how many years we have left. . . .*
>
> *Our last wilderness back pack!*

Jan and Eugene cherished intimacy in their marriage and also with their family. Their journals talk often of boisterous family feasts, having the grandkids over, attending soccer matches and plays and school programs, watching grandkids while parents snuck away for the weekend. This quiet cove, where Eugene baptized his grandson Hans, tethered lives across generations. They loved the family's rich starlit conversations around the firepit, rowdy play in the water, picking huckleberries, hiking in Glacier Park, and climbing those peaks that stood like sentinels over their lives for so many years.

Family holidays at the lake were festivals of joy. Once, with everyone gathered for dinner, Eugene interrupted the banter.

("Everyone stopped and listened if Pop Pop said anything," his grandson explained.) He turned to Drew. "Your father has become a better pastor than I ever was. And you've become a better banjo player than I ever was. I want you to have my banjo." Eugene pulled out his case, with his old Aria tucked into the velvet, and handed it to Drew. In college, Drew played the banjo in a band. They performed a backyard concert on graduation weekend, their swan song gig. Eugene sat quietly in a lawn chair, enjoying the music. "Easiest guy to miss," Drew recalled, "even though he was the best-known person in the place." Eugene's journal revealed the gravity of the exchange. *I don't want to be over-dramatic about this, but I feel like I am getting ready to die—preparing for a good death. A sign: I gave my banjo to Drew a few days ago.*

One weekend when Jan and Eugene kept Leif and Amy's three kids (Hans, Anna, and Mary), they went to lunch after church. Two other older couples from Eidsvold Lutheran walked over to the Petersons' table, gushing. "Oh, you children! You were so good in church today. You were so well-behaved." They oohed and aahed, went on and on. As these effusive folks exited, Hans, ten, said, "Grandma and Grandpa, we're not nearly as good as they think we are."

For years, Eugene regaled the grandkids with stories of Skogen and other trolls who'd traveled with his family from Norway and still resided in the woods around the house. He walked Drew, Lindsay, and Sadie through the woods, concocting new tales, one of which made its way into his illustrated children's book *The Christmas Troll.*

One December, Jan and Eugene sat by their youngest granddaughter, Mary, age ten, at a theater performance of *The Sound of Music.* At intermission, Mary asked, "Grandpa, what do you want for Christmas?"

"Silence," Eugene answered.

On December 22, Leif arrived with an armload of presents,

including a large hatbox addressed to Eugene. Inside rested a single piece of 8½ x 11 inch paper covered in yellow scribbles. In black crayon, it read, "Silence is golden . . . or maybe yellow. Merry Christmas, Grandpa."

"My favorite Christmas present that year," Eugene said.

Eugene relished projects with his boys. Whenever Leif killed a deer, Eugene sharpened the knife and showed his son the butcher's trade. After helping Eric build a fence, Eugene was profuse. *What joy in working together like that—the physical work rhythms, the smell of cedar, the heft of the hammer, the simple craft of getting the boards in plumb, in line. Our camaraderie of work—and the intimacy that derives from it.* When Leif and Eric decided to build a horseshoe pit at the lake, they laid the timbers, "making a work of art out of it." Eugene watched them wielding the chain saw, sledges, and spikes. When they needed to pour the sixty-pound bags of sand, he tried to lift one—and it wouldn't budge. "I grew up throwing 150-pound quarters of beef on my dad's butcher blocks, and now I can't manage sixty pounds of sand." He didn't *feel* like an old man. It shocked him to discover that he was.

But even as an old man, there was still time for him to learn more about what it meant to be a father. When Eric and Lynn's marriage dissolved, Eric poured out his grief to his dad. The intimacy pricked something deep in Eugene. *Eric kept calling me dad, dad . . . And I think I was able to be his father in ways I never was—or never knew how to do. My son, My son . . .*

Jan and Eugene extended themselves to so many, not only family, during these years. Alongside the costly hospitality to the throngs of people who visited the "monastery in Montana," they also gave away vast sums of money. They bequeathed significant amounts to colleges, seminaries, and churches and gave lavish gifts to those in need. For years, they received letters from people who'd heard of their generosity and needed help with their terminal illness or financial catastrophe. They paid for college and graduate studies for numerous students. They provided funds for pastors to have sabbaticals. They gave to a number of nonprofits tackling environmental issues, including one of their favorite organizations, A Rocha. During one of my visits, the *Daily Inter Lake* told the story of a young girl in desperate need of a life-saving medical procedure. The girl's mom had no way of securing the thousands needed. The next morning, I heard Jan on the phone with the reporter, tracking down the mom's contact information to get a check to her to pay her daughter's medical bills.

Despite their desire to pursue a simple, cloistered life tucked away in their remote corner with family and guests, they could not shut out the noise. Requests for speaking (well over three hundred a year), writing, interviews, and endorsements overwhelmed them, like surf pounding relentlessly against a tired shore.

In late 2001, as the nation reeled from 9/11, Eugene traveled to Washington, DC, to speak to the C. S. Lewis Institute, hosted by his friend Craig Barnes. That gathering, filled with thoughtful pastors attuned to God, felt hopeful, purposeful. The following day, he met with thirty staffers at the White House for a weekly Bible study over lunch in the elegant Navy Mess, tucked next to the Situation Room in the basement of the West Wing. Surrounded by mahogany paneling and oil paintings of historic naval vessels, with fresh flowers and white linens adorning the tables, the setting bedazzled.

But the conversation, with its "messianic airs," disturbed him.

They are convinced that Pres Bush is "God's Man" for the hour, which he might well be, but that conviction carries with it no discernment at all, none. Meanwhile, Bush continues to increase his rhetoric of "evil" and now is . . . making speeches all over the country that betray a complete naivete regarding sin and evil (he needs a theologian on his staff!).

One of the staffers, just returned from a meeting in which Secretary of Defense Rumsfeld huddled with a handful of prominent pastors, quipped, "Rumsfeld and Peterson sure have different ideas of what pastors are supposed to be doing these days."

Given Eugene's aversion to the big stage, what friendship would be less likely than Eugene and Bono? After *The Message* New Testament and Wisdom Books released, Bono grabbed a copy. He later wrote,

In the dressing room before a show, we would read [the Psalms] as a band, then walk out into arenas and stadiums, the words igniting us, inspiring us. Some nights I would half remember and invoke the psalmists' words directly over the plangent opening fanfare of "Where the Streets Have No Name"—a song which is an invocation itself. No matter how good or bad a U2 show gets, this is one of those moments when . . . the divine presence in the house is more, not less, likely.

In a November 2001 People of the Year interview, *Rolling Stone* asked Bono what books he was reading. "A translation of Scriptures—the New Testament and the Books of Wisdom," he said, "that this guy Eugene Peterson has undertaken. It has been a great strength to me. He's a poet and a scholar, and he's brought the text back to the tone in which the books were written."

When a friend asked Eugene if he knew Bono had given him a glowing endorsement, Eugene responded, "Who's Bono?" Soon, clippings poured in from around the globe. "I can't believe the number of friends and acquaintances I have who read *Rolling Stone*," Eugene jested. "I thought all they read was the Bible." When he saw the magazine cover, with a provocative Britney Spears rising out of the water, he could only chuckle. *In the interview with Bono he uses the F word in almost every sentence, his favorite adjective. I don't quite know what to think, that I come to the notice of the rock world in company with bosomy Brittany [sic] and effing Bono.*

Jack Heaslip, an Anglican clergyman who'd taught the U2 boys in day school and then became the band's chaplain, contacted Eugene to see if he would travel to Chicago for a visit with Bono. Later, in an interview with Dean Nelson for Point Loma Nazarene University's Writer's Symposium by the Sea, Eugene explained, "I was finishing up the Old Testament at the time, and I really couldn't do it." Dean responded, incredulous, "You may be the only person alive who would turn down the opportunity [to meet Bono] just to make a deadline. I mean, come on."

The crowd broke into laughter before Dean offered an addendum. "It's Bono, for crying out loud."

Eugene paused only for a moment. "Dean, it was *Isaiah*." The crowd roared.

As the full *Message* released, Bono sent a personal video. Though Eugene was still oblivious, his grandkids went bonkers. The grainy video, shot in a spartan living room, showed a young Bono in a lime-green chair offering simple words: "Mr. Peterson, Eugene, my name is Bono. I'm the singer with the group U2 and wanted to video message you my thanks—and our thanks in the band—for this remarkable work you've done. There've been some great translations, some very literary translations, but no translations that I've read that speak to me in my own language. So, I want to thank you for that." The final words can be heard properly only in Bono's warm, tender Irish brogue: "Take a rest now, won'tcha? Bye."

In 2006, Peb Jackson, a consultant working with developing leaders, was in Davos, Switzerland, for the World Economic Forum. He'd met Bono through shared interests in the developing world, and they spotted each other in a hotel bar and chatted for an hour and a half, mostly about Eugene and *The Message.* Peb remembered Bono telling him that one person he wanted to meet was Eugene. Bono didn't know that Eugene had written anything other than *The Message,* and Peb recommended *Run with the Horses.* Several days later, Bono and Peb happened to be in DC at the same time, and Peb scoured the District, locating a single copy in the bookstore at St. Paul's Parish. He waited backstage to deliver the book to Bono. Later, Bono was effusive. "This is one of the most important books for me. I've been passing out copies."

In 2009, Bono's staff reached out to Peb Jackson and Rick Christian again, attempting to arrange a meeting. Eugene agreed, but after Peb showed Eugene a recording of a U2 concert at Slane Castle in Dublin, he regretted the decision. *100,000 people jumping and leaping for 4 hours—and Bono leading the ecstasy,* Eugene journaled.

> *I can't imagine enduring that—but it looks like I'm stuck. Why would Peb (and Rick) think I would want to do this. This celebrity culture leaves me cold—and even repulsed. . . . I'm a month away from my 77th birthday— why do I have to put up with this? . . . [This whole thing is] far too celebrity-impressed for me. And the only reason I'm here is because they think I am a celebrity.*

Bono sent airline tickets for the Jacksons and Christians to bring Eugene and Jan to Dallas for a U2 concert at Cowboys Stadium. Limos picked them up, ushered them through stadium security, and delivered them to a VIP reception with food and drinks. As the concert start time neared, a woman approached their table, asking for Eugene Peterson and Peb Jackson.

As the two men and their wives followed the woman to the door, Rick called out: "Well, I'm his agent."

"I'm sorry," she answered. "We have limited time, but if we're able to arrange something, we'll send a cart for you." As they walked away, Rick turned to his wife, Debbie. "There's no cart coming."

Bono greeted Jan and Eugene, and then staff delivered them to their mezzanine seats, handed them earplugs, and pointed to a hospitality suite for when they needed relief. However, as the bass thumped and lights pulsed, Eugene sat on the edge of his seat, engrossed, until staff arrived again to lead them down to the stage. There Eugene stood, stage right, smiling and covering his ears. Bono leaned into the mic: "I want to thank Eugene Peterson and Peb Jackson." Then Bono read from *The Message*. The morning after, Eugene reflected on the riotous experience: *Immersed in a totally new culture—50,000+ fans, lights, elaborate staging and loud music, everyone singing the songs, knowing the words. I held Jan's hand, asking her to stay close—I felt so an outsider. But as it developed I felt ok—Bono a true prophet, giving an unobtrusive Christian witness.*

The Petersons had a hotel room in Dallas, but Bono asked them to fly with him to Houston, U2's next tour stop, so they could spend time together the following day. After the band hit the final chords of "Moment of Surrender," they rushed to a line of black limos, with Bono and the Petersons in the lead car. The motorcade, with police escort, hit the freeway, red and blue lights flashing. On U2's private jet, Bono chatted with Eugene and Jan, and after a night at the Four Seasons, they joined Bono in his suite. Jan loved him. "Oh, I've *kissed* Bono," Jan said in her best sultry voice. Eugene and Bono spent a chunk of the day alone, and when Eugene returned, Peb asked how it went. Eugene offered three words: "It was precious."

Over the years, Eugene said very little about his relationship with Bono. Even in his journal, he described events and thoughts from the morning at the Four Seasons, but when it came to his private conversation, only this: "Lunch w/ Bono," followed by an entire blank page. Once, when Pete Santucci visited, Eugene was packing a box to ship to Bono. Pete asked if he could drop in a note. "No," Eugene said, "this is a pastoral relationship."

Following Houston, Eugene and Bono corresponded regularly, sharing prayers and discerning their various projects—and yes, Bono's notes were sprinkled with his favorite adjective. They exchanged Christmas cards, and Bono's handwritten art and notes (and a vinyl of one of U2's albums) were strewn about the family room. Bono hoped Eugene might one day write a book for those who didn't consider themselves Christians, "something in the vein of C. S. Lewis for the modern ear." In 2015, Bono's limo pulled onto the Petersons' gravel driveway. Jan and Eugene waited for him on their porch, smiling like parents waiting for their son to come home. David Taylor, who'd received a post as professor at Fuller Seminary, arranged to film a conversation between Eugene and Bono, centered around their shared love of the Psalms. Jan welcomed David and Bono and the film crew with a plate of hot cookies. "Bono kissed Jan on the cheek as he greeted her," Eugene wrote to a friend. "She hasn't washed her face since."

A year later, David was having dinner with Bono in Dallas, and Bono told David his main reason for agreeing to tape the Psalms interview in Montana. "I wanted to confess my sins," Bono said. Bono had requested a private hour with Eugene and Jan before the taping. So, while the crew set up the mics and cameras and ate warm cookies, Jan, Bono, and Eugene sat on the back deck. "I just want you to know," Bono said to David, "that after I confessed my sins to Eugene and Jan, I felt so much better. That was a real gift to me." Though they'd continue to share letters, that afternoon, with the Montana sun shining on their faces and grace shining in their hearts, would be the last hours they would spend together.

A Weathered but Holy Shape

Lord Jesus: I thank you for a life well-lived. Pastoral vo-
cation well done. Books well-written. Marriage . . .
children . . . Regent . . .
  But right now I feel so flawed and inadequate.
  Heal my memories . . . restore me . . . create in me a
clean heart.
                    —Eugene Peterson, journaled prayer

Eugene's reimmersion in Montana's wildness and vast skies birthed a new rush of creativity. He'd long felt crowded and confined by competing responsibilities. *But mostly what I want to do is write. I'm a writer, damn it! Why do I have to fight my way to my desk? Why does everyone want me to do everything else but write—they all think writing is some minor hobby I indulge in at leisure.* He wanted simplicity: to cook a fine meal, play his banjo, serve Jan. And write.

At the desk these final years, crafting beauty out of sentences, Eugene's myriad passions and convictions became a vibrant mosaic. For Eugene, writing was a way of prayer. He had little time for what passed as spiritual writing (overrun with questionable spirituality and mediocre writing) in large swaths of the religious market.

[I am interested in] more what I would call heuristic [writing]—discovering what is going on with our Lord the Spirit and [the] soul, implicitly inviting others into a life of common prayer. . . . Writing that is almost, maybe completely, synonymous with prayer. Writing of this kind is only marginally evident in the Christian community. But there was a time when this was the only way Christians wrote. And look what a legacy those people have given us. Few of our contemporaries, of course, encourage this kind of writing. How could they? As long as a person lives at the informational/motivational level this kind of writing has no value, no interest. . . . [When I write], I am not self-consciously praying. But afterwards there is often a sense of what I can only call "givenness." That the words on the page are not something that came just out of me, but rather while in a kind of receptivity—the way you often say something in conversation with certain people that with other persons wouldn't occur to you.

This way of writing required humility and authenticity. It required the writer to *become the person whose writing is true*. Become *true so you can write true*. Writing *is an expression of living, not knowing: of praying, not knowing.*

For years, he'd dreamed of writing a spiritual theology series, the culmination of his life's work. He struggled with the term *spiritual theology* because he didn't like *spiritual* used as an adjective, as if spirituality were merely some additive to whatever else we're doing (*spiritual* music, *spiritual* books, *spiritual* vocations, and so on). Eugene insisted that to be spiritual is to be connected to what's real, to God: everything finds its essence in God; thus, everything is spiritual. He also disliked how *spiritual* was often spoken as if it denoted a haloed, extra-saintly devotion dismem-

bered from humans at play and work, from creativity, from food
and sex, from genuine life. Eugene decried any pseudospirituality
that had no traction in the butcher shop, among mechanics and
artisans, in the forests and rivers, in the maternity ward or cancer
centers. More, Eugene lamented how *spirituality* had become a
vacuous word, untethered from anything solid, a word we make
to mean whatever we want it to mean. *Spirituality,* Eugene averred,
was "Christ, the God-revealing Christ, who is behind and in all of
this living." Despite his misgivings, he decided to reimagine the
word rather than toss it. Eugene's short description was simple:
*Spiritual theology is what pastors do—give themselves to getting
what we know about God/Jesus lived in the round of ordinary
life.*

In 2000, Eugene mapped titles and descriptions for five books,
all shaped by courses he'd taught at Regent. He hoped to write a
definitive work on spiritual theology for this generation, pulled
from the marrow of his life. These five books would be his heart
and soul:

1. Christ Plays in 10,000 Places. *This is the basic book on
   biblical spiritual theology, which is foundational to all of
   the rest.*
2. Practice Resurrection. *This is the course on spiritual
   formation using the book of Ephesians as the ground-
   work.*
3. Follow the Leader [later renamed The Jesus Way]. *This I
   would describe as a course on spiritual politics using aspects of leadership as they come into being in contrasting
   Jesus with Herod, Caiaphas, and Josephus.*
4. Tell It Slant. *This is the course on spiritual direction,
   which is based on the parables.*
5. Eat This Book. *This is the course on using scripture as
   the formative text for spirituality.*

The project clear in his mind, he considered two publishers: HarperOne and Eerdmans. Mickey Maudlin, editor at Harper, sent a two-page letter, a full-court press. "Eugene was already a hero of mine," Mickey explained. He first encountered Eugene in 1983 when he was a proofreader at IVP. Mickey would read the manuscript out loud while another proofreader scoured the type-set of any mistakes. "That's how I was introduced to Eugene. Reading *Run with the Horses* aloud all day. I still think about Jeremiah all the time." However, Mickey soon realized these ne-gotiations were different. Eugene exhibited a dogged loyalty to Eerdmans, who'd published him when publishers would barely answer his calls (and who never took anything out of print). Even when Harper offered an advance dwarfing what Eerdmans could muster, Eugene stuck with the independent publishing house in Grand Rapids. "That never happens," Mickey said. "We don't lose contracts to small houses. But if Eugene didn't care about the money and didn't care that we could put so much more into pub-licity . . . if the criteria is loyalty, well, then I couldn't compete. That was such a Eugene move." And it was. Eugene generally looked at factors other than the dollar signs in the contract.

Mapping out roughly a book a year, Eugene got to work. As he put down the pen with each volume, he felt as if he'd given birth. After Eerdmans sent him a copy of *Christ Plays,* he immediately opened to the first chapter. Every few pages, he'd call out to Jan, "This is really good!" A few pages more: "I'm embarrassed to say this, but I can't stop reading it." And then again: "I can't believe I wrote this. I didn't even know I *knew* this." Finally, Jan answered from the kitchen: "Gene, shut up."

With the ink barely dry from his spiritual theology, Rick ap-proached Eugene about writing a memoir. Eugene rebuffed the idea, as he had for years. Rick prodded, though, and Eugene reluctantly warmed. When it came time to choose a publisher, he went with Viking because it was a New York house, and he wanted to reach beyond the standard Christian book market. In truth, though, he went with Viking just as much because of a two-hour lunch in SoHo with the editors. While competing publishers pulled out charts and used words like *market* and *demographics* and *platform,* the Viking editors felt like friends. "The book wasn't the agenda at lunch. We just got to know each other." Eugene signed the contract while still nursing reservations about whether he was capable of writing a quality memoir. His concerns proved legitimate. In early feedback, his editor said, "Give me more of you, Eugene—more of your inner thoughts, more description. Take the reader into your life. Less teaching. This is your one shot to tell people your life. Let it rip." Eugene slashed and chiseled. In February 2009, he sent off the manuscript. *I felt like I had a newborn baby,* he wrote to his editor. *Please take care of her. Don't drop her; keep her diapered and warm.* He signed the letter *Mother Eugene.*

Unfortunately, they did drop the baby. Viking judged the memoir lacking. The book wasn't the story they expected, and they canceled the contract.

This time, Mickey and HarperOne landed the book, getting the memoir back on track. Eugene's initial title choice was *Pastor Maybe* (a nod to Anne Tyler's *Saint Maybe*), but when *The Pastor* hit the shelves to wide acclaim, he was stunned. Whether due to age or the intensity of spending a year and a half rehearsing his personal history, after finishing his memoir, Eugene's tank was empty. Now, for the first time in eight decades, there was nothing looming in front of him: no agenda, no books. Only diminishing energy. With the few last drops of blood in his pen, two titles emerged: *Holy Luck,* a collection of poems he had written over seventy years, and *As Kingfishers Catch Fire,* a never-before-published collection of sermons. Rick Christian was instrumental in this endeavor. "Rick helped me do things I could never have done on my own," Eugene said.

This life Eugene had long described as "intently haphazard," one he knew to be riddled with imperfections, had taken on a weathered but holy shape. And now he could reflect on the whole.

> *I keep thinking about "my legacy." I am hesitant to make too much of it. But in all honesty I feel that I have accomplished something major—something almost unique in my generation:* while *the Christian witness has been diluted and fragmented,* while *the American character has been depersonalized and sliding into violence—ugly and vicious,* while *the church has lost its center in Christ, its foundation in scripture, its Trinitarian structure . . . I have been patiently, persistently, and almost unself-consciously working among the ruins, rebuilding the walls of Jerusalem. What I have done quietly, without making any great fuss about it, has, kind of behind the scenes, not making any headlines, slowly, unremarkably, become something like a major change in landscape— looming but unnoticed.*

In high school, Leif joked that his dad had only one sermon, something Eugene always heard as criticism. Years later, Leif found himself in Boulder, Colorado, working on his master's degree in creative writing. He joined a church there, and Eugene asked him about his experience. "I like the church," Leif answered, "but the pastor hasn't found his one sermon." A son's words passed a blessing over his dad's life: One sermon. Congruence.

Eugene never stopped preaching that one sermon, and he never stopped being a pastor. But now his congregation was his friends, with his letters serving as pastoral visits. Ever the pastor, Eugene determined to answer every letter he received. A painstaking task as he typed away like a hen pecking for corn. *At times I feel that I am making things more difficult by refusing email. But then I observe what technology does to the people around me—and I steel my resolve.*

As a monk in church and the world, virtually everything Eugene taught and lived could be gathered into this expansive word he spoke so often: *prayer.* Eugene possessed the discipline of a spartan, spending vast stretches of time in silence and contemplation, praying through the Psalms on a thirty-day cycle, and memorizing most of the Psalter (often in Hebrew) and other great tracts (like Genesis). Whenever people asked for spiritual guidance, he'd explain that he had few answers, no spiritual techniques—but he could help them learn to pray. Teaching people to pray and teaching them to die a good death—Eugene often said these were two essentials in the job description of a pastor.

Apart from mentioning Hans Urs von Balthasar's *Prayer* as the best book on the subject and Edith Stein as a preeminent writer on contemplation, Eugene gave little advice on how to pray. Instead, he walked alongside people as they moved toward God, as they stepped more solidly into their lives—and he gave a name to what they were doing: *prayer.* He chafed against advice because each person's life with God was unique and there was no one-size-fits-all formula. When we pray, he wrote to one inquiring soul, *we don't become more like anyone else, especially the "great ones," we become more ourselves.* An accomplished pastor once explained to Eugene how he was trying to "reproduce himself in the younger generation." Eugene's response: "Isn't one of you enough? Why don't you nurture what is uniquely *them*?"

Eugene considered much popular wisdom on prayer rubbish. He tired of clichés and amped-up rhetoric. *These prayer warrior types seem to think that the only effective way to convince others that prayer is our life blood is to open a vein and bleed all over the carpet. Thank you, I'd rather keep my blood within my veins . . . where it can do its proper work invisibly and with a touch of absurdity.*

Eugene's letters abounded with gentleness and compassion. Many who wrote were disillusioned with church, and they never received a chiding word—but *always* received warmth, kindness, and curiosity. It's remarkable how this man who spent his life as a pastor—and believed in the church with every fiber—attracted so many weary souls leery of the institution. Eugene often found himself in extended dialogue with many who had prickly relationships with the church, such as David James Duncan, the author of *The Brothers K* and *The River Why*—novels Eugene thoroughly enjoyed.

Perhaps it was his outsider sensibility that gave him such a warm heart and welcoming ear. His letter to a reader in Sweden exudes generosity:

> *For some of us a Christian congregation is a space to imagine new possibilities. It is not the only "space" available and it is not for everyone, but for some of us it seems to be our assignment, at least for me it has been.*
>
> *Those of us who choose to remain in the church for the*

most part don't find ourselves in very propitious company.
The impoverished Christian community in which we find
ourselves makes for a lonely business. . . . I learned very
early that the loneliness was unavoidable.

But for cynics and those with acid-soaked pens, which they used to mock or degrade the church, he had sharper words. *There is no church I'm familiar with over the past 2000 years that I would be a member of if it were up to me. . . . Yet I have little time for the anti-church crowd who seem snobbish and who have little sense of the lived way of soul and Christ.*

The number of pastors who sought out Eugene (through letters, visits, and sometimes even crafting entire sabbaticals around his schedule) was staggering. Eugene loved pastors, and he contended that being a faithful pastor within the American consumeristic society required immense grace—and at least a little belligerence. *What most pastors need more than anything else,* Eugene wrote in one letter, *is not encouragement but discernment. Most of what parishioners would consider encouragement is just encouragement to do the wrong thing, the things that make them feel good.*

Alarmed by the beguiling assumptions undergirding most church leadership trends, Eugene cautioned pastors that true ministry typically requires a pastor to operate from the margins. *This is* modest *work. This is not glamorous work, this is behind-the-scenes, ignored, patient servant work. Forget about being relevant, about being effective. Friends, you are living in exile—get used to it . . . The less people notice you the better.*

When one pastor asked Eugene how he arrived at his church's vision statement, he likely didn't expect the answer he received: *If* something like "vision" crept in, I got rid of it as fast as I could. The church I wanted or dreamt of or had a vision for got in the way of the church I had, the church God gave me. No, I'm afraid that I don't have much truck with the "vision statements" that seem to fuel the ambition of pastors these days.

Pastors like Daniel Grothe found their way to Eugene. Daniel moved his family to Colorado Springs to serve at New Life Church, the fourteen-thousand-member church founded by Ted Haggard. Within Daniel's first three years, the church first endured a national headline-grabbing scandal and then a gunman loaded with multiple firearms and one thousand rounds of ammunition stepped onto the church campus, killing two young women before committing suicide inside New Life's building. Beleaguered, Daniel scoured the used-book table at Goodwill, sighting *The Contemplative Pastor* for ninety-nine cents. "I'd never heard of it, but I saw Eugene's name on the spine and thought, *I think that's the guy who translated* The Message." Daniel devoured the book and sent a letter to Eugene, asking if he could visit for a day but assuming he'd never hear back. A few weeks later, a letter arrived from Lakeside, Montana.

Dear Daniel,

Yes, I would be willing to spend a day with you here in Montana. But not so fast. I think it would be better if you spent some time thinking about what is involved. Why don't you take some time to reflect on what "pastor" exactly means to you. And what "church" means to you. Write a couple of pages on each, pastor and church and send them to me.

Daniel wrote the papers, and Eugene liked what he read. Daniel visited Eugene multiple times. Eugene's relationship with Daniel complicates the (easily arrived at) notion that Eugene dismissed all megachurches. He was skeptical, to put it mildly, of the obsession with size and the inevitable limitations to intimacy that come with vast organizations. However, there were always exceptions to the rule, he would say. "It's not impossible to be a true pastor at a large church. It's just very, very hard."

One exasperated pastor asked Eugene how to get his church to understand liturgy and the sacramental life, how to get them to *pray,* for crying out loud. Eugene offered a gentle reply: *Don't spend your time trying to get your congregation to live the truths or the way you want them to do. Instead, you just live this way, with them. It doesn't work very well to impose anything on a congregation.* Eugene resonated with one literary critic's line regarding Thoreau's *Walden: You cannot rush Walden into people's heart—gesture and hint.* Though Sabbath was a cornerstone for Eugene, remarkably he never once preached on Sabbath at Christ Our King. He simply practiced Sabbath, revealing the grace-drenched rhythm in his everyday affairs. Eugene wrote several pastoral letters describing what his Sabbath looked like. And then he simply *Sabbathed.*

"As a pastor, how do you slip through the opposition and make your point?" Eugene asked.

> You do it by being lazy—or what looks like lazy—sitting in your study for half a day reading a book that doesn't have anything to do with your sermon. . . . My father was a butcher. When he delivered meat to restaurants, he would sit at the counter, have a cup of coffee and piece of pie, and waste time. But that time was critical for building relationships. . . . Sometimes I'm with pastors who don't wander around. They don't waste time. Their time is too valuable. . . . To be unbusy, you have to be disengaged from egos—both yours and others—and start dealing with souls. Souls cannot be hurried.

Eugene scorned self-important hero-leaders who acted as if God handed them tablets of stone atop a blazing mountain. To be a pastor, he believed, means one must live with fear and trembling, to cling to hope in God even as she reckons with her own unsteady soul. To be a pastor requires immense humility and self-awareness, clinging to mercy like a drowning man grasps for a buoy. *The strongest sign of authenticity in what you and I are doing is the inadequacy we feel most of the time.*

Eugene aimed his crosshairs at pastoral careerism, where pastors, tempted by ambition or boredom, "abandoned their posts" as they climbed the ecclesial ladder. He loathed the assumption that a larger church (and then another larger church) defined God's preferred trajectory. When he heard one pastor say he wanted to "leverage his ministry," Eugene wanted to pull out his few remaining hairs. However, he carried no iron stance about pastors leaving their churches. Eugene directed his ire at the corporate capitalism run amok in pastoral ministry, but he assumed each pastor's story was unique.

Dean Pinter once found himself mired in an intractable ministry situation. He and his wife, Darlene, drove to spend the day with Eugene and talk to him about their quandary. Darlene dreaded the conversation, certain he'd say, "This is what God has given you to do. Keep at it; stay with your people." Dean and Darlene unloaded their struggles, and as soon as they finished, Eugene leaned forward and answered without hesitation, "Well, looks like you gotta get out of there. Time to go." Darlene broke into tears of relief. This man they admired so much, this man who was so averse to "leaving your place" had seen *their* particular story, was more concerned about their well-being than any commitment to broader ideals.

In a compassionate letter to one beleaguered pastor, he unfolded valid reasons to leave:

There are other conditions that need to be taken seriously and evaluated, conditions that make it difficult for your spouse or children to find affirmation and blessing—that needs to be taken seriously. If the congregation somehow or other makes this problematic (there are many ways this can be done), you need to think seriously about leaving. If your marital or family life is in danger the sooner you get out the better. You can be a doctor or banker or professor and have a lousy marital/family life but not as a pastor. A valid reason to leave.

Another danger symptom is a dysfunctional congregation that has a history of dysfunction. Some congregations are absolutely toxic and it's usually a toxicity that has a history. Sometimes it can be disguised for three or four years, but not indefinitely. An urgent reason to leave.

But maybe the most common reason for leaving is a sense that you simply aren't up to it anymore—fatigue or depression or a change that you aren't equipped to deal with.

Whether in his study or while exchanging letters, Eugene rarely hit any query straight on. Abandoning the idea of rigid perfection allowed him a certain nimbleness. There may even be occasions when what was *pastorally* needed may not be what was *theologically* preferred. "Absolute purity and airtight answers are not high on my priority list," he'd say. One friend came to Eugene, wanting to be rebaptized. "This is not orthodox," Eugene said, "but I'll gladly do it and be with you in this." He led her through the liturgy and baptized her in the lake. I don't know if Eugene would have done this again for any other person. He certainly had no interest in constructing any theological case for rebaptism. However, in *this* instance, with *this* person, this was what he believed he should do. Eugene believed that the Bible often offered less clarity than we want—or at least not the *kind* of clarity we want. And pastoral concerns, especially in matters of the soul, required dexterity and attentiveness that were not served by unbending theological edicts.

At Christ Our King, he had ignored most theological flash fires, burying himself in the congregation and his writing. For instance, he described himself as *a near pacifist but not doctrinaire.* With his church, however, he didn't line up arguments for or against pacifism but rather pastored the people, allowing the gospel to penetrate their lives and trusting the Spirit to help them recognize the implications. *I live in company with Pentecostals and Presbyterians,* he wrote, *Republicans and Democrats, evangelicals and schismatics—I am their pastor, not their policeman.*

In 2006, an earnest twentysomething approached Eugene after a session at a Catalyst Conference in Atlanta and asked if he wanted to go out with him and his friends for a beer. Eugene smiled. "I wish I could, but I have somewhere I have to be." Undeterred, the fellow offered the question he had intended to ask over drinks: "Are you a pacifist?" Eugene paused, contemplating how to answer such a profound question with only a sentence or two, as the line of people wanting to meet him snaked down the center aisle of the meeting hall. "Well, I *want* to be a pacifist," Eugene answered, "but I'm not sure I have enough courage." It was another example of his tendency to care more about specificity than abstraction, more about his own posture than bare positions.

There are wheat and tares, sheep and goats—and while we strive to know and do right, we must live in humility and recognize we cannot always separate the two. These inclinations yielded an open, generous, unanxious posture in Eugene. He didn't approach Scripture or theological questions with fear. Rather, he trusted God's mercy and believed so profoundly in grace that he didn't carry the crushing burden of believing he had to nail every question to the ground.

> *The Bible is inspired and absolutely reliable, Holy Spirit-given, protected and interpreted—so I can relax. That gives me a lot of freedom. I don't need to be overly cautious and nitpicky. I work out of the entire canon of scripture, letting imagination be formed by everything there. Then prayerfully let myself go—wandering, connecting, remembering, whatever. I am much influenced in this by the early fathers (Gregory of Nyssa and Augustine particularly).*

Yet he raised eyebrows in certain corners when he challenged popular conceptions around biblical inerrancy, ones that yielded wooden interpretations and failed to grapple with linguistic complexities.

> *Perhaps the ongoing difficulty is in treating the biblical text as "inerrant." Language always must be understood in context. Words in isolation have no meaning—they only pick up their meaning from the way they are used. And most words can mean half a dozen things depending on the way the sentence works, the tone of voice in which it is spoken. Language is ambiguous, and especially ambiguous when it employs metaphors, which the biblical text does in spades.*
>
> *If God had wanted to communicate with us "inerrantly" he would have used the language of mathematics, which is the only truly precise language we have. But of course you can't say "I love you" in algebra.*

Eugene wanted to spend his life quietly tending his field, but that desire was tested. Multiple times, national Christian leaders approached him, asking him to sign a statement in reaction to some burning matter. He almost always refused, even when he agreed with the content. *I am not comfortable with signing position statements. It seems to me an impersonal way to do a personal thing. I am a pastor who has done everything I can think of to keep what I do personal and local. This doesn't fit into who I am and the way I have gone about pastoral work. Sorry.*

Eugene grew increasingly concerned about the *vigilantes tearing the church to shreds*. When one friend's views on Creation led to a major ruckus with *the Bible Police,* he felt bewilderment and sorrow. *My how these Christians hate one another.* He journaled about a final book he felt he had in him, intending *Jesus and His Friends* to be his response to the viciousness unfolding in the church. Unfortunately, his idea never came to fruition.

When Eugene endorsed William Paul Young's *The Shack,* a book that stirred a tempest over its fictional portrayal of the Trinity, he received immense pushback. After a critical review of *The Shack* in *Books and Culture* that referenced Eugene's endorsement, he sketched out a letter to the editor in response. And what a letter it would have been. In one of the longest entries of his decades of journaling, he defended Young's efforts, while opining on literary criticism, linguistics, historical theology, Trinitarian theology, philosophy, the encroachment of a technological society, and the need for a robust Christian mysticism. He worked on the letter for a week but decided not to send it, saying, *I have no taste for polemics . . . the rancor of the church vigilantes continues to tear the church into shreds. But neither do I want to engage in that fight.*

Apparently, Eugene didn't learn his lesson, later endorsing *Love Wins,* Rob Bell's attempt to integrate Scripture's teaching on hell with God's unconditional love. You can imagine the blow-back. It wasn't that Eugene thought Rob said everything just right. (He called some sections "sloppy writing" and thought Bradley Jersak's *Her Gates Will Never Be Shut: Hope, Hell, and the New Jerusalem,* which he'd endorsed a year earlier, was far better. And actually Eugene's private concern for Bell had more to do with how he would withstand the seduction of celebrity.)

However, Eugene thought Bell broached a subject Christians needed to consider with greater rigor. "I had no idea that my endorsement of Bell's book would evoke so much hate—I just thought he deserved to be listened to." While Bell's breezy style gained a wider audience, it wasn't as though his interpretations were new, at least to Christians who'd read, as Eugene had for decades, the church fathers and Karl Barth.

When Mickey Maudlin asked him to write the endorsement, Eugene didn't flinch. "There were lots of people interested in the book," Mickey remembered, "but virtually no influential person in the church world would touch it. But Eugene did. He wasn't concerned about burning bridges or the institutional fallout. He was his own man. He did what he thought was right."

Fallout indeed. Eugene called the ensuing melee a *barroom brawl with the sheriffs out in full force.*

The controversy swirling around Rob Bell's book Love Wins *is fresh evidence on how cantankerous the American church is. Because of the endorsement I gave to the book, people keep trying to draw me into [the] fracas. And [a] fracas it certainly is. How the so-called Christian community can generate so much hate is appalling. Haven't we learned anything about civil discourse? Will we ever? And it is so debilitating—we have this glorious gospel to proclaim and give away and we gang up against one another and throw dogma-rocks.*

When asked about his own views (a line of thinking that un-derstood the term *universalist* in an older, Christocentric frame), Eugene gave an honest but (for many) unsatisfying answer:

> *All my instincts are on the universalist side—Barth and Mac-Donald and Buechner and many others. But, you're right, the Bible doesn't allow for dogmatism or certainty on it. So what I think is, the ambiguity of scripture is deliberate on God's part. It wouldn't be good for us to be too sure of ourselves in this regard. The tenor and thrust of both scripture and theol-ogy and yes, life itself is universalistic. But no good writer is interested in explaining everything so we have it nailed down, but in involving us in the relationships and plot and imagination of the world he/she is creating. God is the au-thor in this case and there is a lot more going on than a saved/unsaved or hell/no hell in the story that he is pulling us into.*

This is not to say that Eugene harbored no criticisms, far from it. But he felt that most public criticism exhibited more tribalism or self-righteousness than wisdom. When the emergent church gath-ered steam, he listened and felt sympathetic. He liked many of the leaders. However, he saw more than a little immaturity at play.

> *What strikes me forcibly is that they know nothing about the church, except what they don't like about it. They have no sense of what a healthy church looks or feels like. They are inventing the whole thing from scratch. And have no idea of the complexity of congregation and pastoral voca-tion. These "emergent" ideas are all quite wonderful, but they have no foundation to work from, no experience with mature pastors.*

Certain people, though, provoked genuine ire, namely Bishop John Shelby Spong. *He is one of the few people that I would consider a prime candidate for book burning. His writing is so invidious, so malicious regarding the life of the gospel that I would campaign vigorously for a boycott at least.*

And then in 2016, Donald Trump. Eugene vented his exasperation to one friend:

> *Politically we are in the middle of primaries here. . . . I am usually fairly quiet with my opinions politically, but this year makes it more difficult to shut up. Although I do. We have one candidate, Donald Trump, a multibillionaire—he is rude, demeaning to women, foul-mouthed, and unbelievably arrogant. And a lot of people want him for our leader.*

Every morning, Eugene padded down his driveway, breathing crisp air and greeting the birds, to pick up his copy of the *Daily Inter Lake*. He opened the paper on the kitchen table next to his second cup of coffee. Some mornings, he'd sink into his comfy chair to read, propping his feet up on the ottoman. However, this morning ritual disintegrated as candidate Trump gobbled more of the headlines. Eugene became angry and disillusioned. Not knowing what else to do, at one point he considered canceling his newspaper subscription. Eugene couldn't comprehend how his brothers and sisters in faith could support (and with fervor) someone who displayed such lack of self-control, such meanness. He was a man who exhibited the kind of character and morality that in every previous election exemplified exactly what the religious right denounced as absolutely unacceptable, no matter one's politics. But now, rather than denouncing him, these same groups were championing the man who would become president.

However, Eugene offered most of his incensed comments in

private letters, conversations, and journal entries. He simply had no desire to contribute to public controversy. This was partly due to personality. Eugene avoided the limelight and any hint of sensationalism, and he was convinced that in our inflamed age, little good was accomplished with a public fracas. Moreover, he believed that Christians should handle disagreement through human-to-human relationship, not through open diatribes or public denouncements. Eugene believed power should be used by tender hands. He believed that the way to change minds was with open arms rather than closed fists. (Perhaps the beating he had given his first convert worked a lifelong cure.)

An especially revealing insight appears as we encounter Eugene's affinity for a concept he absorbed from the Nobel poet Czeslaw Milosz: *ketman*. Eugene read Milosz deeply and often. Living under the oppressive Communist regime in Poland, Milosz survived by employing *ketman:* a "stance of outer compliance but inner dissent." Milosz appeared amenable to authorities, but this meek exterior masked his subversive freethinking.

In a way, Eugene employed his own version of *ketman* to avoid (as he explained to one friend) *getting "caught" by the people among whom I work and hope to still provide some influence, namely, the evangelicals and the schismatics. [In response to the polarization] in both church and politics in North America . . . the way I have been able to survive is to not provoke or call attention to the non-negotiable positions of the right. . . . I just smile (kind of) and remember a previous appointment. I have always felt cowardly and a little guilty. But now that I have a name for it—ketman!—I feel almost like I am in a secret society.*

When one Christian writer explained to Eugene his attempts to write in a way that was honest to his conviction without putting his head on the chopping block of the "Calvinist and angry" crowd, Eugene commiserated. He introduced him to Milosz and *ketman,* describing his own tightrope: *I've walked this line all my*

life and have been astonished that I have been accepted by so
many various groups that do not accept each other.

One reason Eugene didn't wade into combustible issues was
because in many instances, he'd not arrived at any definitive position on the matter. He was far more comfortable with ambiguity
than most of us, and he generally assumed (a presumption many
interpreted as naive) that people of goodwill could honestly arrive
at vastly different conclusions—and that we simply had to learn
to live together in that awkward reality. Also, Eugene thought that
the hardened, absolutized positions of opposing theological poles
typically framed conversations in ways that lacked wisdom, humility, and a Spirit-inspired way forward. He suspected there were
better questions and wider angles than our intractable skirmishes.
Even more, Eugene had no desire to play the taking-sides game.
For his entire life, perhaps in reaction to the factional Pentecostalism of his childhood, Eugene believed schism and the failure to
love (to believe Jesus things in the Jesus way) were American evangelicalism's greatest sins. He wanted to leave the door open as
wide as possible, open to as many as possible. He wanted to keep
the conversation going.

The controversy that vexed Eugene the most, the one he struggled
the most to understand, centered on the question of same-sex
marriage. As a pastor, whenever Eugene found himself in the living room with parents who were confused over their child's coming out, his main focus was helping them love their child and keep
the relationship intact. *I have had a number of same-sex couples*
in my congregation, he wrote in one letter, *devout Christians and*
faithful to their partners. Evangelical and Bible-believing. This is
hardly a matter of "unrestrained sexual expression." Not that
there is not plenty of such in our culture, but maybe no more

among gays than among straights. Though Eugene had always understood marriage in historic terms, he was most aggrieved by how many in the church reviled the gay community, treating them with disgust and contempt. Whatever one's position on sexuality, the image of God in every beloved human—and the call to love our neighbor as ourselves—was bedrock to Jesus's teaching and Christian faith. Eugene was confused by a sexuality he did not understand and a response by Christians that he could not fathom. In a 2003 journal, he pondered a way forward. *There must be a non-violent approach to . . . homosexuality: an intuitive inclusion, working out ways of healing and grace: paying attention to Reynolds Price and W. H. Auden and G. M. Hopkins and Henri Nouwen . . .* (And then, as if denouncing any inkling of self-righteousness, he scribbled an additional line: *And record this: one drink too many last night.*)

As his Presbyterian denomination fractured over the question of same-sex marriage, his theology never shifted; his greater concern was schism. Keeping his ordination vows ("submission and obedience to my brethren even when I disagree") and heeding Jesus's teaching about the unity of the church trumped disagreements on even important matters.

I have no patience with schism. This dividing the church because we don't like or approve of some of our friends or neighbors is a far more serious heresy than anything posed by same-sex issues. . . . The more "pure" the church becomes the more defiant it becomes to entering into the prayer of Jesus for us that we all be one. Are these friends the "enemy"? Fine, what is Jesus' command regarding the enemy? Love them, right? I took vows in the UPCUSA and I plan to keep them. I can live and respect men and women whom I don't agree with—I have for 53 years now. This is nothing new. But this invective and meanness is new and I want no part of it. I don't think as pastors we are called to be God's policemen.

[The schismatics] cancel out any truth that they are contending for by the hate they vomit in the sanctuary.

In a 2011 letter, he laid out his ongoing thinking:

First, I need to say that [this] is the most difficult area to deal with that I have had to deal with in my lifetime. And I don't have a clear "position" worked out. But I do have some reflections.

Two, it is pretty clear that homosexual orientation as such is not a sin. I think the evidence is pretty clear on that by this time.

Three, it is not at all clear that the citations of homosexuality in the Bible are covered by what is being discussed now by the church. The ancient world was rife with male prostitutes and temples were where they did their business. What Israel and [the] church were faced with was widespread promiscuity associated with pagan religion.

Four, matters of sexuality are very much shaped by culture. Polygamy was common in the Hebrew world—David had nine wives! As for "adhering to scripture" there is a great deal that we commonly interpret contextually: the food laws in Leviticus, for instance; the acceptance of slavery; the rule to stone an adulterer; the death penalty for not honoring father and mother . . . and even more recently, citing Bible verses, adultery (even for the "innocent" party) disqualified a person from any leadership in church.

Five, there are a considerable number of biblical scholars and theologians who are evangelical and take the Bible with utmost seriousness who are convinced that the homosexu-

*ality mentioned in scripture has to do with promiscuity and
pagan religion (as I mentioned above). The biblical world
had no notion of what is being proposed now, same sex
couples committed by marriage covenant to faithfulness.*

*And six—and this is what weighs on me the most, I
think. The American evangelical church has been so mean
towards homosexuals, excluded and discriminated against,
taunted and reviled, that I want nothing to do with the arguments and prejudices that lurk just beneath the surface of
so much same-sex concern. Homosexuals I have been pastor to feel, with much legitimacy, that they have been treated
as lepers. I know same-sex couples who are deeply devout,
follow Jesus faithfully and joyfully.*

*I readily admit that I am not enthusiastic about ordina-
tion. But if our church decides to do that, I will accept it in
the spirit of my ordination vows "to be subject to my brethren . . . and to [further] the peace and unity of the church."*

Further correspondence reveals Eugene's conflict and resistance to declaring some final word:

*I don't have a position on this subject. Yes, I have consid-
ered the biblical evidence carefully and prayerfully. But I
have no certainty. I don't think the biblical evidence is
nearly as black and white as the evangelicals maintain.
And . . , I am highly offended by hate rhetoric in the name
of Jesus. If I had to vote I don't know what I would do—
but I don't have to vote.*

And more:

*I think that this is a most difficult area to make a proper
discernment. . . . Maybe there is more going [on] with*

Christians in the sexual arena these days than I understand.
I am willing to live in uncertainty, without "taking a stand"
(but at the same time "standing with" fellow Christians
who I quite freely admit I don't understand).

In such a weighty, polarized realm, perhaps it's difficult to imagine a wise sage in the twilight of his life—a man who loved Scripture and loved those who suffered at the margins (including those who wrote to him)—confess no certitude. Yet Eugene freely admitted ambiguity. *[These things] are as murky to me as to you. And I have no airtight, clearcut "answers." The difference between us at this point, I think, is I don't feel that I have to have clarity in order to live honestly as a pastor.*

Eugene's correspondence with LGBTQ persons and others (as well as a recorded 2014 Q&A at Western Theological Seminary) reveals Eugene's increasingly nuanced thinking. In one letter, he shared a story of a pastor friend ("as orthodox, devout, and 'proper' as you can imagine"). His friend's daughter ("a solid evangelical Christian") asked her dad to marry her and her same-sex spouse. "And he did it. After another twenty years, she is still married and still evangelical and devout." Hearing his friend's story, Eugene, in one of his letters to me, wrote, *I respect my friend's decision very much, but I don't think I could ever do that.* However, two years later, telling the story again in another letter to me, he offered an addendum: *The longer I thought about it, I decided that I could and would do that if my daughter (or sons) had invited me into that intimacy.*

Even here, Eugene made no sweeping case for same-sex marriage but rather continued to find himself "muddled," a word he picked up from Union Presbyterian Seminary professor Thomas W. Currie's article "Muddled in the Middle" in the *Presbyterian Outlook*, a piece Eugene admired and circulated to friends. Currie described a meeting of the Charlotte presbytery where he found himself "tongue-tied, equally baffled and often offended by those with whom I agree and those with whom I disagree." He affirmed a historic understanding of marriage while insisting that "a faithful reading of Scripture indicates that Jesus seems much more interested in those who are hurting than he is in those who think they have Scripture on their side." While trying to understand the Bible's wisdom, Eugene imagined the faces of actual people (his family) and their particular stories, determining that he would offer a pastoral blessing that he did not entirely understand.

As Eugene receded from the public stage, however, controversy moved further to the margins. He rarely accepted speaking engagements, and his writing slowed to a drip. Except for endorsements —those requests came in droves. Though Eugene declined most, he still read and recommended scores of manuscripts, typically adding a line below his endorsement: "feel free to edit."

Mostly, Eugene watched birds, corresponded with friends, and spent time with family. With Eric's marriage to Elizabeth that brought three new littles (Grace, Isaac, and Eli) into the family, Eugene eagerly looked forward to having children sprinting with vigor about the house again. And Eugene reread old favorites, returning to the novels of Wallace Stegner, Wendell Berry, Marilynne Robinson, and Georges Bernanos. Lots of poetry too: Denise Levertov, Billy Collins, George Herbert, Mary Oliver. "I'd rather read poets than pastors," he said. Eugene loved Jim Harrison and Ted Kooser's remarkable *Braided Creek: A Conversation in Poetry,* which was "an assertion in favor of poetry and against credentials." Concerned with our ecological meltdown, Eugene read Terry Tempest Williams and Rick Bass, who lived in the Yaak Valley, a remote corner of northwest Montana, where Jan and Eugene had friends they loved to visit.

And every Sunday, they sat in the pew at Eidsvold Lutheran. Andrew Wendle, Eidsvold's pastor, told how visitors would sometimes come up to him after church. "I thought Eugene Peterson went to church here," they'd say.

"He does," Pastor Andy would answer. "Eugene and Jan were your ushers."

By late 2015, Eugene's health was deteriorating. He suffered from a leaky heart valve, though at his age, there was nothing to be done other than prescribe medication. His knees, after years of pounding out miles, were constantly aflame. The doctor gave him cortisone shots, and he wore copper-laced braces, but they did little good. For fifteen years, he'd asked, always embarrassed, to be flown business class because just those few more inches offered some relief. Still, on one of my visits, he climbed down on his knees to pull the French press out of the cabinet. "You need to have your own coffee," he said, wincing as he fought to stand. And he had trouble keeping on weight. Eugene's favorite breakfast, since Johns Hopkins days, was fried apples, sausage, and grits. Now, though, Jan added organic heavy cream, pouring him a glass of white velvet each morning. On one rare occasion when he traveled, Eugene boarded a plane and struggled to put his small carry-on into the overhead compartment. A sixty-year-old woman stepped forward. "Let me help you," she said, lifting his bag. *That stuff has been happening a lot.*

And it wasn't just his body. He'd felt frailness in his soul for some time. *I always assumed that as I got older, my faith would get firmer,* he wrote in a letter to his former pastor in Vancouver.

That hasn't happened. Jan preceded me in this. A few years
ago she began voicing doubts, her sense of what she called
"absurdity." Not crippling doubts, really, but no longer the
childlike trust that she was accustomed to. And then it
began happening to me. Not a crisis kind of thing but a nib-
bling at the edges. Instead of more, less. Or at least less of
what I expected. Sometimes it occurs to me that it is my
expectations that need converting but so far that hasn't
happened.

And still, this lifelong desire for congruence between the outward appearance and the inward life: *I'd like to actually be what*
people think I am.

In these late days, Eugene sat for hours in his study. His time went
happily, reading and praying and watching the mountains and the
birds from his monastic perch. And as his and Jan's sunlight
faded, his journal revealed his keen awareness of their reality: *[We*
are entering the] final years of our long obedience. His journals
from this time reveal a man reveling in quiet attentiveness, relent-
less in his desire for God, for holiness, for the Presence. Even his
final journal—the actual pages themselves—evidence his deepening clarity, focus, and ease. The lines are neater, the writing
cleaner. Any hurry had drained, as if all the distractions, even the
noise of a pen brushing against a page, gave way to simplicity,
purity. He had become unbusy.

And though some would assume Eugene's world was growing
smaller, he would profusely disagree. Eugene was immersed in
God's world—and there were vast wonders only a step or two
outside his door. His short walks down the driveway to the gravel

road to pick up the paper provided daily pilgrimages. Eugene once told his friend Bob Jones about his morning walk. "I counted the wildlife. I counted three deer, an elk, two hawks, and 117 earthworms. I was participating in it."

Eugene's spirit was strong, but his body and mind began to falter. In early 2016, he suffered a massive fall. A female guest arrived, and Eugene, eighty-three yet ever the gentleman, insisted on carrying her bags into the house. The heavy bag slipped, flipping Eugene head over heels. He splayed across the flagstone, red pouring from his head. Knocked unconscious, Eugene later remembered nothing. An MRI failed to pinpoint damage, but the scare marked an even more noticeable turn toward cognitive and physical decline.

He never really recovered from the accident. He couldn't drive anymore. The roads he'd maneuvered for seventy years confused him. He struggled with names and details. I remember the awkwardness once when he called me, forgetting almost immediately why we were on the phone. Eugene would have stretches of clarity when you might not recognize his struggles unless you knew him well—but then there were other times when it was obvious to everyone that he was jumbled and lost. Eric and Elizabeth built a suite attached to their house, anticipating the time when Jan would no longer be able to care for Eugene alone. When Jan and Eugene maintained their desire to stay at the lake, Eric and Leif insisted on a standby generator for the ravaging winter—when power can go out for days. After Eugene fell in the shower (twice), Leif and Eric had a walk-in installed.

One afternoon, standing in their kitchen in front of the French press, Eugene spoke slowly to me: "You're catching me at the tail end, just in the nick of time." In a letter to friends, Eric described his dad's condition:

My dad, well into his octogenarian years, is not at his cognitive best these days. He takes longer to process information, he forgets more easily, he is prone to confusion. At the same time, he is as kind and gentle as ever, and remains the holiest person I've ever known.

One afternoon in late 2017, Jan and Eugene and I sat at their table after a lunch of sandwiches and fruit. "How long do you think it will take you to write this biography?" Jan asked.

"I'm guessing three years," I answered.

Jan leaned over, grabbed Eugene's hand, and squeezed. "Can you hold on three years?"

Eugene smiled and let out a short sigh. "I'll sure try," he said. Eugene and Jan sat there, holding hands in the quiet, together facing the unknown, walking into the shadows.

Excitement was brewing, however. *As Kingfishers Catch Fire*, the book Eugene had finished editing several years earlier, hit the shelves. For years he declined most interviews, but his publisher reached out to Jonathan Merritt, a well-known journalist for Religion News Service. At first, Merritt hesitated, thinking a book of sermons from an older pastor would garner little interest among his readers. However, hearing *Kingfishers* heralded as Eugene's last work, he thought an interview offering final words from him would be compelling.

It was fated to be one of Eugene's most profound heartbreaks. Merritt called him from his apartment in Brooklyn, asking questions about *Kingfishers,* about Eugene's leaving public life, about whether he feared death. Merritt asked Eugene his thoughts on President Trump, to which he answered, "Donald Trump is the enemy as far as I'm concerned. He has no morals. He has no integrity." However, two questions at the interview's conclusion lit a firestorm:

RNS: You are Presbyterian, and your denomination has really been grappling with some of the hot button issues that we face as a culture. I think particularly of homosexuality and same-sex marriage. Has your view on that changed over the years? What's your position on the morality of same-sex relationships?

EP: I haven't had a lot of experience with it. But I have been in churches when I was an associate pastor where there were several women who were lesbians. They didn't make a big deal about it. I'd go and visit them and it never came up for them. They just assumed that they were as Christian as everybody else in the church.

In my own congregation—when I left, we had about 500 people—I don't think we ever really made a big deal out of it. When I left, the minister of music left. She'd been there ever since I had been there. There we were, looking for a new minister of music. One of the young people that had grown up under my pastorship, he was a high school teacher and a musician. When he found out about the opening, he showed up in church one day and stood up and said, "I'd like to apply for the job of music director here, and I'm gay." We didn't have any gay people in the whole congregation. Well, some of them weren't openly gay. But I was so pleased with the congregation. Nobody made any questions about it. And he was a really good musician.

I wouldn't have said this 20 years ago, but now I know a lot of people who are gay and lesbian and they seem to have as good a spiritual life as I do. I think that kind of debate about lesbians and gays might be over. People who disapprove of it, they'll probably just go to another church. So we're in a transition and I think it's a transition for the best, for the good. I don't think it's something that you can parade, but it's not a right or wrong thing as far as I'm concerned.

Taken aback by Eugene's candor, Jonathan asked another question, one he hadn't planned:

RNS: A follow-up: If you were pastoring today and a gay couple in your church who were Christians of good faith asked you to perform their same-sex wedding ceremony, is that something you would do?

EP: Yes.

One word. Merritt put down the phone, stunned. He walked into his living room and told a friend, "This changes everything." For days, he agonized over what to do. "I knew what would happen if I published this interview. He would get crucified. But if I didn't publish it, from that day on, I could no longer call myself a journalist." The following week, before stepping into a university writing class he was teaching, Merritt logged on to Religion News Service's website and queued the interview's final installment. Several hours later, when he returned to his phone, texts and tweets and voice mails lit up his screen. The internet raged, a three-alarm fire. Conservative Christians and leaders denounced Eugene. Progressive Christians and leaders rejoiced.

Within hours, LifeWay (at the time, America's largest religious bookstore chain) issued an ultimatum: either Eugene clarify his position or all his books would be banned from their stores. Eugene's phone rang like a tornado siren. Friends called and described the inferno—that he was being placarded and shredded, or cheered, by twenty million people. Eugene was dumbfounded. A man who barely knew how to open his email could not comprehend the social media maelstrom or how his interview (that he remembered only in pieces) had set off such a shock wave. When Rick Christian called, he explained the situation to Eugene and passed along examples of Tweets and social media posts across the spectrum. Eugene, who'd always avoided controversy and schism, had somehow tossed a stick of dynamite.

Confused and distraught, his mind muddy, Eugene tried to understand what was happening and what to do about it. Rick told him he could leave it alone and let others battle it out or he could issue a statement. "I hated to see Eugene so used at the end of his life," Rick explained. "A one-word post with no context triggered LifeWay's heretic alert. And suddenly a man whose prophetic voice is globally esteemed was shoved by bullies into the kind of spotlit corner he always avoided. No conversation. No reasoning together. Just a rush to press and to condemn." Barraged with questions, Rick felt the chaos necessitated some kind of response. However, Eugene, the man who'd written millions of words, couldn't imagine how to start the first sentence. He agreed to have others take a first crack at a statement he could consider. Don Pape, a friend of the Petersons and the publisher at NavPress, who'd also fielded much of the criticism because of their association with *The Message,* worked with one of his editors, David Zimmerman, to start the draft. "We had no desire at all to put any words in Eugene's mouth," Pape said. "We wanted to try to help Eugene by putting some of what we understood of his thoughts on paper so he had something to work with." They passed a working document to Rick, who passed it to Eugene, describing the draft as "wet cement" and reiterating that Eugene could "dump the whole load and start over." Rick explained that whatever went out would be Eugene's words. Over the phone, Eugene asked Rick to edit one section, which Rick did.

And then Rick posted a revised statement with this center line:

To clarify, I affirm a biblical view of marriage: one man to one woman. I affirm a biblical view of everything.

The statement continued,

When put on the spot by this particular interviewer, I said yes in the moment. But on further reflection and prayer, I would like to retract that. That's not something I would do out of respect to the congregation, the larger church body, and the historic biblical Christian view and teaching on marriage. That said, I would still love such a couple as their pastor. They'd be welcome at my table, along with everybody else.

The explosive whiplash was wrenching. Queer Christians who had felt relief and welcome when a giant stepped into their corner felt, only a day later, sucker punched. They were convinced Eugene had abandoned them out of self-protection, greed, or fear of the evangelical machine. Or worse, that Eugene thought so little of them and their pain that he could easily toss (and retrieve) words with no regard for their plight. As Eugene caught an inkling of the anguish inflicted on the LGBTQ community, he descended further into confusion. Angered by the entire mess, Eric drafted an open letter: "While [the revision] was, I am persuaded, well-intended as an effort to calm the waters, in several respects it does not accurately reflect his convictions. In many ways, it doesn't even sound like him." Eric went on to describe his deepest concern:

To have Eugene's pastoral affirmation effectively removed from the gay and lesbian community would be to perpetuate damage to some of the most vulnerable and marginalized constituencies in our church and society. My dad and I care deeply for people in the LGBTQ community: we consider several to be our good, personal friends, and many to be our sisters and brothers in Christ. For any of them to be in doubt about his support of them, or of God's unconditional love for them, would be gravely regrettable.

The transcript of the interview simply shows a one-word "Yes" answer to the question, "If you were pastoring today and a gay couple in your church who were Christians of good faith asked you to perform their same-sex wedding ceremony, is that something you would do?" What the transcript does not reveal is the long pause that spanned between the question and the answer. I could be wrong about this, but I'm quite sure that in that pause Eugene was thinking about one of his grandchildren, considering how he would respond if she asked him to officiate at her wedding. After a lifetime of being immersed in the scriptures and devoted to the way of prayer, after fifty-nine years of pastoral ministry, there was only one honest response. And while the complexity of the question would certainly have benefited from a much longer, more thoughtful conversation, his answer, both then and now, is as close to the truth, as congruent with his convictions and beliefs, as possible: *yes.*

Many accused Merritt of playing provocateur or exploiting Eugene, ignoring his lifetime of dealing with sensitive topics through conversations, with nuance and depth, and neglecting his due diligence given the gravity of the conversation. Merritt believed he was simply doing his job as a journalist: asking pointed questions and letting people speak. "My real issue," Rick said, "is that there was not more back and forth, more questions about what Eugene meant or what has influenced his changing thinking." Merritt agreed with that. "My primary failure," he said, "was that I did not ask a follow-up question, that I didn't ask him how the Bible informed his view. Eugene is known as a Bible person. He's opened up the Scripture for so many. I can't believe I didn't ask that follow-up question, but I was so surprised. And then the interview just ended. I should have asked him more, and I didn't. I regret that." Merritt wrote a piece describing the interview and the aftermath and closed with a gracious line: "Peterson's views on same-sex marriage—whether he supports it or opposes it—have no bearing on my respect for him or his ministry."

In this tragic episode, there were no winners. Only confusion and hurt. LGBTQ Christians suffered, once again casualties in a polemicized war. Christians with a historic understanding of marriage (including some LGBTQ Christians) were confused by vacillating words from a pastor they admired. Merritt suffered, receiving piles of hate mail accusing him of purposefully ambushing Eugene. "I dealt with shame over that for quite a while," he said.

And Eugene suffered. In the months following the controversy, his dementia spiraled, though it would not be officially diagnosed for a couple of months. For the previous year, I'd watched his mental deterioration, and the truth is, Eugene should never have been doing interviews at all.

Amid the fury and after the retraction, Eric was on the phone with his dad, trying to figure out what the next step should be. "I feel so incompetent," Eugene said multiple times. He kept getting confused about who had played what role in the preceding furor. His dementia was full blown. Eric realized that even if there were inaccuracies or misunderstandings, at this moment, his dad and mom needed to be protected. The harm had been done, and there was nothing more that Eugene, confused and heartbroken, could do.

So Eric tucked away his letter, never publishing it. He did email a few words to a small circle of friends:

These recent days, I believe I have seen the church at its worst. My father has been the subject of mean attacks, derisive and dismissive name-calling, and heretical condemnation; these have been both hurtful and disheartening. Worse, and far more importantly, it has been a poor witness to the Gospel of Jesus Christ and a bad reflection on the nature of the Body of Christ. I remind you that the world is watching us, and much of what it has been witnessing would not lead unbelievers to exclaim, "See how they love one another!" At the very least, there have been displays of behavior unbecoming to the baptized. The church can and must do better as it incarnates the Body of Christ across individual differences, especially in matters of adiaphora.

Conversely, I am also quite happy to say that, in the last week, the Peterson family has experienced the church of Jesus Christ at its gracious best. People have given the benefit of the doubt; there has been the exercise of restraint, as well as the extension of forbearance. People have chosen to believe the best about my dad in the face of confusing, contradictory information. To those people I would say that your high regard for him is well-placed, and our family is most grateful for your kind support.

It's a tragedy that in his final public moment, Eugene struggled under the weight of the very thing he'd lived toward his entire life (and what he wrote about in the *Kingfishers* introduction): congruence. Eugene stepped into his last days trusting that his many years and the wide scope of his life and work would tell the final story.

Over the next fifteen months, Eugene faded as his vascular dementia intensified.

He kept picking up copies of his books and underlining in them, as if he was trying to remember what he'd written, who he was. When one friend asked him about *Kingfishers,* he opened it and read a section with a clear, vigorous voice, as if someone had lit old embers. Then he put the book down and said, as if letting his friend in on a big secret, "The person who wrote that is a pastor."

Eugene underwent simple cognitive testing, failing magnificently. The nurse asked him to draw a clock at 3:30. He jumbled the numbers, and he drew the hands in odd spots on the page, outside the circle. The nurse read him an elementary story, followed by simple questions ("Who's the story about? How many children were there?"). Eugene squinted and rubbed his hands on his legs. "I don't know," he said. "He was failing these tests with an F-," Eric remembered, "but he wasn't stressed. He was at peace."

One day, Eric found Eugene alone in the living room with a blank look, caressing a mug of coffee. "How are you doing, Dad?"

"I feel so confused," Eugene answered.

"Yeah, we talked about this, right?" Eric put his hand on his dad's shoulder. "Your mind's not working the way it used to. It will be okay." Eric squeezed, with affection, speaking the first line of Julian of Norwich's blessing: "All shall be well and all shall be well."

Eugene looked at Eric like a light had turned on, words welling up from deep memory and long habit. "And all manner of thing shall be well," he answered.

"Dad didn't know what state he was in," Eric reflected, "didn't know what year of the Lord it was, didn't know his dad built the house he was sitting in, didn't know who the president was. But he knew—in the depths of his soul—the unshakable reality of God's presence." And Eugene, out of that confused, disoriented state, maintained a holy awareness residing at his core, in an interior place completely intact, untouched by dementia. "That life of prayer grooved itself deep inside my dad, and he had full access to that until the day he died. I think in those last months, Dad was simply descending deeper into that interior world that he'd built with God his entire life—only we could not access it with him."

Perhaps this simple interior reality was something being revealed even to Eugene only in these final days. When asked what he considered to be the characteristics of a saint, he had once said, "Humility, number one. Unpretentiousness, having no idea that they're a saint."

The last light was fading. During Eugene's final weekend, Leif and Amy and Eric and Elizabeth kept vigil at the lake. Eric and Leif kept the lantern on the dock burning twenty-four hours, light flickering over the dark water. Eugene took to his bed, declining visibly. Jan held his hand as he drifted in and out of consciousness, walking that precarious threshold between our two ways of being.

In that thin place, Eugene mumbled words—just beyond understanding, words lilting and foreign but with a familiar intonation. Hebrew, perhaps, or, accessing his mother's Pentecostal fire, speaking the glossolalia he'd so longed to burn with in his childhood. From time to time, he opened his eyes, raised his head from his indented pillow, and reached out, stretching to touch someone, interacting with persons very real to him but whom no one else could see.

Eugene startled his hospice nurse when he jolted up and began to stand. "Let's go!" he said energetically. Was it coincidence that these were the same two words that opened the Levertov poem Eugene had, for so long, considered self-description: that dog moving "intently haphazard," sniffing after grace, "every step an arrival"? Was it coincidence that at the end, the words that came so true and quickly to his dying lips were poetry?

Poetry and gratitude. Those final couple of days, he said thank you over and over again. When anyone fixed his pillow or helped him with a drink: "Thank you." Often, he'd simply mumble under his breath, "Thank you." And this was gratitude infused with joy. One afternoon, Eric, Elizabeth, Leif, and Amy were all sitting next to him, lined up on one side of his bed. Eugene opened his eyes, and it took him a moment to gain focus and recognize who was there. Then his eyes went bright, and he broke out in that wide smile. "Wow!" he exclaimed.

Those final hours, Elizabeth sat with him, holding his hand and singing hymns. Sensing the end was near, she called for Eric. Then, the moment—last breaths, new tears, the stepping out into a broader place, a call from a deep, familiar voice, a call to him from a farther shore than we can see. *Let's go.* It was time.

Last words then, barely discernible but sounding like *thank you.*

Then, unhurried and gentle, Eugene went.

At 6:30 a.m. on Monday, October 22, 2018, the lantern on the dock went dark. Eric placed his hand on his dad's head and passed the blessing: "Together, we are witnesses to this glad fact: that in sure and certain hope of the resurrection to eternal life, through Christ Jesus our Lord, I declare that the baptism of Eugene Hoiland Peterson is now complete. 'Blessed are the dead who die in the Lord . . . ,' says the Spirit, 'that they rest from their labors, and their works follow them.' "

Leif, through tears, added, "Sure is nice to have a priest in the family."

Eric returned to his shop to build his dad's coffin. He cut and sanded pine boards, strung white rope for the handles, and affixed a small wooden cross from the Monastery of Christ in the Desert atop the lid. The grandchildren, serving as pallbearers, carried their grandpa's coffin down the center aisle of the church and set the casket in front of the baptismal font. The choir loft was packed with pastors from around the country, all wearing stoles or clerical collars in Eugene's honor (marking themselves as part of his "company of pastors"). Eric stood and, voice cracking, called the congregation to worship. As friends shared memories, Jan sat in the front row, her sorrow broken by moments of laughter. She dabbed her eyes with tissue. Jan caught friends' eyes and smiled. But she carried a hollow ache. For the first time in sixty years, she was alone in church, without Eugene.

Under gloomy Montana skies, the family gathered around the graveside, standing close and braving the icy wind. Drew pulled out Eugene's banjo and led the family in "Heigh Ho to the Fisher Christ," a poem-song Eugene wrote on one of those summer treks to Montana. He sang it often to his children—and then his grandchildren. And now they sang it back.

After final words, they lowered the casket into the ground and tossed dirt on the pine box.

And Eugene's life said *amen.*

Coda

November 11, 2019. It's been just over a year since Eugene crossed that thin threshold, welcomed into the communion of saints. A year since Eric dipped his hands into the baptismal font, splashed fistfuls of water over Eugene's casket, and spoke a final blessing. For months, I put off writing about Eugene's death, not just because the narrative of those final hours provides a natural conclusion. More, I think, I pushed this portion away because I wasn't yet ready to let him go. As long as I was writing, as long as I had not scribbled those grievous words on the page, Eugene was somehow alive in the story. His presence still loomed near.

And this is the bit that has haunted me in the writing: How do I convey *presence*? How do I explain the expansiveness that opened in my soul as I sat with Eugene in unhurried stillness? Or what it was like to be immersed in commonplace rhythms (cooking, filling bird feeders, sitting on the porch in the afternoon sun) and finally understand, without any explanation, what the ancients meant by living a life of prayer? Or how it felt to stand at Jan and Eugene's kitchen window, looking with him over the lake and toward the mountains, trying to see what he saw and realizing that this very act—the watching, the silence—offered the true essence. Eugene lived his own lines of poetry:

> It takes an unhurried while. Then,
> There it is: absences become Presence.

How do I help you encounter his presence? Is this even possible?

I could tell you about my first meaningful conversation with Eugene. We were in Juneau, Alaska, sitting in the blue upholstered booths inside the Travelodge's diner, with plates of huevos rancheros and bacon. Eugene wore the blue jean shirt and boots I would come to love. He ordered coffee but took only a few sips. I was a young and anxious pastor, and I opened my leather journal, ticking off question after annoying question. Eugene smiled, listened, and answered with no frills. Then he smiled and listened more. I can't remember a single question I asked, and I don't recall a single response. But as I left breakfast, my swirling anxiety— all the questions and issues that felt so vexing mere hours before—had melted. Eugene said nothing original, no radiating insight, but he welcomed me into a sphere that I can describe only as immensely human and profoundly holy.

I could tell you about when Eugene led me, years later, down the stone steps, past their kayaks, and into the crawl space under their home on Flathead Lake. That cave held boxes of books and blow-up water toys and several mildly successful rat traps scattered along the floor. Shelves bulged with leather-bound editions of *The Message* and stacks of *Eat This Book* hardbacks—all nibbled through, these Montana rats literally taking Eugene's advice. Stooping through the low entrance, Eugene flipped the switch and the bare one-hundred-watt bulb flickered and sizzled. He pointed to twin black metal cabinets stuffed full of thousands of letters (Eugene always stapled his reply to the original and slid them into a manila folder), manuscripts, calendars, and clippings from high school, college, and decades at Christ Our King. In that dark grotto sat thousands of sermons, volumes of bestselling books, and notes of admiration (criticism too) from prominent figures. And yet, whenever I'd come back up to the house after hours below, Eugene would ask, "Well, Winn, did you find anything worthwhile?" I'd beam. Boy, did I. He'd shake his head, bewildered. "I don't know why anyone would be interested in any of this. Everything has just been a gift." It's powerful to encounter a person of substance and discover, in his most interior world, genuine gratitude and humility. Eugene carried no false modesty, no tempering of his achievements or attempts to appear small. He simply lived in a very large world (*God's* world), and in this largeness, everything, whether mundane or marvelous, evoked wonder. Why highlight his life when there are thousands of glimmering splendors? For Eugene, the gifts were inexhaustible: the glint of fading light over the lake, a line from Mary Oliver, a kiss from Jan, a good joke, an idea from Barth, a bowl of butter pecan ice cream. And in Eugene's company, you'd always find yourself noticing how the most ordinary things shimmered with new and unexpected beauty.

I could tell you about the night of Eugene's funeral—the dark Montana sky and sharp November air. I strolled First Avenue West, the same street where Eugene had roamed on his Schwinn bike, and I stepped onto the porch of a green Victorian house not far from the butcher shop where he wielded a cleaver. Plush brown couches circled the open living room, with large windows and hardwood floors and chairs pulled in from the dining table. Students from Regent and a small number of other friends gathered to tell stories, to remember, to cry and laugh. Boxes of takeout Chinese filled the kitchen, and a bottle of old scotch made the rounds. There were tears. And story after story. But I heard almost nothing about Eugene's books or appearances on large stages, nothing about his awards or influential friends. I heard about out-of-the-way conversations, always more silence than words. I heard about evenings at the Petersons' kitchen table over bowls of soup or long chats by the woodstove after evening prayers. I heard about Eugene and Jan's embrace, about the healing so many felt on the lake, how several affectionately referred to the place as Rivendell.

I could tell you about walking up the stairs to Eugene's study, past the impish small stone gargoyle crouched on the third step, past the black-and-white photo of him seated on a pew underneath the cross in Christ Our King's sanctuary, past the picture of the young woman praying at the Wailing Wall. A thick beige carpet runner covered the stairs, muffling my steps, and I paused at his study door. This must have been a taste of what Eric felt, that young boy peering through the crack and seeing his dad on his knees in prayer. Eugene sat in his rocker, an afghan hung over the back. He faced the water, sun warming his face, eyes closed. No movement. No sound. There was only—how do I say it? Joy. Reverence. Wholeness. Contentment. *Holiness*. This was his cell. This was his cathedral.

Eugene's story cast a long shadow. This son of a butcher. This boy who rode with his mother into sawdust-strewn camps and Grange halls as she preached God's love to loggers and ruffians. This gravelly voiced man who listened, with that earnest smile and tender soul, to whoever sat in front of him. This man who loved watching for the sunrise over the Mission Range or for the osprey swooping into the bay. This man who knew the name of every tree and flower living alongside him and Jan in their monastery in Montana. This man who became a wise and trusted voice in an age of incredulity. Outlets like NPR reached out to Eugene in moments of national crisis, like after the horror of Sandy Hook. One scholarly volume offered a lofty assessment: "Eugene Peterson may be the most influential theological writer in the church today." Numerous institutions extended honorary doctorate degrees to him. Regent College endowed the Eugene and Jan Peterson Chair in Theology and the Arts. And, of course, his stunning publishing career. During his life, Eugene sold roughly twenty-two million copies of thirty-eight books, translated into languages around the globe.

But what mattered to me—to so many of us who knew and

loved him—was something so much deeper, something none of us can really explain. You would just have to sit with the man. You'd have to encounter his warmth, his welcome, the hospitality of his silence. You'd have to encounter the way he *knew* God.

The day before we buried him, I sat in Johnson-Gloschat's small funeral-home chapel, where Eugene lay in his pine coffin. There were three of us spread out, each in our own wooden pew. The heavy gold curtains, maroon carpet, and floral cornucopia would have made Eugene claustrophobic, but he would have loved the stillness. I stepped out of my pew and walked up the short center aisle. I stood over Eugene's body. My eyes were moist. "Thank you," I said. "Thank you."

Discussion Questions

1. Winn has said that what he most hoped for in *A Burning in My Bones* was not to merely catalog Eugene's life but rather to "allow the reader to *experience* Eugene—what it was like to sit with him in his study, to encounter his smile, to hear his raspy voice and his laughter, to have a sense of what it was like to share those long stretches of silence pregnant with God and grace, abundant with human joy and pleasure." Do you think Winn succeeded? Where did you most *experience* Eugene?

2. Montana's Flathead Valley provides more than just the setting in Eugene's story—it functions as a character, a teacher, and an ongoing influence. What's the importance of having the book begin with a map? How do you see Montana's—and Flathead Valley's—ongoing presence in Eugene's life? What memories or questions does this raise about the places in your own story?

3. What is it about Eugene's early life that adds texture to your perception of the man he grew to be? How do some of his younger years (his opinions, disappointments, ambition, wanderlust, competitiveness, or zealous energy) provide a fuller picture?

4. Eugene's mom and dad played very different roles in his life, with much different impact. How would you describe these relationships?

5. Consider the various pastors in Eugene's life (his mother, his childhood pastors, George Buttrick, Alexander Whyte, and other

pastors whose writings he read deeply). What do you notice? How do you see them shaping his pastoral convictions?

6. Eugene reveled in novels and delighted in poetry. What connections do you make between the voracious way Eugene read and the way he lived, pastored, and wrote? Are there any novelists or poets Eugene read that you'd like to enjoy or return to?

7. Eugene used the word *imagination* often. How do you understand what Eugene meant by this, and how do you see this posture of imagination playing out in Eugene's life?

8. Perhaps the most central theme in Eugene's teaching was the unflinching vision of God at the center of life: God as the center of joy, the source of all beauty, the energy behind all human flourishing. Eugene's concern with regard to much in pastoral practice and Christian life was that God was seldom the central character. How do you respond to this vision and this concern?

9. Eugene said that the work of spiritual theology was to "get it lived." How do you see this affecting Eugene's convictions and his resistance to some popular ways we think about—or practice—the Christian life?

10. What struck you most about Eugene's relationships with his family, his friends, and Jan?

11. What part of Eugene's story do you wish you knew more about?

12. Eugene loved Georges Bernanos's novel *The Diary of a Country Priest*. In one of his latter conversations with Winn, as Eugene's own life was nearing a close, he reflected on the dying priest's closing words: "Grace is everywhere." How do you see grace as a ubiquitous presence in Eugene's story? And how was the giver of grace (God) the central vision in Eugene's world?

Acknowledgments

You never know when you first set out on an adventurous task how much help you'll need to see it through. I needed a lot of help. My good friend John Blase told me, after what I thought was my last visit with Eugene, that I needed to be the one to write his story. I listened, and so did Eugene and Jan. John served as my editor for nearly three years, helping me craft sturdy sentences. John, I've marveled at your poetry and story making for years (you're truly one of my favorite writers), so thank you for pouring your skill into these pages.

Paul Pastor took up the editor's mantle, bringing his artful eye and sharp pen to the manuscript. Thank you, Paul, for helping me write a book worthy of Eugene. Thank you to Kathy Mosier and Helen Macdonald for cleaning up my many mistakes (and any errors that remain are entirely mine). I'm grateful for the clear advice and advocacy of Andrea Heinecke, my agent. The photography in these pages allowed us to *see* Eugene—such an essential part of encountering Eugene's humanness. Photographers Martyn Taylor and Todd Holden were particularly generous with their work. And Emily Pastor: my goodness, your sketch of Flathead Valley is everything I could have hoped for. Eugene and Jan would have loved this piece, and I'm certain a copy will hang for decades in Selah House.

One of the joys of researching Eugene's story was the many conversations I enjoyed with an array of diverse, gracious people—each one warm, principled, and thoughtful. I lost count of how many times I got off the phone or finished a lunch and thought, *Eugene and Jan had amazing friends. I'm so glad I get to meet these people.* Even better, a few of their friends have now become my friends too. What an unexpected gift.

So, to Eugene and Jan's many friends I was able to meet, to so many others who helped with research, digging up archives and passing along letters, to everyone who made time for extended conversations and follow-up emails, thank you: Sarah Arnold, David Bauer, Dan Baumgartner, Maria Bitterli, Arthur Boers, Scott Bolinder, Byron Borger, Bruce Bryant, Tracie Bullis, Julie Canlis, Matt Canlis, Alex Chai, Debbie Christian, Rick Christian, Jack Craft, Charles Davidson, Jim Dresher, Craig Fee, Charles Fensham, Karen Finch, Miles Finch, Sister Constance Fitzgerald, Ryan Flanigan, Lu Gerard, Daniel Grothe, David Hansen, Miranda Harris, Peter Harris, Kenneth Henke, Jim Hoover, Dale Irvin, Peb Jackson, Kristen Deede Johnson, Trygve Johnson, Bob Jones, Richard Kew, Toni Kim, Walter Kim, Gisela Kreglinger, Carol Rueck Mann, Mickey Maudlin, Adrienne Meier, Jonathan Merritt, Cherith Fee Nordling, Cuba Odneal, Glenn Packiam, Don Pape, Joyce Peasgood, Drew Peterson, Elizabeth Peterson, Eric Peterson, Karen Peterson, Ken Peterson, Leif Peterson, Sadie Peterson, Dean Pinter, Steven Purcell, Darrin Rodgers, Peter Santucci, Luci Shaw, Simon Steer, Bob Stiles, Jon Stine, David Taylor, Steve Trotter, Walter Wangerin Jr., Prescott Williams III, Jeffrey Wilson, Jonathan Wilson-Hartgrove, Jim Wolff, David Wood, Philip Yancey, Geordie Ziegler, and David Zimmerman.

Thank you to Eugene and Jan's family, and especially to Eric, Leif, and Karen, for trusting me with this task. You were loved. Whatever else I learned by combing through your dad's life and journals, I learned this: you were loved.

My wife, Miska, is my true partner and soul mate, and everything I do carries with it not only my hope and heart but hers too. Thank you for making me a better man, Miska. And Wyatt and Seth, our two sons. Along the grueling way, they both said to me, "Dad, I'm praying for you" or "Dad, I know you can do this." Those words go deep in a father's heart. I love you, Wyatt and Seth.

Notes

Introduction

xv The epigraph is taken from William Blake, *The Illuminated Books*, ed. David Bindman, vol. 1, *Jerusalem: The Emanation of the Giant Albion*, ed. Morton D. Paley (Princeton, NJ: Princeton University Press, 1991), 201.

Chapter 1: Montana

3 The epigraph is taken from Rick Bass, *Winter: Notes from Montana* (Boston: Mariner, 1991), 5.

3 **In 1902:** The family marks this immigration as 1900, though census records suggest 1902. Also, Eugene's grandfather's birth name was Endre Endressen Hoiland, showing up as Endre as late as 1920 census records. However, at some point the family stylized Endre to Andre.

3 **the *Norge* or the *Thingvalla*:** Or they may have sailed on the *Angelo* or the *Hekla (2)*, but passenger records from those years were lost in a fire.

4 **"four general stores":** Harry Stanford, "Kalispell in 1892: A Lusty Infant," in Henry Elwood, *Kalispell, Montana and the Upper Flathead Valley*, 2nd ed. (Kalispell, MT: Thomas, 1989), 55.

4 **served as a pastor:** The *Daily Inter Lake*, Kalispell's newspaper, refers to "Rev. Andrew Hoiland" in an article on July 19, 1917.

5 **"Execution of Fred LeBeau":** Elwood, *Kalispell, Montana*, 84.

5 **"the Garden of Eden":** Elwood, *Kalispell, Montana*, vii.

5 "valleys of Switzerland": Elwood, *Kalispell, Montana*, 2.

5 what we behold: William Blake, *The Illuminated Books*, ed. David Bindman, vol. 1, *Jerusalem: The Emanation of the Giant Albion*, ed. Morton D. Paley (Princeton, NJ: Princeton University Press, 1991), 201.

6 "looking for arrowheads": Eugene Peterson, "Eugene Peterson: The Bible, Poetry, and Active Imagination," interview by Krista Tippett, *On Being*, December 22, 2016, https://onbeing.org/programs/Eugene-peterson-the-bible-poetry-and-active-imagination-aug2018/#transcript.

6 "Jackson County, Missouri": David McCullough, "The Unexpected Harry Truman," in Robert A. Caro et al., *Extraordinary Lives: The Art and Craft of American Biography*, ed. William Zinsser (Boston: Houghton Mifflin, 1988), 28.

6 "work in creation": Paul Evdokimov, *Orthodoxy*, trans. Jeremy Hummerstone and Callan Slipper (Hyde Park, NY: New City, 2011), 23.

7 "*sacred* waters": Eugene H. Peterson, *The Pastor: A Memoir* (New York: HarperOne, 2011), 13.

7 "prayed and practiced": Peterson, *Pastor*, 12.

7 "geography of my imagination": Peterson, *Pastor*, 11.

8 "sometimes wonder still": Peterson, *Pastor*, 10–11.

Chapter 2: Mother: Those Winter Sundays

9 The epigraph is taken from Wallace Stegner, "Letter, Much Too Late," in *Where the Bluebird Sings to the Lemonade Springs: Living and Writing in the West* (New York: Modern Library, 2002), 33.

11 "tears without embarrassment": Eugene H. Peterson, *The Pastor: A Memoir* (New York: HarperOne, 2011), 28.

11 "the best parts": Peterson, *Pastor*, 29.

11 "most colorful cursing": Peterson, *Pastor*, 33.

12 "being a pastor": Peterson, *Pastor*, 28.

12 "it move not": Jeremiah 10:33–4, KJV.

13 "the Christmas tree": This entire story is found in Peterson, *Pas-*

tor, 50–55; Eugene H. Peterson, "Christmas Shame," *Christianity Today,* December 20, 2006, www.christianitytoday.com/ct/2006 /decemberweb-only/151-32.0.html.

15 **"so many boundaries":** Eugene Peterson, journal entry, February 6, 2003.

15 **"love and joy":** Eugene Peterson, journal entry, February 6, 1993.

Chapter 3: The Butcher's Son

16 The epigraph is taken from William Kittredge, *Hole in the Sky: A Memoir* (New York: Vintage Books, 1992), 28.

17 **"into its maw":** Eugene H. Peterson, *The Pastor: A Memoir* (New York: HarperOne, 2011), 36.

18 **"reality of the material":** Peterson, *Pastor,* 36.

18 **"the Killer":** Peterson, *Pastor,* 38.

19 **"sophisticated language":** Eugene H. Peterson, *Subversive Spirituality* (Grand Rapids, MI: Eerdmans, 1997), 205.

19 **"than a store":** Peterson, *Pastor,* 39.

19 **"misfits and oddballs":** Peterson, *Subversive Spirituality,* 205.

20 **"holy place of work":** Peterson, *Pastor,* 39–40.

22 **gifts for Eugene:** Peterson, *Pastor,* 263.

23 **"was my grandpa":** Peterson, *Pastor,* 263.

Chapter 4: The Nature of the Search

26 The epigraph is taken from Walker Percy, *The Moviegoer: A Novel,* 1st Vintage international ed. (New York: Vintage Books, 1998), 13.

29 **"heard from her again":** This story can be found in Eugene H. Peterson, *The Pastor: A Memoir* (New York: HarperOne, 2011), 57–58, and numerous details are given in the 1917 archives of the *Daily Inter Lake.*

30 **"reductions to stereotype":** Peterson, *Pastor,* 59–60.

30 **"my core being":** Eugene Peterson, journal, March 10, 2007.

32 **"tried to imitate":** Peterson, *Pastor,* 47. This story is told in *The*

Pastor, 46–49, and multiple other places. Eugene gave Cecil Zachary the name Garrison Johns in this memoir.

32 **"the other cheek":** Romans 12:14, NIV; see Matthew 5:39.

33 **"first Christian convert":** Peterson, *Pastor,* 48.

33 **"died six weeks earlier":** Obituary, Cecil Zachary, *Daily Inter Lake,* October 16, 2006.

37 **"spectacular upsets":** "Flathead Slates Track Meet with Falls Team," *Daily Inter Lake,* April 26, 1950.

37 **"Key club":** "Sports About Town," *Daily Inter Lake,* May 7, 1950.

38 **"who I've become":** Eugene Peterson, journal entry, September 13, 2006.

38 **"exile's boundary experience":** Eugene Peterson, journal entry, August 5, 1990.

39 **"totally puzzled":** Eugene H. Peterson, *Subversive Spirituality* (Grand Rapids, MI: Eerdmans, 1997), 203–4.

39 **"what he did":** Peterson, *Subversive Spirituality,* 203–4.

40 **"that summer":** Peterson, *Pastor,* 74.

40 **"It still is":** Peterson, *Pastor,* 77.

Chapter 5: Great Promise in Seattle

43 The epigraph is taken from Maria Semple, *Where'd You Go, Bernadette?* (New York: Back Bay Books, 2019), 325.

43 **"inside of me":** Gene Peterson, "Prexy's Pen," *Falcon,* June 3, 1954, 2.

44 **"a learned trait":** Ken Peterson and Miles Finch, conversation with the author, June 27, 2017.

44 **"that kind of person":** Gene Peterson, "Prexy's Pen," *Falcon,* November 12, 1953, 2.

44 **"to use it":** Eugene enjoyed explaining his middle name. Whenever someone would see *Eugene H. Peterson* and ask what the *H* stood for, he'd say, "Hoiland was my mother's maiden name, an old surname connected to family farmland (Highland) that her parents left behind after generations had called it home." Then he'd always pause before finishing. "But Jan says I fabricated the story. She says the *H* stands for *hyperbole.*"

45 **Ken Foreman:** Ken Foreman, *A Coach's Journey: From a Sand Lot to the Olympic Stadium* (Mustang, OK: Tate, 2010). Ken coached at SPU for over forty years, sending six athletes to the Olympics and coaching one hundred athletes to all-American honors. He served as head coach of the women's 1980 Olympic squad and of Team USA for the 1983 World Championships in Helsinki and again for the 1986 Goodwill Games in Moscow.

46 **"than I was":** Eugene Peterson, "Incurably Pentecostal," *Pentecostal Evangel,* April 29, 1956, 6.

47 **"alone to bear":** "Death's Price Is Lowered," *Daily Inter Lake,* September 13, 1951, 1.

47 **"stand for it":** "Poor Sentencing," *Daily Inter Lake,* September 18, 1951, 12.

48 **"justifies his action":** Eugene Peterson, "Schroeter Acted Brilliantly," *Daily Inter Lake,* September 17, 1951, 6.

49 **"Eugene's roommates":** Ed Dillery went on to work for the State Department, serving in an influential post with the United Nations and as ambassador to Fiji during the Reagan administration. Don Goertzen and Jim Bellmore shared the second room. Bellmore spent over a half century as a respected pastor, serving a number of churches before retiring. Goertzen became a beloved school principal, and the *Seattle Times* heralded his wife, Irma, an administrator of the University of Washington Medical Center, as "the first woman in the country to run a major teaching school" (Jonathan Martin, "Longtime TV Anchorwoman Kathi Goertzen Dies After Battle with Tumors," *Seattle Times,* August 13, 2012, www.seattletimes.com/seattle-news/longtime-tv -anchorwoman-kathi-goertzen-dies-after-battle-with-tumors). Don and Irma's daughter Kathi became the revered longtime news anchor for Seattle's ABC affiliate and the first local reporter to broadcast from Brandenburg Gate after the fall of the Berlin Wall (Camille Troxel, "New WSU Building Named for Seattle News Anchor Kathi Goertzen," KXLY.com, September 12, 2013, www.kxly.com/new-wsu-building-named-for-seattle-news -anchor-kathi-goertzen). Elmer Bradley and Finney Stiles occupied the third bedroom. Bradley built large sections of

Tempe, Arizona, and served as Tempe's mayor. Finney spent
thirty years in Asia building radio stations with the Far East
Broadcasting Company, followed by a second career as a successful contractor.

50 **"I can't do this"**: This story is culled from personal conversations,
as well as from Eugene's *Under the Unpredictable Plant: An Exploration in Vocational Holiness* (Grand Rapids, MI: Eerdmans,
1992), 184–85.

51 **"stance of wonderment"**: This story is culled from personal conversations, as well as from *Under the Unpredictable Plant*,
182–86.

52 **"between Tawahsi covers"**: *Tawahsi* (Seattle: Seattle Pacific
College, 1953), 92.

52 **at the typewriter**: Ben later wrote several books, including *Baltha-
zar: The Black and Shining Prince* (Westminster, 1974).

52 **"half-past five"**: Gene Peterson, "Prexy's Pen," *Falcon*, February
11, 1954, 2.

53 **"a warm, responsive girl"**: Eugene Peterson, letter, January 1955.

53 **The farmer**: Foreman, *Coach's Journey*, 138–39.

54 **"synchronized rhythm"**: Gene Peterson, "Prexy's Pen," *Falcon*,
January 15, 1954, 2.

56 **"signed in blood"**: Gene Peterson, "Prexy's Pen," *Falcon*,
January 7, 1954, 2.

57 **a voracious mind**: On occasion, Eugene referred to completing a
double major (at times, "religion and philosophy," and at other
times, "philosophy and literature"), though his transcript officially names only philosophy. It took years and a receding memory to make this murky, because in an article he wrote two years
after college, Eugene was clear: "I majored in philosophy."
(Eugene Peterson, "Incurably Pentecostal," *Pentecostal Evangel*,
April 29, 1956, 6.) His student files reveal extensive courses in
both religion and literature, far more than would have been
needed for general degree requirements. Eugene, it appears, hand-
crafted the equivalent of a double major (philosophy and religion, with a heap of literature on top) and over the decades forgot
the actual details of his diploma. Similarly, Ben Moring once told
a newspaper reporter that his major was philosophy and religion,

when his formal degree was religion. Apparently, these two rigorous overachievers concocted their self-designed studies in tandem. However one pieces this together, philosophy—not religion—was Eugene's academic focus.

58 **"not dull"**: In addition to Eugene's "Prexy's Pen" columns, I've pieced this story together through conversations with Eugene, as well as his interview with SPU's *Response* magazine: "Cultivating the Imagination: A Conversation with Eugene Peterson," *Response,* https://spu.edu/depts/uc/response/new/2011-autumn /features/cultivating-the-imagination.asp.

58 **"Chaucer as companion"**: Gene Peterson, "Prexy's Pen," *Falcon,* April 1, 1954, 2.

Chapter 6: Go East, Young Man

60 The epigraph is taken from Denise Levertov, "Overland to the Islands," in *The Collected Poems of Denise Levertov,* ed. Paul A. Lacey and Anne Dewey (New York: New Directions, 2013), 65.

60 **dog sniffing the wind:** See Eugene Peterson, journal entry, May 17, 2009.

61 **253,000 young men:** "Induction Statistics," Selective Service System, www.sss.gov/About/History-And-Records/Induction -Statistics.

66 **"pass over me":** *The Autobiography of Charles G. Finney: The Life Story of America's Greatest Evangelist—in His Own Words* (Bloomington, MN: Bethany, 1977), 21–22. Pat Robertson, in his autobiography, pointed to this Finney passage, revealing how they were reading it in the weeks prior to their trip where they camped near Finney's birthplace.

67 **"did on Finney":** Pat Robertson and Jamie Buckingham, *Shout It from the Housetops! The Autobiography of Pat Robertson* (Alachua, FL: Bridge-Logos, 1972), 63–64.

68 **"not an exaggeration":** Eugene H. Peterson, foreword to *Inductive Bible Study: A Comprehensive Guide to the Practice of Hermeneutics,* by David R. Bauer and Robert A. Traina (Grand Rapids, MI: Baker Academic, 2011), xi.

68 **"words were holy"**: Peterson, foreword to *Inductive Bible Study,*
   xi–xii.

69 **"English Bible"**: Eugene H. Peterson, *The Pastor: A Memoir* (New
   York: HarperOne, 2011), 89.

70 **George Buttrick**: He once wrote to his mother, "I have heard you
   preach sermons that would rival a good many of the Fifth
   Avenue jobs that I've heard." Eugene Peterson, letter, March 17,
   1957.

70 **"largest Presbyterian church"**: Epigraph, "The Life of Jesus
   Christ: In Ten Pictures and One Thousand Words," *Life,* December 28, 1936, 44.

70 **named by *Life:*** "Great Preachers: These 12—and Others—Bring
   Americans Back to the Churches," *Life,* April 6, 1953, 126–32.

71 **blowing his whistle**: If you dig into the dusty archives in Madison
   Avenue Presbyterian's attic, you'll find black-and-white action
   shots of the basketball league, showing young men in their too-
   short shorts boxing out under the net.

71 **"cliché pass his lips"**: Though Eugene referred to a "year of Sundays," it was actually closer to four or five months. Eugene became an intern at Madison Avenue Presbyterian in the fall of
   1954, and Buttrick preached his first sermon at Harvard's Memorial Church (titled "Man's Hurry and God's Patience") on
   January 2, 1955. Thanks to Buttrick's biographer Charles N.
   Davidson for piecing these details together. This short period
   highlights all the more the power of Buttrick's impact.

71 **"orgy of denunciation"**: George A. Buttrick, *Jesus Came Preaching: Christian Preaching in the New Age* (New York: Charles
   Scribner's Sons, 1931), 163.

72 **"all the more powerful"**: Frederick Buechner, quoted in Ben Pat-
   terson, "Door Interview: Frederick Buechner," *Wittenburg Door,*
   December 1979–January 1980, 17.

72 **"when he spoke"**: John Killinger, "George A. Buttrick: Discipline
   and Style," *Christian Century,* February 1990, 147.

72 **"voice of an old nurse"**: Frederick Buechner, *The Alphabet of
   Grace* (New York: HarperCollins, 1970), 44.

72 **thirsty man to water**: Chad Wriglesworth's article "George A.
   Buttrick and Frederick Buechner: Messengers of Reconciling

Laughter" published in *Christianity and Literature* 53, no. 1
(Autumn 2003) was immensely helpful in orienting Buechner's
relationship with Buttrick and served to point me to numerous
sources.

73 **"touched so deeply"**: Frederick Buechner, *The Sacred Journey: A
Memoir of Early Days* (New York: HarperCollins, 1982), 108–9.
More can be found on Buechner's gratitude to Buttrick in Freder-
ick Buechner, *Now and Then: A Memoir of Vocation* (New York:
HarperCollins, 1983).

73 **"and great laughter"**: Buechner, *Alphabet of Grace*, 44.

73 **"across the face"**: Buechner, *Alphabet of Grace*, 44.

73 **majestic view over Central Park**: Eugene remembered this penthouse as Buttrick's home, the manse owned by the church. However, according to Buttrick biographer Charles N. Davidson,
Buttrick's son David explained that Madison Avenue Presbyterian
never had a manse on Fifth Avenue, though a number of the
church members had Fifth Avenue homes. Likely, Buttrick's
Sunday evening gatherings were hosted by a church member, with
this fact slipping from Eugene's memory. Or it's possible that
Eugene remembered meeting in the Buttrick home at Twenty-One
East Seventy-Ninth Street, only a block from Fifth Avenue—a location that would have afforded a wonderful view of the park
even if not directly on the fabled avenue.

74 **"become gospel"**: Peterson, *Pastor*, 86–87.

75 **"things are . . . nebulous"**: Eugene Peterson, letter, no date.

77 **"released from it"**: Eugene Peterson, letter, no date.

Chapter 7: Getting It Lived

78 The epigraph is taken from Eugene Peterson, letter, February 13
[year unknown].

80 **"sown seed"**: Eugene Peterson, letter, February 13 [year un-
known].

80 **"an adjunct"**: Eugene H. Peterson, *The Pastor: A Memoir* (New
York: HarperOne, 2011), 162.

80 **"real world again"**: Eugene Peterson, letter, no date.

80 **"you can lead them"**: Eugene Peterson, letter, no date.

81 **"across coffee cups"**: Eugene Peterson, letter, no date.

81 **"his friend destroyed"**: Peterson, *Pastor,* 163.

82 **"squeezed out of him"**: Peterson, *Pastor,* 164, augmented by a personal conversation with Eugene.

83 **"getting it lived"**: Peterson, *Pastor,* 90.

83 **"all religious practice"**: Eugene Peterson, "Incurably Pentecostal," *Pentecostal Evangel,* April 29, 1956, 6. This is the first time I found Eugene using *earthy,* a word he used with a measure of disdain but would later employ often and with great affection.

84 **"a Pentecostal service"**: Peterson, "Incurably Pentecostal," 6.

85 **"I write them"**: Eugene Peterson, letter, February 20 [year unknown].

85 **"don't you think"**: Eugene Peterson, letter, January 14 [year unknown].

86 **"about it"**: Eugene Peterson, letter, January 14 [year unknown].

86 **Harald Bredesen**: Eugene described meeting with Bredesen, "a Lutheran minister who has had most remarkable experiences under the leadership of the Holy Spirit. He talked with some of us for about three hours as he recounted spectacular circumstances." As Bredesen (who would be instrumental in guiding Pat Robertson and Pat Boone) spoke, there was "a great hunger for the baptism by most of those present that night." At the end of the evening, Bredesen "asked if we wanted a tarry service for the H.S. next Tuesday night. Everyone wanted to." Eugene wrote on, chronicling each person present that evening and noting how each was prepared for "the Holy Spirit . . . [to] be outpoured in a great way." Among them were Bob Walker ("editor in chief of *Christian Life* magazine, [who] received the baptism and is busily preaching it to close acquaintances"), Pat Robertson ("graduate of Yale Law School . . . now a student at Biblical . . . seeking the baptism"), Donn Crail ("desperate for the Holy Spirit"), and Dick Simmons ("a Presbyterian, confused, discouraged and completely open to the invading presence of the Spirit"). Eugene Peterson, letter, May 12, 1957.

87 **"wait for the headlines"**: Eugene Peterson, letter, May 12, 1957.

88 **"believed it still"**: Peterson, *Pastor,* 214.

89 **"expanded exponentially"**: Eugene shared this story in a conversation with me, as well as in *The Pastor,* 87–89.

90 **"began to be felt"**: Eugene Peterson, letter, November 25, 1956. This notion of a radical or intense spirituality shows up in other letters as well.

90 **silence as an essential antidote**: Thanks to Trygve Johnson, who helped me see this connection.

90 **"revolutionary ways"**: Eugene Peterson, letter, November 25, 1956.

91 **"in the city"**: Eugene Peterson, letter, February 28 [year unknown].

93 **"about it now"**: Eugene Peterson, letter, no date. The line in the letter where Eugene said he was looking forward to a pastorate works against his insistence that he never wanted to be a pastor—and never thought seriously about it—until later. However, is it possible that Eugene wrote this way to his mom (always naming pastoral ministry as a possibility) because he thought it was her expectation or hope? Or was Eugene genuinely more mixed in his desires at this time than he remembered?

94 **"convince the world"**: Eugene Peterson, letter, February 5 [year unknown].

94 **"for lone wolves"**: Adapted from Peterson, *Pastor,* 91.

94 **"no ties please"**: Eugene Peterson, letter, May 5, 1957.

95 **"Near Eastern studies"**: Wikipedia, s.v. "William F. Albright," last modified February 3, 2020, https://en.wikipedia.org/wiki/William_F._Albright.

97 **"vibrant with energy"**: Peterson, *Pastor,* 64.

97 **"lectures and seminars"**: Peterson, *Pastor,* 64.

Chapter 8: The Long Married

101 The epigraph is taken from Thomas Merton, *The Seven Storey Mountain* (New York: Harcourt, Brace, 1976), 150.

103 **"Delta's most progressive citizen"**: "Vincent G. Stubbs, Delta, Victim of a Vicious Horse," *York Daily,* September 29, 1905, 6.

103 **"to the porch"**: Janice Peterson, *Becoming Gertrude: How Our*

Friendships Shape Our Faith (Colorado Springs: NavPress, 2018), xiv.

104 **Alabama College:** Alabama College is now the University of Montevallo.

105 **Bob's Jeep:** This story is pieced together from conversations with Eugene and Jan and from sections in *The Pastor.*

107 **"such idiocy":** Eugene H. Peterson, *The Pastor: A Memoir* (New York: HarperOne, 2011), 94.

109 **"ingenuous response":** Eugene Peterson, letter, January 20, 1958.

110 **"this presbytery":** Eugene Peterson, letter, June 2, 1958.

112 **"professor on sabbatical":** Peterson, *Pastor,* 19.

113 **Wiseman:** Jerry Van Marter, "Bill Wiseman Is Dead at 91: Tulsa Pastor Mentored Generations of Justice, Peace Advocates," Presbyterian Church (USA), July 15, 2010, www.pcusa.org /news/2010/7/15/bill-wiseman-dead-91.

114 **"pastoral prayers":** "Dr. William Johnston Wiseman, S.T.D., D.D.," *Tulsa World,* July 16, 2010, www.tulsaworld.com/archive /dr-william-johnston-wiseman-s-t-d-d-d/article_253e3563-5c19 -52de-8b58-7b01eea6820f.html.

116 **"crowded sidewalk":** Peterson, *Pastor,* 21.

116 **"waffles and yogurt":** Peterson, *Pastor,* 68.

117 **"stifling sectarianism":** Peterson, *Pastor,* 69.

118 **"sing and pray with":** Peterson, *Pastor,* 96–97.

118 **"prospect without Jan":** Peterson, *Pastor,* 97.

Chapter 9: I Think I'm a Pastor

120 The epigraph is taken from Frederick Buechner, *Wishful Thinking: A Seeker's ABC* (New York: HarperCollins, 1973), 73.

122 **"go barefoot":** Eugene H. Peterson, *The Pastor: A Memoir* (New York: HarperOne, 2011), 114–15.

123 **inkling of interest:** Peterson, *Pastor,* 105–6.

124 **"financial services":** Peterson, *Pastor,* 112.

124 **"you will speak":** Pieced together from multiple stories and conversations.

126 **"American stereotypes"**: Peterson, *Pastor,* 114.
128 **confessing his fiction:** Much of this story can be found in Peterson, *Pastor,* 198–200, as well as in Eugene H. Peterson, *Under the Unpredictable Plant: An Exploration in Vocational Holiness* (Grand Rapids, MI: Eerdmans, 1992), 77–80.
129 **"for my vocation"**: Peterson, *Under the Unpredictable Plant,* 80.
130 **"hymn-of-the-month"**: This is a scattered collection of notes from the 1975 issues of *Amen!*
130 **adored Elvis:** To protect pastoral confidences, Eugene, within his writing, chose to alter the identities of some individuals. At times, I have done the same.
130 **"scraping a chalkboard"**: Peterson, *Pastor,* 121.
130 **"*get* to choose them"**: Peterson, *Pastor,* 128.
132 **"to worship God"**: Peterson, *Pastor,* 136, 141.
134 **"doesn't it? Ha!"**: Jan Peterson, letter, February 13, 1965.

Chapter 10: Staying Put

135 The epigraph is taken from Scott Russell Sanders, *Staying Put: Making a Home in a Restless World* (Boston: Beacon, 1993), 54.
135 **"my blood stream"**: Eugene H. Peterson, *The Pastor: A Memoir* (New York: HarperOne, 2011), 202–3.
137 **"a failed pastor"**: Peterson, *Pastor,* 203–7.
138 **"God refreshed them"**: Eugene Peterson, letter, March 28, 1968.
139 **"don't see it"**: Eugene Peterson, letter, May 13, 1968.
141 **"cross-country workouts"**: Peterson, *Pastor,* 233.
141 **"say anything"**: Peterson, *Pastor,* 234.
141 **"Marathon Monday"**: Jay Apperson, "He Preaches on Sunday, Runs in Marathon Monday," *Harford Sun,* April 15, 1984, 18.
141 **"felt like it"**: Peterson, *Pastor,* 234.
142 **"contemplative pastor"**: Peterson, *Pastor,* 210–12.
144 **"this damn church"**: Peterson, *Pastor,* 145.
145 **"they lost interest"**: Peterson, *Pastor,* 148.
146 **"participant in the story"**: Peterson, *Pastor,* 227.
146 **"autobiographical to me"**: Peterson, *Pastor,* 200.

Chapter 11: Pure Mercy

148 The epigraph is taken from Annie Dillard, *Holy the Firm* (New York: Harper & Row, 1977), 62.

148 **Karen had been counting:** Eugene H. Peterson, *The Pastor: A Memoir* (New York: HarperOne, 2011), 277. In *Under the Unpredictable Plant,* Karen tells him he's been gone thirty-eight nights, but in *The Pastor,* it's twenty-seven.

150 **and walked out:** This story is pieced together from conversations and *The Pastor,* 277–79.

153 **"week ago Saturday":** Eugene Peterson, letter, December 23, 1969.

153 **"culture of hospitality":** Peterson, *Pastor,* 258.

154 **"small hallway closet":** And there were copious awards: multiple Gold Medallion and Platinum Book Awards, a Book of the Decade award, a Readers' Choice award, several Book of the Year and Author of the Year awards, SPU's Alumnus of the Year, and the David Steele Distinguished Writer Award—just for starters.

154 **Newman answered:** Peterson, *Pastor,* 224.

155 **"to be fixed":** Peterson, *Pastor,* 226.

157 **"the two of us":** Eugene Peterson, letter, April 16, 1968.

157 **"having a coke":** Eugene Peterson, letter, May 27, 1969.

160 **"to beat him":** Eugene Peterson, letter, April 14, 1980.

162 **shared letters:** Eric Peterson published these letters in *Letters to a Young Pastor: Timothy Conversations Between Father and Son* and in a companion volume, *Letters to a Young Congregation: Nurturing the Growth of a Faithful Church* (both NavPress, 2020), containing letters Eric wrote to his church, Colbert Presbyterian.

163 **"I am experiencing":** Eric Peterson, letter, April 25, 1991.

164 **"A second chance":** Eric Peterson, letter, April 26, 1991.

165 **"didn't see me":** Eugene H. Peterson, *Traveling Light: Modern Meditations on St. Paul's Letter of Freedom* (Colorado Springs: Helmers & Howard, 1988), 148.

166 **"through the winter":** Jan Peterson, letter, August 23, 1974.

167 **"way with me":** Eugene Peterson, letter, February 6, 1968.

Chapter 12: Words Made Flesh

169 The epigraph is taken from Barry Lopez, quoted in Fred Bahnson, "The World We Still Have: Barry Lopez on Restoring Our Lost Intimacy with Nature," *Sun,* December 2019, www.thesun magazine.org/issues/528/the-world-we-still-have.

169 **"vocation was bipolar"**: Eugene H. Peterson, *Under the Unpredictable Plant: An Exploration in Vocational Holiness* (Grand Rapids, MI: Eerdmans, 1992), 48.

169 **"your glory. Amen"**: Eugene Peterson, journal entry, January 7, 1986.

170 **"how to live"**: Peterson, *Under the Unpredictable Plant,* 47.

171 **"at that time"**: Peterson, *Under the Unpredictable Plant,* 57.

171 **"make happen"**: Peterson, *Under the Unpredictable Plant,* 60.

172 **"not an analyzer"**: Luci Shaw, "A Conversation with Eugene Peterson," *Image,* no. 62, https://imagejournal.org/article/conversation-Eugene-peterson.

172 **"pointed applications"**: Stephen Board, letter to Eugene Peterson, December 16, 1975.

172 **"at your essay"**: Harold Lindsell, letter to Eugene Peterson, February 12, 1976.

173 *Growing Up with Your Teenager:* Eerdmans now publishes this book under the title *Like Dew Your Youth: Growing Up with Your Teenager.*

173 **"to sell it"**: Years later, Eerdmans reissued *Five Smooth Stones.*

175 **"to be noticed"**: Eugene Peterson, journal entry, October 29, 1984.

175 **"not an achievement"**: Eugene Peterson, journal entry, February 25, 1985.

176 **"not entirely free"**: Eugene Peterson, journal entry, October 6, 1984.

176 **"let on to me"**: Eugene Peterson, journal entry, October 7, 1984.

177 **"ideas and information"**: Eugene Peterson, journal entry, October 8, 1984.

177 **"much more deliberately"**: Eugene Peterson, journal entry, October 8, 1984.

177 **"play my banjo"**: Eugene Peterson, journal entry, January 1, 1985.

178 **"more than enough"**: Eugene H. Peterson, *The Pastor: A Memoir* (New York: HarperOne, 2011), 293.

179 **"an integrating dream"**: Eugene Peterson, journal entry, May 18, 1989.

179 **"vocation as a pastor"**: Peterson, *Pastor,* 28.

180 **"he expressed them"**: Eugene Peterson, journal entry, June 21, 1993.

180 **"crowded, uncreative"**: Eugene Peterson, journal entry, January 10, 1985.

180 **"wanting me to do"**: Eugene Peterson, journal entry, March 28, 1985.

181 **"nearly 100 countries"**: Steve Chawkins, "Russ Reid Dies at 82; Creator of Pioneering World Vision Infomercials," *Los Angeles Times,* December 14, 2013, www.latimes.com/local/obituaries /la-xpm-2013-dec-14-la-me-russ-reid-20131215-story.html.

182 **"by prayer"**: Eugene Peterson, letter, August 28, 1985.

Chapter 13: Living at the Margins

183 The epigraph is taken from Wendell Berry, *The Memory of Old Jack* (Washington, DC: Counterpoint, 1999), 143.

183 **"the integration of worlds"**: Eugene Peterson, journal entry, April 6, 1985.

184 **"though temporary"**: Eugene Peterson, journal entry, May 18, 1985.

185 **"something quite different"**: Eugene H. Peterson, *Working the Angles: The Shape of Pastoral Integrity* (Grand Rapids, MI: Eerdmans, 1987), 9–11.

185 **"brain both"**: Eugene Peterson, journal entry, May 18, 1985.

186 **"better about it"**: Eugene Peterson, journal entry, June 2, 1985.

187 **"back to obedience"**: Eugene Peterson, journal entry, January 1, 1986.

187 **"get it right"**: Eugene Peterson, journal entry, January 29, 1986.

188 **"cottonwoods and willows"**: Eugene Peterson, journal entry, October 9, 1986.

188 **"middle of a parish"**: Eugene Peterson, journal entry, October 9, 1986.

189 **"few of them"**: Eugene Peterson, journal entry, May 24, 1985.

191 **"home than here"**: Eugene Peterson, journal entry, August 21, 1988.

191 **"be a saint"**: Eugene Peterson, journal entry, July 13, 1988.

191 **"your vocabulary"**: Eugene Peterson, journal entry, October 23, 1994.

192 **"in action"**: Eugene Peterson, journal entry, October 15, 1992.

193 **"Christ Our King"**: Eugene Peterson, journal entry, July 15, 1988.

193 **"for very long"**: Eugene Peterson, journal entry, August 15, 1988, pieced with additional entry.

193 **"wounds of loneliness"**: Eugene Peterson, journal entry, July 21, 1988.

194 **"they are making"**: Eugene Peterson, journal entry, May 14, 1990.

194 **"top number"**: Eugene Peterson, journal entry, July 2, 1990.

195 **"like this—overwhelming"**: Eugene Peterson, journal entry, March 11, 1989.

Chapter 14: The Long Obedience

196 The epigraph is taken from Wallace Stegner, *The Spectator Bird* (New York: Vintage Books, 1976), 203.

196 **"you've ever seen"**: Thank you to Tracie Bullis for this colorful story.

197 **"deliberately decided"**: Eugene Peterson, journal entry, July 27, 1988.

197 **"my icon spouse"**: Eugene Peterson, journal entry, August 23, 1988.

197 **"in me"**: Eugene Peterson, journal entry, July 17, 1990.

198 **"heaven's envoy"**: Eugene Peterson, journal entry, August 1, 1988.

199 **"indulgent of them"**: Eugene Peterson, journal entry, July 5, 1990.

199 **"after Eugene"**: This is different from some of Jan's journal entries, where she said she believed the woman had no guile and was not attempting to drive a wedge in the marriage or do anything sordid.

200 **"myself, to myself"**: Eugene Peterson, journal entry, May 14, 1990.

200 "with his enthusiasms": Jan Peterson, journal entry, November 28, 1990.
201 "self-censoring": Eugene Peterson, journal entry, November 22, 1992.
201 "over the cliff": Jan Peterson, journal entry, November 27, 1990.
202 "onto thin ice": Eugene Peterson, journal entry, January 25, 2005.
202 "rejection—of divorce": Eugene Peterson, journal entry, January 25, 2005.
202 "might have occurred": Jan Peterson, journal entry, December 28, 1990.
202 "gracious rescue": Eugene Peterson, journal entry, September 15, 2005.
202 "and love me": Jan Peterson, journal entry, June 1, 1991.
204 "hopes and expectations": Eugene Peterson, journal entry, July 9, 1988.
205 "ways of holiness": Eugene Peterson, journal entry, August 15, 1988.
205 "in this pen": Eugene Peterson, journal entry, July 22, 1988.
206 "I cannot live": Eugene Peterson, journal entry, February 4, 1988.
206 "from writing *well*": Eugene Peterson, journal entry, April 5, 1989.
206 "Too ambitious? Prideful": Eugene Peterson, journal entry, June 5, 1989.
206 "into the parish": Eugene Peterson, journal entry, April 18, 1991.
209 "Jesus Christ": Eugene Peterson, *Amen!*, July 24, 1991.
209 "might be fulfilled": Eugene Peterson, journal entry, July 24, 1991.
209 "mind and body": Eugene Peterson, journal entry, November 28, 1992.

Chapter 15: So Lucky

213 The epigraph is taken from Eugene Peterson, journal entry, June 21, 1994.
215 "life into harvest": Eugene Peterson, journal entry, May 24, 1990.
215 "koine American": Eugene Peterson, letter, October 9, 1990.
219 "worth doing here": Eugene Peterson, journal entry, October 6, 1990.

219 "Hearty company": Eugene Peterson, journal entry, October 10, 1990.

220 "trusted with this": Eugene Peterson, journal entry, March 29, 1992.

220 "lose their shirts": Eugene Peterson, journal entry, April 19, 1992.

221 "working in the 'corner' ": Eugene Peterson, journal, September 10, 1992.

221 "form a democracy": Richard Foster, quoted in "The Chrysostom Society: A Brief History," September 28, 1999, unpublished.

222 "bear fruit": Eugene Peterson, journal entry, March 3, 1993.

223 "guru-itis": Eugene Peterson, journal entry, September 12, 1990.

223 "marriage and vocation": Eugene Peterson, journal entry, December 17, 1992.

223 "trek to Moriah": Eugene Peterson, journal entry, December 28, 1992.

224 "to find that": Eugene Peterson, journal entry, December 28, 1992.

228 "be prayed for": W. David O. Taylor, "A Prayer for Beginnings and Endings," *Diary of an Arts Pastor* (blog), April 17, 2016, https://artspastor.blogspot.com/2016/04/a-prayer-for-beginnings-and-endings.html.

230 "into the picture": W. David O. Taylor, "In Memory of Eugene Peterson (1932–2018)," *Diary of an Arts Pastor* (blog), October 24, 2018, https://artspastor.blogspot.com/2018/10/in-memory-of-Eugene-peterson-1932-2018.html.

230 "kept himself aloof": Taylor, "Prayer for Beginnings and Endings."

231 "the bivouac, the danger": Eugene Peterson, journal entry, May 3, 1993.

232 "the imagination": Eugene Peterson, letter, April 12, 2001.

232 "non-recognition": Eugene Peterson, journal entry, April 17, 1993.

232 "talk of the town": Eugene Peterson, journal entry, July 5, 1993.

233 "not a professor": Eugene Peterson, journal entry, November 12, 1995.

233 "aspect to it": Eugene Peterson, journal entry, December 3, 1993.

233 "more than I live": Eugene Peterson, journal entry, July 24, 1996.

233 **"teach on it"**: Eugene Peterson, journal entry, January 30, 1997.

233 **"out of circulation"**: Eugene Peterson, journal entry, April 20, 1996.

234 **"I'm interested"**: Eugene Peterson, journal entry, June 6, 1996.

235 **"the Beam-decision"**: Eugene Peterson, journal entry, March 9, 1992.

235 **"into the vow"**: Eugene Peterson, journal entry, March 12, 1992.

235 **"only solution"**: Eugene Peterson, journal entry, April 12, 1993.

236 **"that way too"**: Eugene Peterson, journal entry, October 31, 2009.

236 **"sharp or taut"**: Eugene Peterson, journal entry, date unavailable.

236 **"in body"**: Eugene Peterson, journal entry, December 31, 1994.

236 **"night's rest"**: Eugene Peterson, journal entry, July 16, 1995.

237 **"evangelical ethos"**: Eugene Peterson, journal entry, date unavailable.

238 **"over-use of the term"**: Eugene Peterson, journal entries, November 13–14, 1993.

238 **"clear-cut for me"**: Eugene Peterson, journal entry, May 25, 1995.

239 **"reverent being present"**: Eugene Peterson, letter, May 11, 2005.

239 **"as a dying person"**: Eugene Peterson, journal entry, August 5, 1997.

Chapter 16: Monastery in Montana

240 The epigraph is taken from T. S. Eliot, "Little Gidding," in *Collected Poems: 1909–1962* (New York: Harcourt, Brace, 1963), 208.

241 **"tin ear"**: Eugene Peterson, journal entry, no date.

242 **"vernacular American"**: Eugene Peterson, letter, December 9, 2006.

242 **"the better"**: Eugene Peterson, letter, September 6, 2000.

243 **"felt like doing"**: Judges 21:25, MSG.

243 ***Jeopardy!* question"**: The question was "*The Message* Bible brings a prize-winning heifer to the prodigal son's feast instead of this familiar phrase."

244 **"Bye"**: Letter to Eugene Peterson, August 5, 2002.

244 **"witches, etc."**: Eugene Peterson, email, June 2, 2015.

245 **"on your side":** Eugene Peterson, journal entry, March 15, 1994.

245 **"in our culture":** Eugene Peterson, letter, August 14, 2002.

246 **"you are ready":** Eugene Peterson, email, June 2, 2015.

246 **"all the time":** Eugene Peterson, journal entry, September 7, 2006.

247 **"humous of Montana":** Eugene Peterson, journal entry, September 3, 2009.

248 **"a stray dog":** Eugene Peterson, journal entry, date unavailable.

248 **"prominent among them":** Eugene Peterson, journal entry, date unavailable.

249 **"mature holiness now":** Eugene Peterson, journal entry, June 16, 1993.

249 **"the sensuality":** Rodney Clapp described this same scene with Eugene that I—and surely numerous others—encountered.

249 **"God, pray":** Eugene Peterson, journal entry, August 1, 2005.

250 **"prepare to die":** Eugene Peterson, journal entry, March 18, 1997.

250 **"to be *herself*":** Eugene Peterson, journal entry, April 12, 1993.

250 **"husband/father/writer/prayer":** Eugene Peterson, journal entry, June 21, 1993.

251 **"these next years":** Eugene Peterson, journal entry, March 14, 1992.

251 **"same old thing":** Eugene Peterson, journal entry, June 30, 2006.

252 **"wilderness back pack":** Eugene Peterson, journal entry, August 6, 2005.

253 **"few days ago":** Eugene Peterson, journal entry, January 1, 2010.

254 **"derives from it":** Eugene Peterson, journal entry, September 12, 1993.

254 **"My son, My son":** Eugene Peterson, journal entry, date unavailable.

256 **"on his staff":** Eugene Peterson, letter, March 8, 2002.

256 **"not less, likely":** Bono, foreword to *The Message 100,* by Eugene H. Peterson (Colorado Springs: NavPress, 2015).

257 **"books were written":** "People of the Year: Bono," *Rolling Stone,* November 16, 2001, www.atu2.com/news/article/people-of-the-year-bono.html.

257 **"effing Bono":** Eugene Peterson, letter, January 23, 2002.

257 **crowd roared:** Eugene Peterson, interview by Dean Nelson,

Writer's Symposium by the Sea, Point Loma Nazarene University, February 23, 2007, YouTube video, 13:33–13:56, www.youtube.com/watch?v=FaaIui7cESs.

258 **"a celebrity"**: Eugene Peterson, journal entry, October 3, 2009.

259 **covering his ears**: While rock concerts were new for Eugene, music was a deep love of Eugene's. From the cornet to the banjo, to the many nights Jan and Eugene spent together at the symphony, music was always essential. "I don't think [it can be] emphasized too much the role that music plays . . ." Eugene wrote, "music as an artistic expression of man's feelings, thoughts and culture." Journal entry, date unavailable.

259 **"unobtrusive Christian witness"**: Eugene Peterson, journal entry, October 13, 2009.

260 **"modern ear"**: Bono continued to talk about *The Message*. In an interview following his harrowing bike accident, he referred to a portion of Psalm 18 as "one of those psalms of David that has been translated into a modern idiom by this man called Eugene Peterson—great writer." Jann S. Wenner, "Bono: The Rolling Stone Interview: U2's Frontman on the State of His Band, the State of the World and What He Learned from Almost Dying," *Rolling Stone,* December 27, 2017, www.rollingstone.com/music/music-features/bono-the-rolling-stone-interview-3-203774.

Chapter 17: A Weathered but Holy Shape

262 The epigraph is taken from Eugene Peterson, journal entry, February 5, 2008.

262 **"at leisure"**: Eugene Peterson, journal entry, October 21, 1995.

263 **"occur to you"**: Eugene Peterson, letter, April 21, 2008.

263 **"praying, not knowing"**: Eugene Peterson, journal entry, December 24, 1994.

264 **"this living"**: Eugene H. Peterson, *Christ Plays in Ten Thousand Places: A Conversation in Spiritual Theology* (Grand Rapids, MI: Eerdmans, 2005), 3.

264 **"ordinary life"**: Eugene Peterson, letter, May 23, 2002.

264 **taught at Regent**: A publisher approached Eugene about collect-

ing and editing his class notes, but he wasn't interested in that. He'd agreed to allow *The Unnecessary Pastor,* cowritten with Marva Dawn, to be culled from notes, and he didn't care for the results. "I can write better than that," he said.

264 **"text for spirituality"**: Eugene Peterson, letter, August 22, 2000. Once he completed the mammoth project, Eugene provided retrospective context for the "comprehensive re-orientation" he had aimed for: "(1) a Trinitarian theological framework for everything; (2) a rigorous biblical orientation in both OT and NT texts; (3) an incarnational focus in Jesus; (4) a hermeneutic that takes seriously the way metaphor and story work in contrast to the literal that evangelicals often get hung up on; (5) an immersion in the reality of church (not the individual) as the context in which all this is carried out. And all of it in a conversational, relational language that any layperson can understand." Eugene Peterson, letter, November 14, 2013.

266 **slashed and chiseled:** Eugene read this quote in *Emperor of the Earth* and felt resonance with his attempt to tell his own story: "I had to return to myself, to learn how to outline my own hidden convictions, my own real faith, and through this to pay witness. It's a lot of work and I haven't yet learned how to do it." Czeslaw Milosz, *Emperor of the Earth: Modes of Eccentric Vision* (Berkeley: University of California Press, 1977), 14.

267 **"but unnoticed"**: Eugene Peterson, journal entry, August 29, 2009.

268 **"steel my resolve"**: Eugene Peterson, journal entry, June 12, 2009.

269 **"become more ourselves"**: Eugene Peterson, letter, September 6, 2006.

269 **"touch of absurdity"**: Eugene Peterson, letter, September 5, 2004.

270 **"loneliness was unavoidable"**: Eugene Peterson, letter, January 2, 2012.

270 **"soul and Christ"**: Eugene Peterson, letter, date unavailable.

270 **"feel good"**: Eugene Peterson, letter, date unavailable.

270 **"you the better"**: Eugene Peterson, journal entry, August 9, 2006.

271 **"these days"**: Eugene Peterson, letter, March 20, 2008.

271 **"them to me"**: Eugene Peterson, letter, December 2, 2008.

272 **"gesture and hint"**: Eugene Peterson, letter, date unavailable.

272 **"cannot be hurried"**: "The Business of Making Saints: An
Interview with Eugene H. Peterson," *Leadership Journal,*
Spring 1997, 23, 26–27, www.christianitytoday.com/pastors/1997
/spring/7l220a.html.

273 **"most of the time"**: Eugene Peterson, letter, date unavailable.

274 **"to deal with"**: Eugene Peterson, letter, June 5, 2013.

275 **he should do:** This should not be misconstrued to mean that
Eugene thought people could do whatever they felt like doing.
One dynamic speaker who was paired up with him at a seminary
conference troubled him. He wrote, "I was pounding away on the
need to take all our experience, whatever it is, with absolute seriousness, honoring and giving dignity to whatever comes into our
lives. But that it is never authoritative for the living of our lives—
only God is sovereign authority. Meanwhile she was pounding
away in alternate lectures that our experience is our only authority . . . and scripture must be conformed to and submitted to that
authority." Eugene Peterson, letter, February 11, 2000.

275 **"not doctrinaire"**: Eugene Peterson, letter, date unavailable.

276 **"Augustine particularly"**: Eugene Peterson, letter, date unavailable.

276 **"in algebra"**: Eugene Peterson, letter, October 24, 2006.

277 **"work. Sorry"**: Eugene Peterson, letter, April 14, 2008.

277 **"that fight"**: Eugene Peterson, journal entry, January 27, 2010.

278 **"dogma-rocks"**: Eugene Peterson, letter, March 18, 2011.

279 **"pulling us into"**: Eugene Peterson, letter, March 22, 2000.

279 **"mature pastors"**: Eugene Peterson, letter, September 5, 2006.

280 **"boycott at least"**: Eugene Peterson, letter, February 22, 2000.

280 **"for our leader"**: Eugene Peterson, letter, February 23, 2016.

281 **Czeslaw Milosz: *ketman*:** Eugene learned this concept from Milosz's *Captive Mind.* He explored this concept in multiple places,
but his most in-depth and extended conversation along these
themes was with Arthur Boers.

281 **"inner dissent"**: Thanks to Arthur Boers for this concise summary of a tricky concept.

281 **"secret society"**: Eugene Peterson, letter, date unavailable.

282 **"accept each other"**: Eugene Peterson, letter, June 23, 2012.

283 **"among straights"**: Eugene Peterson, letter, date unavailable.

283 **"many last night"**: Eugene Peterson, journal entry, October 14, 2003.

284 **"God's policemen"**: Eugene Peterson, letter, March 6, 2012.

284 **"the sanctuary"**: Eugene Peterson, letter, January 8, 2010.

285 **"unity of the church"**: Eugene Peterson, letter, March 18, 2011.

285 **"have to vote"**: Eugene Peterson, letter, July 20, 2011.

286 **"I don't understand"**: Eugene Peterson, letter, July 17, 2011.

286 **"honestly as a pastor"**: Eugene Peterson, letter, October 8, 2012.

287 **"on their side"**: Thomas W. Currie, "Muddled in the Middle: Reflections on a Presbytery Vote," *Presbyterian Outlook* 193, no. 9, June 27, 2011, https://pres-outlook.org/2011/06/muddled-in-the-middle-reflections-on-a-presbytery-vote. Currie's conclusions ran sideways of most everyone: "The people on the 'right' who have 'Scripture on their side' know something important, something they do not always articulate or express well, and that is, that following Jesus Christ costs something. They are also right to be suspicious of the ways in which our church accommodates a culture of sexual permissiveness. They may not perceive so clearly the ways in which their use of Scripture or even attitudes toward human sexuality are also captive to the culture. We Presbyterians, even we conservative Presbyterians, divorce a lot. We have affairs. Most abuse of women and children is not instigated by homosexuals. There is precious little room for anyone to throw rocks.

And the people on the left know some important things too, namely, that Scripture is never enough, that the Word became flesh, not a disembodied principle or a moral idea but flesh, and the church is not finally a debating society or the collection of the righteous but the dysfunctional family that Christ insists upon calling his own body. These issues are never 'settled' and they have the capacity to cause deeper hurt and great bitterness."

287 **marriage to Elizabeth:** After Eric and Lynn's divorce, Eric married Elizabeth.

287 **"against credentials"**: Ted Kooser and Jim Harrison, *Braided Creek: A Conversation in Poetry* (Port Townsend, WA: Copper Canyon, 2003), back cover.

288 **"happening a lot"**: Eugene Peterson, letter, date unavailable.

289 **"hasn't happened"**: Eugene Peterson, letter, February 20, 2006.

289 **"think I am"**: Eugene Peterson, journal entry, May 27, 2007.

289 **"our long obedience"**: Eugene Peterson, journal entry, June 20, 2009.

291 **"I've ever known"**: Eric Peterson, letter, July 17, 2017.

291 **"no integrity"**: Jonathan Merritt, "Eugene Peterson on Donald Trump and the State of American Christianity," Religion News Service, July 11, 2017, https://religionnews.com/2017/07/11 /eugene-peterson-on-donald-trump-and-the-state-of-american -christianity."

293 **EP: Yes.**: Jonathan Merritt, "Eugene Peterson on Changing His Mind About Same-Sex Issues and Marriage," Religion News Service, July 12, 2017, https://religionnews.com/2017/07/12 /Eugene-peterson-on-changing-his-mind-about-same-sex-issues -and-marriage.

296 **"as possible: *yes*"**: Eric Peterson, letter, July 17, 2017.

297 **"or his ministry"**: Jonathan Merritt, "RNS Best of 2017: Eugene Peterson Backtracks on Same-Sex Marriage," Religion News Service, December 31, 2017, https://religionnews.com/2017/12/31 /Eugene-peterson-backtracks-on-same-sex-marriage-2.

300 **"they're a saint"**: *Peterson: In-Between the Man and the Message,* directed by Greg Fromholz, produced by Emma Good and Nathan Reilly, executive producer Don Pape (Colorado Springs, CO: NavPress, 2016), YouTube, 18:43, www.youtube.com /watch?v=LaMgIvbXqSk.

300 **interacting with persons:** "My interpretation," Eric said, "is that he was in a very thin place, and the veil between earth and heaven had been removed. The clouds were parted for him, and he saw people we can only presume were welcoming him into paradise."

300 **"step an arrival"**: Denise Levertov, "Overland to the Islands," in *The Collected Poems of Denise Levertov,* ed. Paul A. Lacey and Anne Dewey (New York: New Directions, 2013), 65.

302 **"the Fisher Christ"**: The text of this song is available in *Holy Luck,* though for that volume he changed the poem's title to "Ballad to the Fisher King." Eugene H. Peterson, *Holy Luck* (Grand Rapids, MI: Eerdmans, 2013), 74–75.

Coda

303 **"absences become Presence":** Eugene H. Peterson, "Hospitality," in *Holy Luck* (Grand Rapids, MI: Eerdmans, 2013), 46.

306 **"church today":** Jason Byassee and L. Roger Owens, eds., *Pastoral Work: Engagements with the Vision of Eugene Peterson* (Eugene, OR: Cascade Books, 2014), back cover.

ABOUT THE AUTHOR

In addition to *A Burning in My Bones*, WINN COLLIER has authored four books (*Restless Faith, Let God: The Transforming Wisdom of François Fénelon, Holy Curiosity,* and *Love Big, Be Well*) and contributed to numerous other volumes. He has written for multiple periodicals including *Christianity Today, Christian Century, Relevant,* and the *Washington Post*.

A pastor for twenty-five years, Winn was the founding pastor of All Souls Charlottesville in Virginia. He now directs the Eugene Peterson Center for Christian Imagination at Western Theological Seminary in Michigan. He holds a PhD from the University of Virginia, where he focused on the intersection of religion and literary fiction. Winn and his wife, Miska, a spiritual director, live in Holland, Michigan, with their two sons.

winncollier.com

THE EUGENE PETERSON CENTER
FOR CHRISTIAN IMAGINATION

God, give us eyes to see the wideness of your world,
shimmering with beauty and holiness.
Stimulate our imaginations, infusing us with
courage and hope.
Surround us with friendship.
Plant us as seeds of resurrection.

Amen.

Western Theological Seminary, Holland, MI
petersoncenter.org